Textuality and sexuality

Textuality and sexuality

Reading theories and practices

edited by Judith Still and Michael Worton

MANCHESTER UNIVERSITY PRESS

MANCHESTER and NEW YORK

distributed exclusively in the USA and Canada by ST. MARTIN'S PRESS, New York

1117686 /5

Published by Manchester University Press
Oxford Road, Manchester M13 9PL, UK
and Room 400, 175 Fifth Avenue,
New York, NY 10010, USA

*Distributed exclusively in the USA and Canada
by* St. Martin's Press, Inc.,
175 Fifth Avenue, New York, NY 10010, USA

British Library Cataloguing-in-Publication Data
A catalogue record for this book is available from the British Library

Library of Congress Cataloging-in-Publication Data
Textuality and sexuality: reading theories and practices / edited by
    Judith Still and Michael Worton.
        p.   cm.
      ISBN 0-7190-3604-6. – ISBN 0-7190-3605-4 (paper)
      1. Feminist literary criticism.   2. Reader-response criticism.
    3. Sex in literature.   4. Women in literature.   I. Still, Judith,
    1958–   .   II. Worton, Michael, 1951–   .
    PN98.W64T44 1993
    809'.933538 – dc20   92-21096

ISBN 0 7190 3604 6 *hardback*
ISBN 0 7190 3605 4 *paperback*

Printed in Great Britain
Bell & Bain Limited, Glasgow

Contents

Acknowledgements

We should like to express our gratitude to the British Academy for a grant which made it possible for parts of the Introduction to be researched in Paris. We should also like to thank friends with whom we have discussed ideas, and who have provided much support while this volume was in preparation, especially Joanne Collie, Keith Fairless, Diana Knight and Vinod Patel. Several of the ideas in our Introduction were discussed with students of the Postgraduate School of Critical Theory, Nottingham University and students of the Department of French, University College London – to whom we also extend our thanks.

Judith Still and Michael Worton

Introduction

Judith Still and Michael Worton

Foucault's *Introduction* to his *History of Sexuality* suggests that one of the ruses of power in the modern period is to make us believe that power is monolith⋅c, operating only by uniform techniques of repression and silencing.[1] Such a belief deludes us into confidence that coming out into the open, talking about sex, will bring about our liberation. Foucault attacks such naive (or self-interested) confidence, persuading us that the economy of power is both more all-encompassing and less homogeneous. However, while asserting that sex can be seen to have long been an obsessive focus of discursive concern, if discourse is defined sufficiently widely (embracing architecture or ritual practices for example), Foucault himself performs further analysis. His performance implies that even if we reject the simplifications of the Repressive Hypothesis we should not abandon our interrogation of (discourses about) sex simply because such interrogations have long been one of the techniques of the dominant figures in a series of dyads (priest–confessant, analyst–analysand, teacher–pupil, parent–child and so on). The Introduction to the present volume will shamelessly and pleasurably pursue knowledge relating to sexuality as a textual construct, while seeking to avoid the trap of hypostasising sex as *the* secret. The field which we are attempting to cover is a vast and proliferating one. We shall not in fact attempt to *cover* it, particularly not in the sense of casting a totalising blanket (or shroud) over it even if the connotations of copulation for the purposes of breeding with it might, in this context, be usefully, ironically perverse. Instead, in this Introduction, we shall adopt a strategy of scattering or dissemination of seed(s).

We have wilfully, as well as playfully, chosen to speculate on, first, our understanding of the term *textuality* in the hope that this will inform our more specific excursions into sexuality. Second, we turn to the question of defining woman; *woman* is a term which will necessarily be used throughout this book, and yet we do not want either *woman* or *man* to be terms which go without question. Even if there is no answer to the question, the act of questioning is, we hope, a significant gesture in itself. We also briefly consider why one should want to use or to question the word *woman* in view of the pitfalls and pleasures associated with it. Next we turn to a more recent, but also problematic and necessary, rallying cry – 'feminism'. Our account of feminisms is necessarily selective, but we hope that it gives a flavour of some debates and of ways in which theories of textuality must invade any account of feminist thinking. After feminisms, we address the belated and controversial domain which, significantly, hardly has a title, to wit, 'men's studies'. Here it is even less clear which great names to evoke, and we have simply sampled the range of issues: for example, how and why some women are made 'masculine', the role of initiatory rites in the construction of ideologies of manhood, the problematics of display and effeminacy, the dialectical counter-model for the West of the Hindu concept of man, and, above all, issues in homosexuality. The field of men's studies is vast and largely uncharted, so we have chosen a variety of areas, all of which we regard as pressure points. However, our overriding concern has been to consider how visual and, especially, verbal codes function as operatives of (self-)labelling.

What is textuality?

Textuality is often used in modern critical theory as if it were synonymous with *textness*. However, the latter term implies that texts have some inherent quality, whereas we would wish to argue for a greater recognition of their dynamic mobility and their contingency. After all, the process of reading from left to right and from top to bottom is by no means shared by all cultures, and differing socio-cultural experiences and expectations influence the ways in which printed works are seen to be 'authentically' textual: for instance, in some African societies which have an essentially oral tradition, published works have only fairly recently come to be accepted as more than inadequate, bastardised versions of stories which the listener knew but which the story-teller embellished and personalised each time s/he told them. For centuries, though, Western theories of what a text is have focused on the importance of the published version and on the usefulness of manuscripts and variants. Both palaeographers and practitioners of what is now known as genetic criticism are committed to the exercises of decoding texts and following their genealogy through what are seen as earlier, 'primitive' versions of what will be the masterpiece, the masterwork. Yet they thereby not only accord to the text a certain authority but also suggest that the meaning of the text is bound to its author in perpetuity – as if there were a natural indissoluble bond, as if the text were the child of the author. The critical revolutions of Anglo-American New Criticism and French Structuralism shifted the emphasis away from the author to the text, but, creative and challenging as these approaches are, especially in their inclusion of the reader's role, they nonetheless continue to give primacy to the visually available text. Our main objection to much Structuralist criticism arises from its insistence on the text's autonomy and self-sufficiency – and its post-Formalist fascination with closure. Narrative closure is seductive, because it appears to make a text 'manageable' for the reader, but closure is, we would argue, impossible, since texts are always going to be read in different contexts – and with different personal and collective agendas and presuppositions.

Each written text comes into being through a process of transposition, whereby empirical and *local* concerns with (vocal) emphasis, speed (of enunciation), intentionality and subjectivity are translated into the prevailing written code. In this sense, the text can be seen as a translation or transcoding of elements which are personal to the originating writer. The importance of the aural, indeed the sensual (and therefore the subjective), in the writing/creative process cannot be ignored. Yet we must remember that every subjectivity is grounded in and founded by some form of subscription to, and engagement with, a prevailing collectivity and a contingent ideology.

In the choruses in Milton's *Samson Agonistes*, for instance, virtually every line has two co-existing scansions, thereby drawing attention to the formal nature of the text as much as to its content. Gerard Manley Hopkins's use of what he termed sprung rhythm was an attempt to approximate in poetry the movements of natural speech in order to create a tone of sincerity and emotional involvement. While this technique makes possible a sense of intimacy between reader and text, it also evokes other, 'hidden' rhythms and texts. Interestingly, in a description of the technique, his vocabulary has an aggressivity reminiscent of Bloomian theories of the anxiety of influence: 'the secondary or "mounted rhythm", which is necessarily a sprung rhythm, overpowers the original or conventional one and then this becomes superfluous and may be got rid of; by taking this last step you reach sprung rhythm'.[2] The surface simplicity of a Hopkins poem proclaims its own originality but also implicitly calls up preceding texts (notably *Samson Agonistes* which he greatly admired). In other words, its textness gives way to textuality – which is a process, a dynamics.

Modern experiments with such visual features as layout, different typefaces and images undoubtedly foreground the text as more than a direct or transparent vehicle for communication: one thinks, for example, of Mallarmé's *Un coup de dés*, Apollinaire's Cubist poems, Breton's incorporation of photographs and drawings into *Nadja* not as illustrations but as *part* of the text, Beckett's *Malone Dies* where the words dribble off the last page, Monique Wittig's *The Lesbian Body* where the I is 'scarred' (*I*; j/e), and Kathy Acker's typographical experimentations in *Blood and Guts in High School*. However, this focusing on textness does more: it engages the reader in a work of speculation, in the productivity that is textuality, wherein memories of other texts and images are collated with the text you have in front of yourself.

Another technique, that of explicit rewriting, discloses the impossibility of textual closure. In Baudelaire's prose poem 'L'Invitation au voyage', he not only expands (on) his verse poem of the same name, he also uses the exact words of the refrain in the verse poem, but in a different order: this highlights the 'artificiality' of prosody, since the conventions both of poetry and of prose are questioned. Borges's 'Pierre Ménard, author of *Don Quixote*' suggests that the rewritten version of a text is ironic and consequently superior to the original; Michel Tournier's rewritings for children of his *Friday* and of his *The Four Wise Men* are in his view anti-ironic, simpler and thus superior. However one regards rewriting, it is clear that it challenges the authority of any single text and of any single author, engaging the reader in a labyrinth of reference.

Textness cannot therefore be seen as some sort of fixed, universal quality. Every text is, of course, initially created in a particular situation and by a particular writer, but many other forces are at work at the time of its writing – and its successive readers will redefine and reposition it, maintaining it in a state of fluidity, of textuality.

As Kristeva has asserted in *La Révolution du langage poétique*, every text is under the jurisdiction of other, and often alien or hostile, discourses which impose upon it a context which it seeks to transform (p. 339). This is a partial definition of textuality as a process.

We would add that readers are an integral part of this process and that their (mobile and questioning) interventions are necessary if the text is to enter into the *agon*, the arena of debate and change that is textuality.[3] For historical, religious, cultural, political and, indeed, psycho-social reasons, the (Western) reader continues to be anxiously fascinated by the problem of origins. Source-criticism, genetic criticism and theories of influence undoubtedly have value for an understanding of how texts come into being, but they tend to privilege the individual text(s) chosen for examination, whereas we believe that there is a need to interrogate such privilege – and to inscribe explicitly into textuality the role of readers as at least equally important as texts and authors.

Heidegger's concept of art is of some help here. He states that the artist is the origin of the work of art and that the work is the origin of the artist, adding that, although interdependent, they *exist* through art – which precedes both of them.[4] Heidegger replaces the concept of *natal* or causal origin with *nuptial* origin, which is a phenomenon of *aletheia* (or unveiling/unconcealedness): origin is the presence of what is always-already present. Subtle and persuasive though Heidegger's argument is, it nonetheless tends to essentialise 'Art' (and, crucially, it leaves no place for the reader). As writers and/or as readers, we discover the 'presence' of a text within our own plural moments of presence, recognising that the 'now' is inescapably an amalgam of past, present and future – all of which are states we create projectively, fictively as much as we remember or know them.

The major thrust of our argument is thus that we reject essentialism, be it of text, art or woman/man. Texts, like individual women and men, are socially constructed, whatever may be their features of specific individuality. Textuality implies the relative and mobile form of a structuration (i.e. a structure which is not fixed but constantly changing), from which significations can be produced by a subject – which is itself partly constructed by encounters which can themselves be understood as textual. In other words, our use of the term textuality insists on the following points:

(i) the accessibility of material to significations;
(ii) the inessential quality of signification (i.e. meanings are not fixed for all time even though some meanings persist over considerable time periods);

(iii) the potential fluidity of textual structures (including social net-
      works) over time and place;
(iv) the permeation of (textual) relations by power;
(v) the *intertextual* quality of textuality.

These assertions arise in part from our understanding of intertextuality.[5] Kristeva's coinage *intertextuality* refers not only to written
sources of influence, but also, and more importantly, to *codes* such
as the courtly code of chivalry which intersects medieval texts.[6]
Drawing on the Kristevan theory of intertextuality, Barthes suggests
in *S/Z* that we as subjects are made up of networks of crossing codes.[7]
This point, which may seem reductive, can be glossed with reference
to Althusser's writings on ideology.[8] The codes may be referred to as
texts, and yet (as Althusser says of ideology) they are also *material*
in that they involve practices. In fact the apparent opposition between
texts and material reality is a false one, as suggested even by the
restricted meaning of the term *text* where a Shakespeare text, say,
may appear to be essentially immaterial and yet can exist and be
known to us only via artefacts (books) or practices (theatre).

In order to make this argument more comprehensible and its political
import more obvious, we are approaching textuality via one particular
area, namely sexuality. This is not because we are insisting, with
some Freudians, that sex is inevitably the prime motor force and is
necessarily the charged lens through which we experience the world.
But we would claim, with Foucault, that sexual practices and identifications have been in different ways at different historical moments
a particularly charged domain of ethical problematisation. The construction of the self as subject is, today, a construction as sexed and
sexual subject.[9]
   Some of the primary and crucial codes which construct us as
subjects are those which shape our sexual identifications. While
these identifications are in general riddled with confusion and contradiction, many subjects wilfully assert and cling to an identity such
as 'a straight man' – to take a common example of our times. The
epithet 'straight' implies that those who do not conform to the subject's practices and self-perception are 'bent', 'deviant', 'queer'. Yet
even an apparently more neutral paraphrase ('a heterosexual male')
poses problems, for, as many feminists have pointed out, heterosexuality is 'as learned and institutionalised as "democracy" or

"socialism" or "scientific methods" or [...] "literary standards"'
(Gillian E. Hanscombe, *Heterosexuality*, p. 8). Because of the difficulty
of forging and sustaining a coherent identity in the field of sexuality,
the assertion may be all the more fiercely passionate. It may involve
a denial or repression of other identities in self and others. This
forging of sexual identity is a continuing process – both in social
exchange and in intercourse with texts.

Reading and writing in the more general sense of these terms
are among the most frequent of our activities. Subjects decipher the
world, social situations, themselves, as well as texts in the narrow
sense. Simultaneously these interpreting individuals, in making
sense of the material which surrounds them, write plots for themselves to figure in, and script first themselves and then others as
characters in the scenario. However, it must not be forgotten that
these acts of self-script-writing necessarily involve using the language
of others and that the scenarios are meant to be seen, transcoded
by others. The construction of a subject may well be understood
as an aesthetic act; Foucault has illustrated, with respect to Plato's
Greece and Seneca's Rome, how asceticism can be a form of self-
stylisation. Oscar Wilde redefined the aesthetic concept of the dandy
in order to present homosexuality publicly, and many contemporary
lesbian and gay theorists and activists have recourse to established,
socially accepted artistic icons in their presentations of 'difference'.
Perhaps one of the most powerful statements about identity is to
be found in Gertrude Stein's *Sacred Emily* where she writes: 'Rose
is a rose is a rose is a rose'. She is simultaneously evoking the male-
determined *topos* of woman as a rose and echoing in positive terms
Heraclitus' aphorism 'You never step twice into the same river'
which proposes that exact repetition is impossible. Stein's multiplication of exact equivalences ironically questions the Aristotelian
principles of identity, non-contradiction and the excluded middle
that still continue to dominate Western metaphysics and politics:
it suggests and shows that every identity is multiple, and, more
importantly, fractured. A woman always is and is not a woman,
a man always is and is not a man: the biological, the social and the
aesthetic are constantly interfering with the identity the subject
may wish to establish.

Defining 'woman'/defining 'man'

Western metaphysics, the system of thought in which we are caught,
desires to be firmly based on binary oppositions of the true–false,
1–0 kind.[10] For example, we understand what a cat is as much by
reference to what a cat is not as by reference to some essential feline.
Any Goethian or Romantic concept of the 'eternal feminine' is actually
grounded in the shifting but consistently hierarchical structure
masculine–feminine, and the norm of the everyday woman is set
against the norm of everyday manhood. Consequently the question
about the definition of 'woman' is also a question about the definition
of not-woman, that is to say, man – and just as 'woman' can be a
difficult term for feminists, so the appellation 'man' increasingly
poses problems today for many heterosexual and gay men who are
suspicious of the presupposition that manliness equals machismo
or proclaims virility.

The reference to a general pattern of binary thinking may disguise
the peculiarity of the emphasis laid on this particular opposition.
The labelling of human subjects m or f happens at birth if not before
(despite the hidden 1–4 per cent born with degrees of hermaphroditism[11]) – the first question 'is it a boy or a girl?' is echoed by each
friend and family member and continues in social intercourse to be
a primary factor in summing up an individual. Extraordinary barriers
are put in the way of anyone wishing to change the sex given on
their birth-certificate; there is a major investment in the security
of sexual identity. This is not to say that the political structure
cannot tolerate, and even enjoy, some playfulness around sexual
identity; just as the fixity of feudal structures welcomed the occasional
and delimited carnival transgression, so a bourgeois family with
absolute faith in sexual difference can celebrate the comedy of male
drag artists on television. In 'Choreographies', Jacques Derrida re-
marked: 'What remains undecidable concerns not only but also
the line of cleavage between the two sexes' (p. 181). In this Introduction we want to analyse that cleavage – which is perhaps a
wilful split deriving from a union. First of all, we shall consider
the defining of woman along four axes: the cultural axis, the economic
axis, the biological axis and the psychic axis.[12]

The cultural axis

It is assumed by many feminists that it is in the cultural domain, understood in the most general sense, that gender is constructed. While analysis of this domain should have the virtue of being historically specific, it can easily be invaded by ahistoricity, by a discourse of 'women have *always* been represented as ...', or can be subject to certain forms of historical narrative such as history as progress. The constructivist position permits a certain optimism, which can be liberating if it doesn't fall into complacency, as it constructs a domain in which many women have felt that they can intervene and effect change of some kind. In *The Second Sex*, Simone de Beauvoir charts the way in which small human animals are *made* into women, and her approach has proved very popular with 'Anglo-American' feminists whether they are working in social science, literature or other fields. Historical and (even micro-)cross-cultural research is useful in persuading us that the definitions of the 'real man' and the 'real woman' change, but it often begs the question whether on some level (say, that of biology) a fixed residual difference remains between men and women, that is to say, whether the cultural difference is 'textual' but a 'real' difference exists in a (non-textual?) materiality. Research work within the sphere of culture must ultimately address that question. If the process of gender construction is taken to be superstructural, then the study of that construction has all the attendant problems of the (more or less dependent?) relationship of superstructure to (material) base. Our understanding of that relationship will affect our view on what can be changed and how it can be changed. For instance, can we take the optimistic line that sexist attitudes can be altered by means of superstructural measures, say, banning sexist advertising, magazines or jokes?[13] Or must there be some fundamental shift (economic or biological) before attitudes will follow suit?

It is clear that the cultural superstructure of legislation is important from a number of perspectives: the definition of male and female in law (naming), the political domain (for instance 'equal opportunities'), the role of the state (whether perceived as the representative of dominant forces or as a site of conflict), and the influence of what Althusser calls Ideological State Apparatuses on the structuration of gender identity. Social codes, however, contribute even more than legislation to the structuration of sexual identity. In *S/Z* Barthes indicates how femininity is 'recognised' according to certain cultural

codes in Balzac's 'Sarrasine', and indeed in all 'realist' fiction which
teaches its readers about 'life' even as it is informed by the intertext of
the social codes which have already written its readers. The femininity
of Sarrasine's beloved Zambinella is *proved* by three interlocking
proofs: the narcissistic (if I, masculine, love her then she is a woman),
the psychological (a 'womanly' trait, such as timidity, induced from an
episode with a snake or a champagne cork, proves that she is a woman)
and the aesthetic (only woman is beautiful). Balzac's stories often
depict subversively extreme situations in which culturally-conditioned
recognition is mistaken: the beautiful, timid opera singer is a castrated
man ('Sarrasine') or the violent rival lover who keeps the hero's
mistress in luxurious confinement is a woman ('The Girl with the
Golden Eyes').[14] However, these crossings of the boundary of antithesis can be understood as punished by death or at least by the end
of desire.[15] Barthes's interrogation of stereotypes both in literature
and in 'real' life results in his (politically provocative) conviction
that events and, more importantly, classes of people can be – and
are – reduced to a pure denotation which 'seems both to establish
and close the reading' (*S/Z* pp. 8–9). At the heart of Barthes's thinking
lies the problematic concept of transparency which is a social construction rather than a given. His insistence on the inevitable nar-
rativisation of all events and encounters aids us to understand how
and why every stereotype (woman, man, black, lesbian, gay, or
whatever) may be presented as if it were believable and transparent,
for it functions like a realist text, seeming to refer to some objective,
empirically verifiable truth. However, as John R. Leo has pointed
out, 'this apparently simplifying denotation works as a connotation,
one which seems to designate persons and groups ahistorically and
yet which assimilates new meanings over time'.[16]

Culture (high or low) in a narrow sense has been extensively
treated by feminist theorists: written texts by Beauvoir, Millett,
Schor, Gilbert and Gubar to name but a few, and paintings by, for
example, Griselda Pollock.[17] In this volume Jan Montefiore analyses
the popular cultural form of schoolgirl fiction and the forms in which
it has been parodied. It may at first sight seem that schoolgirl stories
are conservative in every sense, and that debunking them is therefore
a subversive gesture. However, Montefiore shows that, on the one
hand, the mental escape to a woman-centred universe may have some
positive aspects for the female reader, who should not be imagined
to be naively wishing to be in a boarding school in real life, and,

on the other hand, that masculine irony at the expense of these all-female worlds may be maintaining hierarchies rather than breaking them down. Rosalind Coward analyses the myths of diets and other fashion, health and beauty discourses in women's magazines as well as the myths of romantic love or of the perfect home and garden in *Female Desire*. It is clear that both capitalism (forever needing to expand markets and to interpellate the consuming as well as the producing subject) and patriarchy (forever reinventing repression) have a purchase on these myths. Beauty products sell at high profit margins, and it could be argued that women are duped into spending time and energy in the competition to objectify themselves for men (although it should be remembered that men are increasingly the victims of a similar dupery in their desire to match up to the expectations of women). And yet it is not quite so simple: feminine pleasure in the ornamentation of body or environment should not be too swiftly dismissed as vain and trivial relative to masculine pride in productivity or creativity. Furthermore, in criticising the consumption of popular cultural fictions, we should ask ourselves what kind of reader of romantic fictions or problem pages we should imagine. A similar question about the degree of resistance and creativity with which readers are endowed has been raised in the debate around feminist film studies engendered by Laura Mulvey, and continued by Teresa de Lauretis, Stephen Heath, Ruby Rich amongst others – that is, is Hollywood or commercial cinema necessarily conservative with respect to gender positions? Is avant-garde cinema, which breaks with mainstream formal techniques, necessarily more radical? How active in producing the filmic text could the (female) spectator be?

Emphasis on the construction of gender can result in the bolstering of another myth, that of feminine passivity, of women composed or written by social forces which men control – or alternatively the belief that both sexes are programmed. While literary theorists from Plato and Aristotle onwards have tended to cast the reader in the passive and therefore 'feminine' role, and while most (male) social philosophers until the twentieth century presupposed that women were both marginal and dependent, feminism has alerted us to other ways of dealing with presuppositions of passivity. We would argue that the best hypothesis is that of a dialectic between construction (reading as being written) and action (reading as writing) in the human subject. (Relative) autonomy would in this scenario thus be fostered by the illusion of coherence, unity and freedom.

The economic axis

An alternative hypothesis to those which emphasise the cultural construction of gender is one that argues that it is women's economic dependency throughout history which makes them 'women' (feminine), and, conversely, that being born a woman has a strong influence on your economic position. The economic axis is regarded as important by most feminists, but its degree of importance is an area of contestation. The strongest economist positions argue that change in the mode of production is the major prerequisite for any real change in the structure of sexual difference. Within this argument there are two major camps: socialist feminists who argue that classic class struggle is prior to sexual struggle (and so a socialist revolution is a prerequisite for sexual equality), and those who claim that sex constitutes a class. Economist positions lead to questions such as: do women have a particular function under capitalism, for example as a reserve army of labour or as the chief agents of the reproduction of the means (and relations) of production? This kind of economic question can be used to differentiate between the position of lesbians (women in economic terms) and that of gays (men in economic terms).[19] The economic assumptions (and engagement with Marxism) of those who take less purely economist positions are often ignored. For example, Cixous, Irigaray and Kristeva would all claim that a change in the political economy is one of the necessary pre-conditions – alongside a transformation in the construction of the subject – for new forms of sexual difference.

The case that what determines the superstructure of masculine and feminine identity is the economic base is strongly argued by the sociologist Christine Delphy.[19] She regards herself as a materialist, in the sense that she holds to the postulate that the way in which life is materially produced and reproduced is the base of the organisation of all societies, and that history is the story of the domination of various social groups by others. She refuses to reserve the Marxist method for the analysis of the capitalist mode of production, wanting to expand it to cover all modes of exploitation, arguing that the struggle between labour and capital is not the unique dynamic of society. The other dynamic is the struggle between men and women, regarded as classes in the Marxist sense, that is to say defined by their relation to the (patriarchal) mode of production.[20] It is thus the economic exploitation of women by men, husbands' appropriation of their wives' labour, which gives rise to sexual division as a social and psychological reality. She argues that it is marriage not childcare which oppresses women, and that one should not confuse biological reproduction with the reproduction of labour power nor with social reproduction in general. Motherhood is not a natural fact giving birth to exploitation, but a social construct created by exploitation. For Delphy, it is crucial to relate the ideological (in its materiality) to the economic. Institutional structures give rise to psychological structures of sexual division, which are also concrete, objective and exterior. However, it is the existence of exploitation which requires the constitution of an exploited population which in turn requires the creation of a sexist or racist or classist ideology; in other words, the material exploitation has logical primacy. If we accept with Delphy that there are two systems of oppression (capitalism and patriarchy), each with its own material base, we might also want to ask whether (as in Shulamith Firestone's reading of Marx and Engels) there could be an eventual withering away of sex distinctions since Marxism suggests that class distinctions could ultimately vanish.

The fact that sexual difference can be observed may thus be explained on grounds other than those of an innate divide between the sexes; however, even the observation of 'sexual difference' should perhaps not go unchallenged. We need to ask to what extent sexual difference is produced by the observing and recording subject (the reader and writer) as much as by the object of study? This question is of interest to many areas of research; Dale Spender has analysed the problems in work on the difference between men and women's speech, such as the assumptions that women are more facilitating, apologetic, tentative, use 'I' less often, make general assertions less often, or speak less than men when both sexes are present.[21] One of the problems with this linguistic research as with much social science research is the difficulty in controlling for class, racial and regional differences. Differences between American black working-class men and women, whether with respect to language, social interaction or employment history, are quite differently structured from differences between British Asian middle-class men and women.

Analysis of labour markets involves decisions about how to divide up the population (unless it is assumed to be broadly homogeneous), and frequently the division will be made on the basis of sex since it is a common observation that women's labour supply is far more elastic than men's.[22] However, it may be the case that the significant difference is between married women and all other adults, or, in the UK, between women with a child below a certain age and all other adults, or, in France, between women with more than two children and all other adults. These issues complicate any sense that two monolithic blocks (males and females) can be opposed one to the other. Of course, typically, we have emphasised the heterogeneity of women and assumed that all men conform to a 'masculine' model.[23] Again the question of what is most significant about the supply of labour is crucial. Is it participation in the market of any kind which is the key division – in which case the large majority of women are no longer radically differentiated from men? Or is it the mode, duration, wage-earning capacity and status on which the observer should focus attention? And how do these relate back to issues of language production?

The biological axis

The biological sexual distinction between male and female is often assumed to pre-exist as some natural reality prior to the more problematic construction of gender. This assumption is made not only by anti-feminists who wish to argue from biology that, for example, men are naturally more active (needing to penetrate in order to ensure reproduction) and women more passive (needing only to be penetrated), but also by many feminists. The majority of these latter have argued that biological difference is something to be overcome, that it is a natural inequality, but one which is less significant as society makes progress in mastering brute nature. Variations on that position are to be found in, for example, Simone de Beauvoir, Shulamith Firestone or Michele Barrett.

An alternative approach, encapsulated in the *Parole de femme* of Annie Leclerc, is to celebrate that difference on the grounds that it marks female superiority – giving birth, lactation and so on can be presented as the supreme pleasures (*jouissances*) available to human kind. Her work is notorious for its account of the 'orgasmic' pleasures of menstruation, for example. This represents a shift away from orgasm as something you 'achieve' in heterosexual intercourse – which might seem quite liberating – but we might ask whether she simply unloads even more guilt on to women – one of feminism's constant problems or paradoxes as Coward points out in her soul-searching Introduction to *Female Desire*. The difference between male and female or masculine and feminine orgasms has preoccupied a surprising number of late twentieth-century theorists, and we shall return to this briefly with respect to Derrida and Spivak.

Leclerc argues that what we really need is a change in values – from masculine ones of death to feminine life-giving values.[24] But whether you love it or hate it, whether you consider it to be of major significance or of fairly minor significance – is it necessary to accept biological difference as something which goes without saying? Such an acceptance appears dangerously close to essentialism – the belief in immutable essences. Leclerc seems the closest to 'essentialism' of all the French feminists who are regularly charged with this crime.[25] In *The Poetics of Gender* Jane Gallop produces an extraordinary reading of Leclerc as the author of a lesbian love-letter in *La Venue à l'écriture*.[26] Gallop celebrates Leclerc's unexpected desire for the other (working-class) woman, although ends with a sad reminder of the perils of essentialism. In fact Leclerc's essentialism – if that is what it is – seems to us to be part of her prioritising of hetero-sexuality even in this highly ambiguous love-letter. The end of loving women/woman is to love men.[27]

There are at least three ways of problematising sexual biology: the continuum argument;[28] the mutability argument, in other words how biology is affected by class (for example, the influence of diet and environment on size, or the role of fashion), by chemistry (e.g. reproductive technology), or by surgery (does a life-saving hysterectomy affect status as a female?); and the textual argument (the mental relationship with the body or how we read our bodies).

The psychic axis

In considering the psychic axis of sexual difference, we need to ask if the unconscious is fixed for all time or if it is mutable. Louis Althusser is one Marxist theorist whose work implies that the Freudo-Lacanian Unconscious with which we are familiar might be co-terminous with certain forms of social organisation. On that basis we need not assume that the Freudian masculine libidinal economy organised around the phallus and the castration complex – where women are a deviation from that apparently fixed norm – is an eternal formation even if we accept it as a relatively accurate account of the patriarchal, capitalist moment with which we are familiar. Freud's theories continue to dominate psychoanalytical discussions of sexual (self-)identification, much more than, for example, Jung's *Aspects of the Feminine* and *Aspects of the Masculine*. The reason for this is that Freud is an

Author in Foucault's terms, whereas Jung is a writer – and necessarily, as Bloom would say, a late-come writer. In 'What is an Author?', Foucault argues that a writer is an Author because s/he establishes an endless possibility of discourse (and of divergences). In other words, an Author is necessarily both a depersonalised and an ideological figure which enables readers to mark – through projection – their fear of the proliferation of meaning and a functional principle which determines how they choose, limit and exclude information and responses. Freud is and does all this, hence the proliferation of responses to his work. In *Creativity and Perversion*, Janine Chasseguet-Smirgel offers one of the most challenging interrogations of Freud's work and of his theory of phallic monism which stipulates that the boy-child attributes a penis to all human beings, women included. Her re-reading of 'The Wolf-Man' is particularly important for its contestation of the nature and function of passivity. While Freud insists on the discovery of the vagina and the biological significance of masculine and feminine and 'in a rather curious way [...] asserts that the observation of the coitus *a tergo* (from behind) brought the Wolf-Man to the conviction of the reality of castration', Chasseguet-Smirgel chooses to present what she calls 'an *economic* theory of the building up of the imago of the phallic mother' (p. 44). Her argument that, 'because of human helplessness, sexuality changes into psycho-sexuality' (p. 54) is particularly convincing, and enables us better to understand some of the apparent inconsistencies in Freud's work. She reminds her readers of Freud's demonstration in 'Analysis Terminable and Interminable' that passivity towards a man may be felt as a castration, whatever form this passivity may take – in other words, 'feminine' passivity need not necessarily involve (or even wishfully presuppose) actual penetration. Freud himself said of his clinical work with male patients that his most difficult, indeed almost impossible, task was 'to convince a man that a passive attitude to men [...] is indispensable in many relationships in life' ('Analysis Terminable and Interminable', p. 252). Chasseguet-Smirgel's analysis shows how social feelings are sexualised; we would add that it is important also to recognise how sexual feelings and impulses are socialised. If almost all male patients are haunted by the fear of passivity, then passivity is not inherently 'feminine' but is part of the shared (psycho-sexual) human condition. By recognising this fact, both women and men may thus resexualise – and ultimately retextualise – themselves, and so inscribe themselves in a new psycho-social order.

Freud can certainly be read as revolutionary and not only in his own historical moment; many of his claims still seem highly radical and counter-intuitive (in other words, counter to what we have absorbed as 'normal' and 'commonsense'), for example, his expansion of sexual feelings, presenting 'perversions' as part of normality, his reading of the body as text, his (literary) analysis of everyday speech, parapraxes and dreams.[29] However, a reading of Freud as presenting a model of development will appear normative (an assertion that we should all progress towards healthy genital maturity), whereas a structural reading is more liberating.[30]

A number of feminist theorists have read Lacan as more productive for feminist thinking than Freud largely because of his insistence on the linguistic structure of the subject.[31] He may be understood to suggest in *Encore* that we can take up sides (either on the side of the phallic function or on the side of the 'not all') and that masculine and feminine subject positions are available to either sex without illness being the necessary byproduct. However, *Encore* and other texts may also be understood to argue that femininity is unrepresenting and unrepresentable – an even more extreme formulation than Freud's claim that women find it less easy than men to sublimate. Lacan asserts that of her essence woman is 'not all' (*Feminine Sexuality*, p. 144) $\bar{\forall}x = \phi(x)$ – and therefore has a supplementary *jouissance*, beyond the phallus – but then the term 'woman' embraces male mystics. Lacan is often read optimistically as inaugurating a shift from Freud's biological penis to the phallus as signifier, but other close readings challenge the notion that the phallus is not welded to the penis.[32] A number of French feminists have responded to the Lacano-Freudian symbolic anatomy with attempts to re-evaluate (the experience of) the female body so that it is no longer a black hole in the symbolic system – for instance Irigaray replaces Lacan's flat mirror with her speculum.[33] A major question may be to do with how we (want to) read the texts of psychoanalysis – should the resisting reader simply take the best and leave the rest, calk her own formulations on to those of the father-figures, or argue back?

Why ask the question?

Simone de Beauvoir – often perceived as the founding mother of
modern feminism – argues that the Hegelian Self–Other (Master–
Slave) dialectic shapes all our relations. Man has been able to appropriate the position of the subject/the same and has constituted Woman
(also the Jew, the Black, the Homosexual) as Other.[34] Shulamith
Firestone asks whether biology is cause or effect of that structure.
The acceptance of body as cause seems surprisingly pessimistic (and
counter to the arguments of those French feminists often charged
with 'essentialism'); Firestone escapes pessimism by appealing to
science to modify biology or at least biological functions. However,
the problem of who determines the agenda of science would return us
to social structures of power. Not only Beauvoir but feminisms in
general have consistently addressed themselves to questions of difference and of hierarchies. Derrida's argument that binary oppositions
are always hierarchical and violent is already familiar to feminists –
accustomed to 'reason versus emotion', 'light versus darkness' or
'mind versus body' being called into the service of 'masculine versus
feminine'. This metonymic slippage from one reductive binary to
another, this slippery ideological structure which privately embraces
contradictions despite its public espousal of logic, implies the importance of taking time and analysing definitions.[35]

Feminists may ask the question (what is a woman?/what is a
man?) because of the tension between opposition to essentialism as
the notion of fixed sexual identities, and the desire to be able to
talk about and appeal to 'women' and women's experience, women
writers and readers. Contemporary feminists often do not want to
fall back into a universal identity (humanity) – knowing that the
neutral usually returns to the masculine. But if we don't accept
uniformity (perverse sameness), or the fixed difference promoted in
contemporary social ideology, what do we demand? Pragmatists may
simply work at gradual reform of the fixed opposition whereas utopians
project a radical alterity (an outside of the social structures we know).
Those influenced by Derrida's theories of *différance* may look at a
moment when there would be a plurality of sexes and not just the
familiar two.

Feminisms recurrently ask whether it is more *useful* or more
dangerous to be able to talk about 'women'. The generalising grand
narrative has its problems but so does the kind of specificity which

reduces to units of (less than) one. For emotional reasons it is important for women to be able to talk about 'women'. We might also
accept the rallying call 'women' (as Kristeva does) for narrow but
important political purposes such as legislation on abortion or rape.
But on a theoretical level Kristeva's insistence that woman can
never be defined means that no definition has happened once and
for all – precisely, analysing 'woman' is to be always in a state of
'moving on'.[36] Against Kristeva's reluctance Irigaray claims, however, that the building of a place for women in the Imaginary and
the Symbolic orders is more necessary than a rush to deconstruct
a sexual difference which has never really existed other than as a
masculine projection. For women have not yet existed: all that we
know is a monosexual (masculine) economy. Therefore women in
general have not yet loved themselves as women, nor have they been
able to love other women (particularly mothers) since women have no
home in the Symbolic order.[37]

We would argue that reading and writing in the more restricted
sense represent a focus and distillation of the everyday strategies of
survival and pleasure for the would-be coherent subject. Consequently
it is not surprising that the business of sexual identification (a process
which involves clinging to ego ideals as well as constructing others as
Other) pervades both explicit and implicit theories about the creative
process, about reading precursors and becoming a poet or teacher
onself. The analysis of theories of textual reception and production
must take into account the structured relations of inequality which
frame reception and production, as exemplified in, say, the models
of Socrates the teacher or Homer the father of poets. Those power
relations are suffused by the family romance, which shapes and
colours the terms of the *agon*, by castration, guilt, games of exclusion
and inclusion, and desperate self invention and assertion. The apparent
homogenisation of intertextuality (reducing everything to text) can
provide a way of relating common drives in different practices and
their associated fantasies.

What is feminism?

The work of feminists and theorists of sexuality (particularly those
who combine social theory with psychoanalysis) is highly relevant
to an analysis of theories of textual reception and production. At the

same time, these theories are very useful in tackling questions such as the gendering of style and content. Are certain forms masculine or feminine?[38] Are certain contents oppressive to women? Does the context of production (including the biological sex of the author) or the context of reception (including the sex of the reader) affect the answers to these questions? Are certain modes of reading masculine or feminine, filial or parental? Moreover, theories of textual production and reception can help us to analyse the construction and interpretation of 'femininity' or 'masculinity': our relations to our bodies, domestic structures (sites of reproduction?), and lover–beloved relations.[39]

Just as women (or men) are falsely represented as *one*, so feminisms are wrongly represented as one. And yet any division is flawed. The problem of the level of analysis is intractable: from humanism's 'man' to stand for us all to 'we women' to 'black women' to 'British lesbians of Afro-Caribbean origin' – any one of these generalisations may well seem to hide more differences than is tolerable. Strategic reasons for remaining (temporarily) at a given level of analysis may include psychic and emotional needs, political needs or intellectual needs. We should not, however, forget to interrogate these 'needs', recognising to what extent they stem from the way in which our 'selves' or the political domain in which we operate have been constructed, making us want to huddle together with others, or create insiders and outsiders, carve up and categorise. Feminisms can be divided up in a number of different ways which rightly or wrongly give the impression of camps or sides; for example, temporal divisions can be made (early, late, first wave, second wave, third wave), geographical divisions (French, Anglo-American, first world, third world), political divisions (liberal, Marxist, ecologist), conceptual divisions (equality, difference, unified subject, *différance*) and divisions of sexuality. Some of these constructions re-deploy features familiar from the masculine–feminine opposition (Anglo-Saxons are rational while foreigners are excitable, fashionable and passionate), or from the oppositions patriarchy uses against women (political lesbians are pure while women who enjoy pornography are stupid sluts).[40] Drawing on Marx, we could comment with Toril Moi that 'all forms of radical thought inevitably remain mortgaged to the very historical categories they seek to transcend' (*Sexual/Textual Politics*, p. 88). This raises the question of the construction of history; the way in which a mass of past events becomes a narrative transmitted by educational and other media is obviously of interest to theorists of textuality – its ideological biases and exclusions have made it a crucial domain politically for feminists as well as for colonised peoples or those interested in the class struggle.

There are problems of *translation* in a number of senses, for example how certain French terms get translated into English, which texts or fragments of texts are translated into which languages and where they are published.[41] Another problem of translation or conceptualisation stems from current debates in cultural and socio-economic periodisation, and the question of the interrelationship between style and the human subjet. A number of thinkers set up divides or oppositions, either chronological or conceptual, between less and more radical forms. Moi's *Sexual/Textual Politics* introduces feminist literary theory in terms of the divide between the (Anglo-American) intellectual tradition which privileges realism, and the French 'modernist' tradition which wishes to disturb representation but which can fall back into essentialism or political ineffectiveness. Feminism has productively deployed the discourse and practice of emancipation, but certain kinds of contemporary feminism no longer wish to be caught in 'Enlightenment' humanist values without challenging their underpinnings because the universal human subject has so often been evoked in order to further the practices of patriarchy, capitalism and imperialism. Fredric Jameson sets up a chronology in which what is sweepingly termed Enlightenment thinking or modernity is coextensive with the rise of capitalism, and modernism is the cultural form representing the crisis of modernity. For Lyotard (who does not – unlike Jameson – accept a cultural chronology), modernist writing is defined as writing which is nostalgic for an adequate (re)presentation of what we conceive, whereas postmodernist writings (one of Lyotard's provocative examples is Montaigne's *Essays*) celebrate the faculty of conception.[42] Jameson and others present French poststructuralist thinking as an example of postmodernism, and yet much poststructuralist (including 'French feminist') work engages in analyses of modernist writing which are not concerned to emphasise any distinction from 'postmodernism' but rather from 'realism' or 'monologism' – if pure examples of such categories even exist. Barthes's work in *S/Z* suggests that everything we read is a modestly plural classical readerly work since the writerly text would be us writing, structuration *without* structure, a limit. We would argue that in practice any of these grand divides are hard to sustain absolutely, and that the interest must lie in the way in which the divisions are productive for thinkers privileging a given category. In other words, Lukács's optimistic claims about realism may be quite wrong, as are, from the anti-realist side, those of Alain Robbe-Grillet – and yet the claims may be (re)generative.

We shall now turn briefly to the texts and the figure of Simone de Beauvoir who, despite the work of so many women before her (which *she* recognises), is usually figured as the mother of modern feminism. *The Second Sex* (first published in 1949) is a founding work arguing that 'woman' is constructed from a professedly materialist (Marxist existentialist) – although not a 'feminist' – standpoint. Existentialist ethics can be seen as an enabling fiction of the potential to change your life, to shape your own destiny.[43] But is this a masculinist privileging of rationality, freedom, projects, creativity, the world of paid work (as opposed to the body, emotions, mutual dependency, procreation, the home)?[44] Is the very language of existentialism suffused with masculinity and an image of the feminine as reified, slimy, sucking passive holes?[45] Beauvoir's analysis of feminine masquerade (e.g. 'the woman in love' in *The Second Sex*) – may indeed be set against an ideal of authenticity, but in Beauvoir's fiction there is an underlying anxiety that 'our' authenticity may also be role-playing, albeit in a more self-questioning form.[46]

There are a number of questions related to reading Beauvoir and the passions invested in this. Some energy has gone into the construction of a character: the free-living/loving left-bank intellectual – to be faced with a double bind that she is either too dependent on her man (intellectually), or not dependent enough (materially) and so could not sympathetically understand the problems of the majority of women – housewives and mothers. In *Feminist Thought and Simone de Beauvoir*, Moi shows how conservative male readers have set up Beauvoir as the little girl or the schoolmarm against the philosopher Sartre. Beauvoir is often criticised for her alleged acceptance of dominant patriarchal (and/or Sartrean) definitions and categories such as instrumental rationality or universality – and her alleged rejection of the female body, nurturing values and so on. In 'She Came to Stay', Moi has argued that we can usefully analyse some attacks on Beauvoir by indebted women readers as analogous to those on the Kleinian Mother; works about her turn frequently to an autobiographical, even 'true confessional' mode. There is often little sensitivity to stylistic considerations in the demand for 'positive images' and perfectly correct positions; for example, instances of what could be free indirect speech in *The Second Sex*, i.e. accounts of what is

generally held to be the case, or what is now the case (but not necessarily for all time), are sometimes read as prescriptive or approvingly
rather than critically descriptive. Sensitive accounts of female bodies
and female desire in *The Mandarins* (Anne) are sometimes overlooked in the angry or sorrowful reaction against Beauvoir's dissection
of the horror of unreciprocated desire and dependency (Paule).

Kate Millett is one example of an ambivalent daughter to Beauvoir;
she wrote a passionate indebted obituary in *The Observer* on the
occasion of Beauvoir's death, and yet makes almost no acknowledgement of *The Second Sex* in *Sexual Politics* despite the great proximity
of some material, not only on major figures such as Freud and Engels
but even in her choice to follow Beauvoir in her analysing of D.H.
Lawrence.[47] Many women readers have been distressed by Millett's
focus on male-authored texts only, and by her desire to read them
polemically, identifying an author with his characters, cutting and
misquoting. But is this ventriloquising, parodying and aggression
strategically useful at a given moment in the history of feminism,
when daughters have to learn not to be dutiful? Millett has a tendency
to unify the enemy, that is to say, patriarchal ideology if not men
in general, rather than emphasising cracks and fissures or contradictions – but again this can function as a powerful strategy of
reading. Readers can identify with the myth of the sole hero(ine)
doing battle, even if – or perhaps because – the myth has a certain
patriarchal style.[48] The 'or perhaps because' is where one of the chief
issues lies. Feminists have had problems arising out of their (natural?
patriarchal?) wish to lay down the law, or at least guidelines, about
what is correct behaviour in feminists. Good conduct may at one
historical moment involve abjuring the trappings of conventional
femininity and styling oneself in a masculine way or it may involve
wearing femininity with pride – whether on the grounds that many
traits deemed feminine would be of value to both sexes or in the
desire to mark sexual difference. This applies to rhetorical style as well
as to other modes of relating to others; some elements of language are
coded as masculine and feminine. While the opposition traditional
versus avant-garde cannot simply be mapped on to this, there is
some overlap. Breaking forms may be a courageous masculine act of
aggression, but degrees of formlessness are usually coded feminine.

Germaine Greer is another ambivalent daughter: where are the
references to Beauvoir in *The Female Eunuch*? Mary Wollstonecraft
(at a safe historical distance) is one of the few women to be quoted

with frequency; Juliet Mitchell is 'clearly deficient on the tactical side' (p. 297), 'Mrs Friedan' is patronised (p. 295), and Millett fares little better (p. 346). Greer does question the gratitude that we are obliged to feel towards mothers (p. 150) as damaging to women who thereby become locked into femininity as self-sacrifice. Perhaps Greer's Bloomian desire to be first – most recently with respect to her discovery of the menopause (about which Beauvoir has writtten so sensitively) – and to be a liberated woman in order to bed more men and want to leave them before they want to leave you, should simply be read as part of that historical moment of abjuring the conventional trappings of femininity. While that brand of feminism was not immune to the reactionary strategy of innoculation,[49] what strategy cannot be used against itself? – hence, Barthes or Derrida would say, the need to keep moving on. Patriarchy, like capitalism, is not an oak-tree – it can bend, adapt and absorb contradictory positions. Since *The Female Eunuch* Greer has done other work which uncovers and celebrates matrilinear genealogies, for example in painting.[50]

We shall now turn to a very different example of 1970s feminism. Monique Wittig is a controversial figure for her radical lesbianism and her loving portrayals of female violence in, for example, *Les Guérrillères* and *The Lesbian Body*. Wittig's radical claims include the assertion that lesbians are not women, since 'woman' is defined relative to 'man' and presupposes heterosexual relations ('The Straight Mind', p. 110). Her writing, she says, exists in a context of total rupture with masculine culture. It is written about women and for women; all positions in the language game (addresser, addressee, referent) are female. The gender female is a whole in itself for Wittig; there is no search for androgyny or bisexuality. This does not mean that she privileges femininity in quite the same way as some Anglo-American cultural feminists have done, seeing the feminine as naturally peaceful, tender, gentle-affectionate and sensitive. Wittig challenges these conventional norms; she not only reveals the violence done to women (entering language) but also turns the violence back on to language – the body of the text, of the word – and the body in the text. She asserts in 'The Mark of Gender' that part of her work as a writer is the destruction of gender in language, since grammar is the mark of what appears to be an ontological distinction between the sexes, and, more importantly, contributes to engineering it.[51] While she maintains that economic and political change is essential (and she regards herself as a materialist), she argues that this will never be achieved without change in the structure of language. In *Les Guéril-lères*, *elles* is universalised as the absolute subject of the world, in a way which is difficult to reproduce in translation; the use of 'the women' does not convey the same message. Likewise her scarred *j/e* is more troubling and violent than an italicised *I*.

Where Wittig's all-female communities wage war on men (*Les Guérillères*), feminist separatists have been able to celebrate her writing with less difficulty than when they encounter the detail, the semi-accuracy, of her slashing and mutilating her female lover in *The Lesbian Body*.[52] The reader's emotional, even physical, response to these imaginary dismemberments makes us ask questions about our visceral relation to language. *The Lesbian Body* collapses the system which differentiates between metaphor and textual reality, masculine metaphors of women, in texts exchanged between men, become metamorphoses of women: instead of being like a bird a woman becomes a bird.[53]

On a formal level Wittig's writing is sometimes presented as a break with male tradition:

> Gone are the single narrator, unity of tone, precision in space and time, the celebration of the individual, inter-relationship of major and minor characters and the resultant hierarchical forms that shape most male writing. Gone also are all the usual kinds of linear, logical structure and binary oppositions attributed to rational 'apollonic' thought.[54]

However, Wittig's (post)modernist style has its own male tradition – a problem which Cixous handles by insisting on the 'bisexuality' of male writers who fit her definition of *écriture féminine* – this is not an option acceptable to Wittig.

Wittig's works have utopian elements; for instance, she evokes a new kind of writing under the protection of Sappho in which language fuses body and mind, a community of equals, and an economy of abundance. Utopian thinking (or poeticising) has proved influential in a variety of kinds of feminism – Charlotte Perkins Gilman is just one important example. Equally, utopian forms of socialism, such as that of Charles Fourier, have sometimes proved more amenable to the rethinking of sexual difference than, say, Marxist forms.[55] We shall now turn to one recent utopic intersection of textuality and sexuality, that which is sometimes termed 'French feminism'.

Feminism and libidinal and textual economies

Thinking about sexuality has persistently returned to economic considerations. In *The History of Sexuality*, volumes II and III, Foucault examines the classical Greek and Roman desire to profit in the domain of *aphrodisia*, for example, to expend less energy or vital fluid and to gain more pleasure and healthy offspring. In the eighteenth and nineteenth centuries, worries around masturbation were often expressed in economic terms.[56] Freud's deployment of economic metaphors such as those of investment and disinvestment (particularly in his metapsychological writings) has been related to a scientific and 'masculine' desire for quantification and to a masculine anxiety about loss. Freud emphasises (for instance in his work on jokes) that the energy circulating within the psyche should be kept at the lowest possible level. Hélène Cixous argues that psychoanalysis describes the man who wants to 'gain more masculinity: plus-value of virility, authority, power, money or pleasure, all of which reinforce his phallocentric narcissism at the same time' (*The Newly Born Woman*, p. 87). In her own language, Cixous brings out an analogy between two kinds of *homo economicus*: capitalist man described by Marx and libidinal man described by Freud. The Freudian psychic economy is built around the necessity of (the fear of) castration for entry into the symbolic order, the order of the name, of interdiction, of the law of the father. The question which contemporary French thinking provokes is: to what extent can we, and should we, imagine something other, a non-castrated subject, a non-phallo-morphic language, *jouissance* (maternal giving) rather than ejaculation (economic reproduction)?

Cixous celebrates a feminine economy as opposed to the masculine one.[57] She argues that the terms *feminine* and *masculine* as she uses them are not anatomical, that they could be replaced by adjectives of colour for example, and that her work aims precisely at getting rid of such expressions.[58] However, she continues to use them and has thereby contributed to an increase in their currency, even if she problematises simple biologism by including male writers such as Kleist or Rilke in her examples of feminine generosity. This feminine economy is at once intrapsychic (built around *jouissance* not around castration), intersubjective, a political economy and, most famously, a literary economy known as *écriture féminine*. Cixous suggests the possibility of a de-censored relation to the body 'jusqu'au bout' (a term which conjures up Marguerite Duras) – which feeds into *écriture féminine.* The difference between the two economies is in the relation to the gift. Cixous claims that for historical reasons women are more likely than men to display feminine traits, and that, in (rightly) fighting repression and exclusion in the name of equality, they must not abandon feminine *jouissance.* Masculine castration entails the desire to appropriate on all levels to the point of wishing to incorporate the other, to contain and imprison the other, whereas a feminine economy takes the other into the self and is taken into the other also; it is a kind of mutual knowing or fluid mingling. Cixous, unlike Wittig, does not privilege the lesbian but rather what she calls 'bisexuality' – not the imaginary plenitude of the androgyne but the multiplication of the effects of desire's inscription on every part of the body and of the other body (*The Newly Born Woman,* p. 85).

In *La Venue à l'écriture* and elsewhere, Cixous emphasises the role of the body and of desire in reading and writing.[59] She describes the act of writing as having by loving, not by possessing or keeping: touching letters with her lips and breath, caressing with her tongue, licking with her soul (*La Venue à l'écriture,* p. 12) or as a continual process of giving birth (to herself). Reading is eating, sucking, being fed, kissing, loving and, again, being born incessantly (p. 19). Thus writing becomes the madness of suckling your own mother (p. 20), as well as endless *jouissance,* a sexual pleasure for writer and reader. Other texts and other tongues are not only nourishment but impregnation (p. 21). The question has often been posed: is there in Cixous and other French feminists a privileging of presence and the voice, of speech, and of the maternal which could be quite conservative?[60] We hope that it is clear in these examples from *La Venue à l'écriture* that, while Cixous persistently refers to the female anatomy and to female bodily functions, her biology is a fantasmatic one in which mothers are also lovers, impregnators and children. While some male writers have imagined being fathers to themselves, or fathers to their fathers, Cixous converts writing and reading into a feminine 'bisexuality' which fears passivity no more than activity, loss no more than receiving (the gift of) the other. This may be utopic, but it does not seem to us that it is productive to attack it on the grounds that it is thinking which seeks to return women to the patriarchal home and motherhood in a literal sense.

One of the worries sometimes expressed about the focus on maternity is that it reinforces the social bias towards the heterosexual norm. While volumes II and III of Foucault's *History of Sexuality* show that heterosexuality has not *always* functioned as a norm in the way that it does in the modern period, Sarah Kay's article, in this volume, analyses textual constructions of reproduction as normality in the medieval period. There the privileging of *natural* reproductive sex already involves a disparaging of homosexual practices. As Kay point out, the Middle Ages are frequently passed over in silence as dark and mysterious: historical summaries often leap from the sunshine of Greece and Rome to the glorious Renaissance overlooking the body of texts in between. This tradition could be compared to the desire to have an entirely masculine genealogy, which involves the censoring of the mother's body. The strength of homosocial bonding is such that within any particular text or tradition preaching reproduction a number of strategies work to exclude or objectify the female – including, in Kay's example, the invocation of goddesses. Another instance of the image of Venus being exchanged between men is in the Darwin letter which Gillian Beer analyses in this volume. Our concern to struggle against the imprisoning of women or men in the Malthusian couple must be attentive to the range of patriarchal strategies (denigrating, overlooking or fetishising the maternal function or the female body), but also open to the ways in which we can use them against themselves.

In Cixous's earlier writings, her chief examples of *écriture féminine* were male writers.[61] Some readers overlooked this, assuming that Cixous was a biological essentialist; others have noted it and find it uncomfortable, either because it seems dismissive of women predecessors or because of the feminisation of the male. Greg Woods, in this volume, takes exception to the application of the adjective 'feminine' to male writers (particularly if they are gay), arguing that Cixous is insufficiently attentive to the historical residues in her terminology. Both Woods and Sandy Petrey analyse the ways in which certain cultural assumptions are made about what writing as a man might entail, for example, a certain reserve. Cixous would no doubt claim that that is why she can use 'feminine' for a style which refuses reserve – but Woods wishes to argue that this simply reinforces conventional categories despite Cixous's wish to revalue these. More recently Cixous's preferred example and lover/beloved has been the Brazilian writer Clarice Lispector.[62]

Cixous's own prose fiction is often very difficult for the reader in its lack of sentence structure, punctuation, characters and so on –

the familiar props for the reader accustomed to conventional forms. The case can be made that conventional forms are socio-politically conservative, but avant-garde writing is inaccessible and consequently elitist. Against this last point, it may be argued that radical change requires hard work, patience and some pain – it cannot be expected that the reader will find the instant pleasure of easy consumption when incited to co-produce the text.

Marguerite Duras is one contemporary writer who to some extent meets the formal criteria for *écriture féminine*,[63] and yet whose writing is more accessible for the reader. Duras's greater accessibility may of course make her more appropriable by the forces of reaction; the recent film from her novel *The Lover* could be perceived as a vehicle for eroticism derived from the fetishisation of the pubescent female and Orientalist exoticism. (Equally the spectator could read the film more productively as a play on activity and passivity, which resists any simple equation of passive object with feminine, or passive object with oriental, in its depiction of the passion between the Chinaman who is older, sexually experienced and economically potent yet both enthralled by, and fascinating to, the poor young white girl and the powerful elderly writer she becomes.) Duras's writing can be claimed for *écriture féminine* because of its seemingly uncensored relation to the body, to sexuality and to pleasure, its representation of desire which goes to the limit ('jusqu'au bout'), which is not held back by economic considerations, which imposes itself as necessary. The superabundant generosity of Duras's female characters who give themselves (sexually, emotionally), and yet always have more to give, recalls Cixous's feminine economy. Duras's writing, like her characters, is traversed by otherness such as the madness of the beggarwoman (a figure totally outside linguistic communication) or of the vice-consul in *The Vice-Consul* – their passionate shrieks and peals of laughter echo through the text. The body erupts in this way via the voice or in convulsive vomiting or weeping like a hysterical mime of passion (in the sense of both love and suffering unto death). Duras plays with racial difference as well as sexual difference and the inhumanity of exotic nature – for instance, the relentless invasive sea, or the unbearable heat. Her texts are punctured by silences and gaps and by inviting ambiguities both on the level of individual words (a 'poem in a word' as Duras herself puts it) and of plot and characterisation.

Luce Irigaray is another 'French feminist' – sharing much of

Cixous's diagnosis of the masculine economy. Her work is a quest for a new feminine Imaginary, which is sometimes critiqued on the grounds that it is a denial of the Symbolic (necessary for differentiation and therefore to escape psychosis according to Lacanians). We would rather accept Margaret Whitford's argument, that it is a step towards symbolising the relationship to the mother's body.[64] Again the relation to the gift is crucial. Irigaray uses the (female) body, tropes of sexual intercourse and pleasure in her attempts to symbolise anew; for example, she writes of a kiss which is not 'open' in the sense of being the opposite of 'closed', but 'entr'ouvert', a structure which might remind us of Barthes's *The Pleasure of the Text*, the pulsing, the now half-open (or is it half-closed?) flickering of *jouissance*. We choose to refer to this example of lips rather than the much discussed two lips of *This Sex Which is Not One* because it seems to us that by glossing the one with the other it becomes clearer than Irigaray is not biologistic.[65] This (half-)openness escapes classical economies: it cannot be produced (or reproduced), thus it is not a commodity. An *infinite* exchange is set in motion by this half-openness, which is to be distinguished from the closed (finite) system of classical economy. This kiss between two pairs of two lips escapes definition as heterosexual or lesbian:

> But when lips kiss, openness is not the opposite of closure. Closed lips remain open. And their touching allows movement from inside to outside, from outside to in, with no fastening nor opening mouth to stop the exchange.
>
> An exchange of nothing? Which is not without value. Unless you count as nothing the interest accruing to openness. The economy of which does not easily appreciate the price. What is the utility of an open non-object? (*Elemental Passions*, p. 63)

For Irigaray, as for Cixous and Leclerc, the relation to the mother is crucially important.[66] It has, she argues, been left unsymbolised – psychoanalysis and philosophy both rest on the murdered mother. Symbolisation of the maternal relation is essential if women are to be able to love themselves, other women and men. Irigaray's work involves both attempts to map out and open up the future and analysis of psychoanalytic, linguistic and philosophical material which closes out any feminine elements. We shall now turn briefly to other attempts to deconstruct and refeminise philosophy.

The feminisation of philosophy

Jacques Derrida does not attempt to provide a programme for feminism, and yet his writing in general, his analysis of hierarchical binary oppositions, has proved fertile for some feminists, and in certain texts, such as *Spurs* or the interview 'Choreographies', he does address femininity (in)directly. The series of metonyms (of which *différance* is the best known) which he deploys to unsettle the metaphysics of presence includes 'woman' and other words which conjure up female-ness such as 'hymen' or 'invagination'. These words contribute to a resexualisation of philosophy, a discourse which has long wilfully presented itself as objectively neutral, disembodied and dispassionate – in other words, man's talk – where philosophers will claim that man is universal and feminists may beg to differ. Derrida does not propose that, for instance, the hymen or invagination are proper to women (or man). Woman enters *Spurs* as *écriture* rather than as written. Derrida analyses Nietzsche's styles, the woman in Nietzsche, which prevents him from fixing woman in one place (such as truth, deception or affirmative artistry). Men wish to know the difference between truth and lies, and may figure woman as either; but woman is a sceptic who dissimulates, disturbing the phallic economy of castration.

Feminist theorisations or poeticisations of a non-phallic economy are indebted to Derrida (as he is indebted to them); for example, he writes: 'There is no such thing as the essence of woman because woman averts, she is averted of herself [*écarte et s'écarte d'elle-même*]. Out of the depths, endless and unfathomable, she engulfs and distorts all vestige of essentiality, of identity, of property' (*Spurs*, p.51). In 'Choreographies', an interview with Christie V. MacDonald, Derrida explains that dance/madness/joyous disturbance is a step back from history, even revolutionary or feminist history, in so far as it is oriented towards the reappropriation of woman's own essence or truth and therefore phallogocentric. But it need not imply an abandonment of laborious feminist struggle. Kristeva seems to make a similar point:

> A woman cannot 'be'; it is something which does not even belong in the order of *being* [...] In 'woman' I see something that cannot be represented, something that is not said, something above and beyond nomenclatures and ideologies. There are certain 'men' who are familiar with this phenomenon; it is what some modern texts never stop signifying: testing the limits of language and sociality – the law and its transgression, mastery and

jouissance – without reserving one for males and one for females, on the condition that it is never mentioned. ('Woman Can Never Be Defined', pp. 137–8)

Gayatri Spivak has both welcomed and critiqued Derrida's use of concept-words such as hymen or dissemination.[67] She is suspicious of male deconstructionists adopting the position of the feminine before women have had the chance to assert themselves as subjects. The double displacement which she identifies as Derrida's strategy may be less liberating for women who are (for example, in psycho-analytic terms) already doubly displaced (for example, from the clitoris and from the mother). A term like hymen, conjuring up male property rights over women, virginity and wedlock, may be an inauspicious or revelatory choice. Derrida has, of course, selected hymen because of its paradoxical cultural baggage – and perhaps he considers that the tension resulting from the fact that this baggage cannot easily be discarded is a productive one. Spivak also challenges Derrida on the grounds that he relates woman to the simulation of orgasm, and that he is envious of this uniquely feminine ability. It seems to us that this is an overly literal reading of Derrida's play on *se donner* and *se donner pour* in *Spurs* which is a reformulation of the feminine economy in which women both give (themselves) with superabundant generosity and yet are reserved in that they can act a part. It also seems to us that it is to fall into masculine myth-making to assume that only women fake orgasm since, leaving aside the domestic, male actors presumably do precisely this when required. Spivak has also critiqued Kristeva and other 'French feminists' for a privileging of the vagina and womb which (once again) represses the clitoris – the female organ of pure un-productive pleasure which is literally cut off in some cultures, sym-bolically in others, in order to ensure 'normal' accession to womanhood as maternity.[68]

A different point against Derrida is made by Irigaray; she argues that it is too soon to move to plurality of sexes or sexual *différance* since we have not yet experienced two sexes or sexual difference but only the monosexuality of 'man'.[69] Derrida tries to open up thinking on sexual difference which would not be 'sealed by a two' ('Geschlecht: Sexual Difference, Ontological Difference', p. 80). However, as he is well aware, there is no stepping outside of the (linguistic) structures which we inherit even before birth. Male philosophers can write like women but not as women nor as Woman.

The question is open whether the attempt to take on a feminine subject position is yet another appropriation.

And/so ... what about men?

While the terms *feminism* and *feminists* are now familiar in both popular and theoretical discourses, there are no equivalent terms for the study of men's condition(s) or for those who engage in such studies or in socio-political activism for men's liberation. Our placing of this section after extended consideration of women and feminisms is therefore deliberate – in that it reflects the late-come nature of men's studies. It was not until the mid 1980s that men's studies and gay studies emerged as major fields of enquiry, largely as a result of the pluralising of feminism into feminisms and of the exploration of gender theory.[71] Both the term and the concept of 'gender studies' cause a certain anxiety for some feminists. For example, Janet Todd writes in *Feminist Literary History*: 'There is a danger that the study of men, masculinity or homophobia in literature will aim to supersede feminist criticism with its political aim and dimension, will cause not a swerve from and return to feminist issues and women's writings, but a straightforward march out of them' (p. 134). It will be evident from the preceding pages of this Introduction that we view gender studies as a productive means of expanding the ways in which we can analyse sexual difference and problems of social marginalisation. However, we also recognise the political need to maintain a separation (*not* a separatism) between women and men and between gays and straights in fields such as publishing and academic institutions: the 'archaeological' impulse behind the Virago Press, for instance, must be maintained if the canon of texts is ever to be changed, and the specificities of women and gays must be reflected in course structures in teaching institutions – and indeed in the appointments made to posts.

Our Western societies, of course, continue to be patriarchal, so men apparently need to do little, since they are still largely in control of the institutions that determine and regulate both acceptable attitudes and permissible behaviour. However, if they wish to engage in feminism or in explorations calked on feminist researches, they are faced with major problems. Stephen Heath has described men's relation to feminism as 'an impossible one', and Elaine Showalter

has convincingly argued that 'The way into feminist criticism, for
the male theorist, must involve a confrontation with what might
be implied by reading as a man and with a questioning or a surrender
of paternal privileges'.[72] This abdication or interrogation of male
power is undoubtedly desirable, and it is equally imperative for men
to (re-)discover and to define masculinity – which is not as natural,
transparent and unproblematic as many men (and women) have
assumed it to be.

In this context, one thinks, for example, of the hysteria displayed
in 1992 by (mainly male) British politicians and journalists in their
arguments against reducing the age of consent for male homosexuals
to 16 or at least 18, and of the hysteria which marks the discourse
of recent European and American demands for the quarantining or
imprisoning of people with AIDS and even those who have the HIV
virus. Our choice of the term 'hysteria' is wilfully ironic, because
its etymology associates it with the womb and therefore with women.
Originally, it was thought to be a disturbance of the uterus, hence
the 'fact' that women were more liable than men to the disorder.
Histories can often be significant, if sometimes amusing: medieval
gynaecology believed the uterus to be a small animal that lived
essentially on sperm and that, when this was not provided, travelled
through the woman's body in search of some similar nourishment.
It therefore found and ate the cells of the brain, leading to loss of
control (hysteria). Ludicrous as this belief seems to us in an age when
anatomical, neurological and psychoanalytic knowledge is so advanced,
hysteria is still considered to be a feminine weakness (even Freud in
his psychopathological work viewed it as a mainly feminine condition).

In the examples of political responses we have given, there is
clearly a hostility to males who are not proven men, a fear that the
myths of male supremacy and self-control might crumble, and,
crucially, a fear of difference-within-sameness – which corresponds
to a defensive anxiety about the possibility of the loss of manliness.
So are we really being over-manipulative in our application of 'hysterical' to the workings of homophobes who, against the bulk of medical
evidence, insist that AIDS is a 'gay plague'?

In her analyses of the metaphors of illness, Susan Sontag exposes
how (male) military metaphors inform discourses on suffering. In
Illness as Metaphor, she writes: 'Punitive notions of disease have a
long history, and such notions are particularly active with cancer.
There is the "fight" or "crusade" against cancer; cancer is the "killer"

disease; people who have cancer are "cancer victims". [...] And conventions of treating cancer as no mere disease but a demonic enemy make cancer not just a lethal disease but a shameful one' (p.57). In *AIDS and its Metaphors*, Sontag goes further. Exploring the ways in which Western culture has for centuries used the metaphor of 'plague' to designate what are (sometimes wrongly) perceived as epidemics, she argues that 'AIDS has banalized cancer' (p.44) and reminds us that plagues 'are invariably regarded as judgments on society' (p.54). This political manipulation of the 'plague' metaphor has occasionally been challenged – as, for example, in Albert Camus's *The Plague* which literalises the metaphor in order to expose the ways in which politics and religion collude to maintain their societal power. In our insistence on Camus's literalisation of the plague, we clearly diverge from Sontag's view that his use of plague is 'more epitome than metaphor, is detached, stoic, aware – it is not about bringing judgment' (*AIDS*, p.60). However, while *The Plague* might attempt, on an existentialist level at least, to avoid the issues of justice and love, it nonetheless clearly presents resistance as a masculine activity: Oran is a domain in which both homosociality and manliness are privileged.[73]

Rhetoric is an essential arm in the weaponry of those either in power or desperately seeking power, therefore we must be aware that, by dis-covering tropological manoeuvres, we may fall into the trap of merely supplanting one rhetoric by another. In this respect, Sontag's discursive strategy is admirable, for it combines transparency with intertextuality: she ends her analysis of the socio-textual manipulations operated by discourses on AIDS with an 'assault' on the predominance of military metaphors (such as invasion, ravaging and overcoming) and with a provocative plea for the replacement and relocation of such metaphors: 'The body is not a battlefield. The ill are neither unavoidable casualties nor the enemy. We – medecine, society – are not authorized to fight back by any means whatever ... About that metaphor, the military one, I would say, if I may paraphrase Lucretius: Give it back to the war-makers' (p.95). Sontag's exposure of the military metaphors used in medical and political discourses on illness undoubtedly helps to counter the stigmatisation of AIDS sufferers, and therefore has a therapeutic function both for individuals and for society. We would add that the reference to 'the war-makers' unveils the extent to which men continue to impose their language, even in areas where it is patently – and historically – inappropriate. One cannot imagine such renowned medical carers as Florence Nightingale, Edith Cavell or Mother Teresa using the terminology of warfare to describe their work, but they have all used it in their various struggles to gain funds. Does this mean that women are allowed to function politically only if they are perceived as surrogate men?

'Masculine' women

In the ancient world, such powerful leaders as the Queen of Sheba and Cleopatra were described in terms of their femininity and seductiveness. This emphasis, however, in no way detracted – or was meant to detract – from their political power or acumen; rather, it was a recognition of their difference, of their specificity. In the modern period, and especially in Europe, responses to female executive heads of state have testified to a desire to make of them surrogate men. Elizabeth I of England had, for historically understandable reasons, to collude with her courtiers' wish to present her as a man's (military) heart in a woman's body: she had, also, constantly to legitimise her right to govern and to prove herself her 'father's daughter', and to convince a nation that had hardly advanced beyond the fiercely male feudalism of the Middle Ages that a woman could make the right decisions. Queen Victoria, who reigned over the vastest empire the world has seen, was initially much criticised for being over-influenced by Prince Albert and then, after his death, for being 'the Widow of Windsor'.[74] Indeed, it can be argued that it was not until she re-entered the public sphere after her prolonged mourning that she could become (perceived as) a true monarch – because she was now asexual, because she had (re)appropriated the right to legislate on moral, if not on political, issues – as kings were expected to do.

In the contemporary period, major national and international power-brokers such as Indira Gandhi and Margaret Thatcher were presented both by their opponents and by their supporters as essentially male politicians. Another 'father's daughter', Mrs Gandhi was frequently compared with Pandit Jawaharlal Nehru, but usually in order to insist on how much sterner than he/she was. It was not until well after the assassination of her son Rajiv, her (dynastic) successor as Prime Minister, and after the refusal of his widow Sonia to head the Congress Party, that studies of Mrs Gandhi began to focus on her personal roles as daughter and mother and to recognise both that her 'masculinity' was politically constructed by the virility cult associated with the fight for Indian independence and that her 'femininity' was an equally potent element in her wielding and maintaining of power. Margaret Thatcher is perhaps the most discussed woman politician of the past decades. Renowned in political and diplomatic circles for her exploitation of flirtatiousness, of 'feminine wiles', in her dealings with heads of state such as Reagan, Gorbachev and Mitterand, she was (and is still) portrayed as the 'strongest man in British politics'. Despite the recurrent mocking references to her biological father, lampoonists throughout the world seek above all to accord her a genealogy consonant with what men expect politicians to be: she is the 'Iron Lady', i.e. the spiritual descendant of the Duke of Wellington, or she is the men's-suited, cigar-smoking reincarnation of Winston Churchill known to viewers of *Spitting Image*.

By contrast, Edith Cresson may briefly have been Prime Minister of France, but her fall from power had perhaps less to do with her efficiency or political nous than with the way in which she was portrayed by a hostile national and international press: was she Mitterand's mistress? how could she possibly say that most English men are gay? why does she want men to whistle at her in the street? Although these questions may seem silly and irrelevant, they were posed – and analogous questions would not have been posed to male politicians and speculated upon. Mme Cresson's major error was to assume that women had politically 'come of age' and that they no longer needed to act like/as men.

In other words, women are not allowed to be (seen as) women in politics. These examples are, of course, selective, but it is useful to point out that Mrs Gandhi and Mrs Thatcher, two of the most important political figures of the past two decades are women-defined-as-men, women who were both feared and admired for their tenacity, ambition and aggression and described as more masculine than their ministers. If women can be better men than men in the political arena, what happens then to men? And, more importantly, how does this affect the categories of manhood and manliness which are assumed by many men to be taken for granted, inviolate, permanent?

The question of who or what 'men' are must therefore be addressed. Indeed, can 'men' be any longer a useful category in political debate or, indeed, in theoretical speculation? Does a biological description actually define any individual or any group? In other words, is it not time to undo or to deconstruct the violent hierarchies of man/woman,

male/female, straight/gay, active/passive? (We have deliberately put
the 'patriarchal' terms first in these 'oppositions' in order to underline
ironically how thinkers tend automatically to privilege what Adrienne
Rich calls 'the oppressor's language'.)

These questions are important, because they challenge the language
of gender, of sexuality, or 'sexness' – and threaten the 'taken for
granted' syndrome which assumes that we all know what a man is.
Feminism as a plural and often self-interrogating, even self-aggressing,
movement increasingly chooses to blur the distinctions between the
social needs and the personal desires of women, so that some progress
towards recognition and equality may be made: lesbians speak on the
same platforms as straight women, publish in the same journals and
books, are regarded as 'sisters'. The concept of sisterhood has been
widely accepted by feminists and incorporated into their activist
and theoretical work.[75] The same does not hold, though, in the
domain of men's studies, where straight men are often nervous about
being aligned with gay men: for a variety of cultural and historical
reasons, 'brotherhood' is understood by many people as connoting
a closed circle, be it one of Christianity, Freemasonry or ethno-politics
as in reggae and 1990s rap.

It is clear that we see gender as a socially constructed category, one
might even say a symbolic category. The political, economic and
psychoanalytic slants of much recent feminist theory inevitably
mark contemporary men's studies, but it is useful also to approach
the question of what a man is from an anthropological point of view –
which creatively problematises the nature versus nurture and essentialism versus constructionism debates. In the preface to his important
study of the ideology of masculinity, *Manhood in the Making: Cultural
Concepts of Masculinity*,[76] David D. Gilmore points out that, while
most societies have some idea about 'true' manhood and while men
in very different cultures share analogous concepts and/or anxieties,
one of the main problems he encountered in researching his book
was the fact that 'there is no recognized place to look up "manhood"
as a cultural category' (pp. xi–xii). In terms of Western politics, this
void is hardly surprising, since Western cultures remain phallocentric,
even phallocratic (indeed, Irigaray has argued provocatively that
Western society is essentially homosexual, even paedophilically
homosexual, in its exercise(s) of power and in its choices of what
to allow to be said and of what should remain silent). However,
the evident – and imposed – lack of reference to masculinity and

manhood in the databases of ethnography and anthropology is both revelatory and worrying. Gilmore asserts that 'there is something almost generic, something repetitive, about the criteria of man-playing [...] in many societies', although he is careful to propose 'a ubiquity rather than a universality' of societal imagings of the man (pp. 2–3). So why the silence? Is a taboo at work?

A first answer is that men do not *need* to speak of themselves because, in Western culture at least, language as both a political and a linguistic structure already privileges men/the male. A more convincing answer, however, may be that men do not *want* to speak of themselves – for fear of losing the authority conferred by centuries of control over social practices and over language. Yet to become a 'man' is to become socialised: biological sexing is not sufficient, the boy must choose to accept the precepts and limitations of his society – and so privilege societalism over individualism. Although we disagree somewhat with Gilmore's early statement that 'manhood ideals make an *indispensable* contribution both to the continuity of social systems and to the psychological integration of men into their continuity' (p. 3; our emphasis), we endorse his concluding remarks on how gender ideologies pressure people into acting in certain ways and on how manhood is a *script* which has more to do with society's needs than with the individual's needs or desires (p. 224).

Becoming a man: initiation

Beauvoir's assertion in *The Second Sex* that one is not born a woman but becomes a woman can, and indeed should, be translated into male terms. This, however, poses a problem for men. While Beauvoir argues that women (as *adult* females) should discover, establish and give agency to their specificity, the history of men encourages men to believe that the essential moment is the rite of passage from boyhood to manhood. In other words, once he has become a man, the male need have no more anxieties! In many ancient cultures (and still in several non-Western societies), the passage from boyhood to manhood is marked by initiations based on physical ordeals, such as circumcision which is performed in public and without anaesthetic. In *The Worlds of a Masai Warrior: An Autobiography*, Tepilit Oli Saitoti reveals how, just before the ceremony, he was warned not even to blink because 'The slightest movement on your part will mean you are a coward, incompetent and unworthy to be a Masai man' (p. 142). For the Masai, manhood is therefore equated with courage – although it should be noted that this courage must be moral as well as physical, since the entry into manhood is also entry into the tribe as a responsible protector. While circumcision, or, more accurately, female excision which involves both clitoridectomy and the severance of the vaginal lips, is performed on Masai girls, they are not expected to show an equivalent stoicism. Indeed, while many scream or try to escape and while warriors may be called to hold down the victims, they are not stigmatised by this 'weakness' as are boys, because, as Melissa Llewelyn-Davies shows, their ability to endure pain silently is 'of little public significance' ('Women, Warriors, and Patriarchs', p. 351).

The Masai justification for excision is bound up with concerns with property and control over dependants, but, although aware of the risks involved in imposing Western concepts on, and even in juxtaposing Western concepts with, African cultures, we would also suggest that the practice of excision offers a physical (and societal) manifestation of Freud's theory of how one becomes a woman. In 'The Transformations of Puberty' where he discusses sexual activity in childhood and adolescence, he writes: 'in order to become a woman a further stage of repression is necessary, which discards a portion of infantile masculinity and prepares the woman for changing her leading genital zone' (On Sexuality, p. 159). Freud's views are determined by his belief that 'Anatomy is Destiny' ('The Dissolution of the Oedipus Complex', On Sexuality, p. 320), although even he admits to a 'suspicion that the choice between "innate" and "acquired" is not an exclusive one' ('The Sexual Aberrations', On Sexuality, p. 51). In his perception of womanhood and manhood as states that can be defined in biological terms, Freud is both following nineteenth-century notions and offering to twentieth-century men the possibility of leaving aside the anxiety of how to become a man once one has passed puberty, hence the importance of translating Beauvoir's radical proposition into male terms.

The role of the public gaze is crucial for all initiatory ceremonies, but boys are expected to *perform* actively whereas girls merely *submit* to the knife: so when boys become men, they assume the mantle of activity; when girls become women, they assume the mantle of passivity. Despite the specificities of Masai culture, its ritualised separation of the equations man = active and woman = passive is found *mutatis mutandis* in most societies. Yet there is little biological justification for this division. Referring to the work of the biological anthropologist Melvin Konner, Gilmore writes that 'testosterone (the main male sex hormone) predisposes males to a *slightly* higher level of aggressivity than females' (*Manhood*, p.22; our emphasis), but he concludes by arguing that 'men are innately not so very different from women and need motivation to be assertive' (*Manhood*, p.230).

In 'The Transformations of Puberty', where he argues that an understanding of bisexuality is essential for an understanding of the sexual manifestations in men and women, Freud writes in a foot-note added in 1915: 'Every individual [...] displays a mixture of the character-traits belonging to his own and to the opposite sex; and he shows a combination of activity and passivity whether or not these last character-traits tally with his biological ones' (*On Sexuality*, p.142). His psychoanalytical speculations therefore complement anthropological and sociological findings: manhood is recognised to be a scenario, a symbolic script which males are expected to follow to the letter. Despite his insistence on separating the masculine and the feminine principles (the *animus* and the *anima*), Jung too accepted in his psychological and psychoanalytical speculations that both these principles are to be found within each human psyche. Interestingly, though, while he argues in 'Initiation and the Develop-ment of Masculinity' that life is a continuous series of initiations and that genuine development will inevitably result in the renuncia-tion of pretensions to heroic mastery, he insistently privileges the masculine by suggesting that it is coterminous with 'bright conscious-ness' and that the feminine, the *anima*, can compensate in the second part of one's life for the loss of ego (seen as a 'descent'). (See *Aspects of the Masculine*, pp.25–36.) Furthermore, in his essays on the feminine, there are virtually no references to initiation(s). This is undoubtedly due to Jung's association of the masculine with con-sciousness, both personal and cultural, but it is none the less worryingly phallocentric. Both Freud and Jung were, of course, working and writing in a society before feminism achieved even the degree of recognition it is grudgingly accorded today, but their common marginalisation of female initiations/rites of passage is still sufficiently marked to witness to an anxiety about sexual (and gender) difference.

Initiations have a double function: they permit the individual to 'grow up', to enter the world of adults, and they confirm the solidity, the 'safeness', of the community within a community into which initiates are admitted. However, we would insist on the fact that such passages are more than social. In Africa, South America and aboriginal Australia, the rite of passage is not just a single, once-and-for-ever transitional event; it is often marked visually, *textually* by tattoos, scarification, piercing of body parts, or body painting. In other words, it is not enough to have become a man or a woman – a mark must be left for others to read, the body must be a text. We would thus argue that initiations should be seen as entries into textuality as well as into adult sexuality.

Here it is useful to refer to religious initiations in modern Western culture. In Christian communities, a child can be confirmed at any age as long as s/he can satisfactorily answer all the questions of the relevant catechism. In Jewish communities, the ritualisation of rites of passage is even more textually grounded. Judaism may be matrilinear in 'genetic' and familial terms, but one of its main initiatory ceremonies is the Bar Mitzvah, whereby a boy of about 13 years publicly shows his manhood by being able to recite and comment on passages from the Torah. The term Bar Mitzvah means 'son of commandment, man of duty', thereby conjoining the expectations of dutiful filiation with those of responsible adulthood. This conjunction is analogous to that presupposed in African and Moslem circumcision ceremonies, but there is a major difference. Jewish boys are circumcised in the first weeks after their birth in order that they may (passively) re-enact the pact made with God by the Chosen People. Their public entry into manhood, into cultural fitness, is thus left until they can show manhood not through physical courage but through their ability to read, to engage with the textual past and present of their religion. (Within the Reform movement, there is the Bat Mitzvah, an equivalent ceremony for girls. On one level, this marks a progress away from the sternly patriarchal nature of Judaism, but it should be noted that the ceremony for girls is calked on that for boys.)

Testicular and effeminate men

In the modern secularised West, there remains in many domains a residue of the equation of manhood and manliness. This residue is frequently coded and consequently forgotten by many of those who use what they think are neutral terms. For instance, the notion of testimony which is central to Western jurisprudence and legal practice first arose in Roman law – but we tend to forget the functional and etymological link between testimony and testicles (in Ancient Rome, no one could give evidence unless he was properly hung, i.e. unless his testicles were there – and in the right place!). Another example is that of the Pope who, allegedly even today, must be medically examined before the public proclamation of his election in order to ensure that *Habet* (he's got them, i.e. testicles). This widespread belief 'testifies' to an anxiety that a woman might ascend to the throne of St Peter, as did the apocryphal ninth-century Pope Joan (John VIII) who is said to have died in childbirth. So the supreme Catholic pontiff must paradoxically prove his masculinity – in order to be able to deny active sexuality to his priests. Furthermore, the central Christian concept of virtue is etymologically linked to the Latin *vir* (man, soldier) and *virtus* (valour, moral excellence): in order to be a worthy Holy Father, the Pope must be sexed, so that he can demonstrate his manliness by exerting self-restraint.

Our two testicular examples show that in Western culture masculinity is not, *pace* Freud and the post-Freudians, only phallocentric. Indeed, as we shall see in greater detail later, the reference to (metaphorised) testicles is one of the ways by which gay men differentiate themselves through discourse from straight men: possessors of a penis and so presumed to be endowed with a phallus, many gay men *say* their difference as men within a male-determined culture by focusing on a different portion of their genitalia, thereby denying the authority of phallic power. One of the major problems for contemporary Western males is the equation of masculinity with virility. Fathers are still to be heard saying to their teenage sons who are being bullied or are reluctant to participate in sports: 'Show me (or us or them) that you're a man'. These sporting activities are, however, phallically hierarchised. Activities such as ballet and ice skating which are equally strenuous but associated with artistry (and therefore with femininity) are considered to be less masculine than football, rugby, basketball, baseball or boxing. In an increasingly secularised society, the sports field and the locker-room have become the sites of initiatory rites which may operate through 'feminine' gossip and mockery, but where the virile, phallic father still rules: 'his' text is the script to be followed by his sons, even though this text is usually one dictated by a phallocratic society rather than by his own empirical and intuitive experiences.

The cult of virility is certainly not universal, but the economic and cultural supremacy of the West, and especially of the USA, tends increasingly to impose this cult as a model of manhood. From Heming-way onwards, the American 'virility school' of writing has insisted on the importance of achieving manhood through passing tests of courage and deprivation – in a context of homosociality, as defined by Eve Kosofsky Sedgwick (see *Between Men*, pp. 1–21). Hollywood films have almost systematically legitimised the view that boys/young men must 'win their spurs' through acts of individual bravery – which are proofs that they are worthy to be protectors of their tribe. However, the virility cult of Westerns has been developed more worryingly in the various series of *Rocky*, *Rambo* and *Terminator* films, all of which ally virility with imperialism and even with racism. (*Rocky 4* is a particularly noxious example of cultural and political imperialism masquerading as a presentation of the nobility of boxing.) Constantly, there is the need to *show*, to prove against all odds that one is a man – and a man is someone who both conforms to and supports the dominant ideology. As Leonard Kriegel states in his survey of American male attitudes: 'In every age, not just our own, manhood was something that had to be won' (*On Men and Manhood*, p. 14).

Kriegel's perspective is, of course, determined by the material he chooses to analyse; he focuses on 'white' America and therefore takes no account of such fascinating, if problematic, cases as the Cheyenne *berdache* who is an 'honorary woman', an androgynous, almost transsexual figure much respected in his/her tribe.[77] This disregard for native Americans is analogous to much British sexo-anthropological work which determines manhood in Eurocentric terms and therefore often assumes that, for example, Indian men were 'feminised' or 'castrated' by the imperatives and practices of colonial rule. These arguments have an undoubted value and force, but, as we shall explore later, Hindu culture offers a creative alternative to the manhood-as-virility presupposition, precisely because of the specificity of its cosmology which even the British Raj could not efface.

While implicitly recognising that not all men are 'real' men, Western men are reluctant to admit that biological maleness has little to do with manhood. This reluctance may well be the result of the centuries-old tradition of maintaining male hegemony by refusing to throw the (problematic) notion of masculinity into the forum of genuine public debate – which might then have to be censored ... Masculinity has always spoken itself and been spoken about, yet this very garrulousness conceals an anxiety as to what it might really be, as to whether it can be defined, hence the manipulative force of silence-within-discourse. At one point in his subtle consideration of the relations between sexuality and the discourses that ignore, permit or determine it, Foucault writes: 'power is tolerable only on condition that it mask a substantial part of itself. Its success is proportional to its ability to hide its own mechanisms. [...] For power, secrecy is not in the nature of an abuse, it is indispensable to its operation' (*History of Sexuality*, I, p. 86). Even today, many heterosexual men who mouth the rhetoric of solidarity with 'minorities' nonetheless choose to believe that sexual politics is essentially about the rights of women and gay men and has little to do with them. In an essay in which he makes clear that he is writing as a heterosexual man of the left, Jonathan Rutherford challenges this complacency: 'Heterosexual masculinity shifts its problems and anxieties, defining them as belonging to others'.[78] While this modern self-protective projection of insecurities on to those perceived as other is a manipulation of silence, it is also blind and deaf to the many historical interrogations of the social place of gender. For instance, as Lawrence E. Klein points out in this volume, eighteenth-century women were perceived as a force for politeness, so when men sought to appropriate politeness, this raised questions about male identity and led them to regender it in a masculine way to insure themselves against effeminacy.[79]

There is, in fact, a long tradition of 'effeminate' men: Elizabethan courtiers, fops, exquisites, beaux, dandies and, more recently, 'gender-benders' such as Boy George. While this 'effeminacy' may in various historical periods have been exploited by some gay men, its main importance lies less in its appropriation of femininity than in its theatricality, in its performativity and consequent non-referentiality.[80] There must always be a political sub-text to extravagant (or, conversely, minimalist) visual ornamentation or to cross-dressing. However, we would point out that the adoption by men of 'feminine' dress codes is usually determined and accompanied by a concern with display, with the ways in which aesthetic – and, ultimately, ontological – beliefs can be proclaimed by the ways in which the body is dressed and presented for public scrutiny. Displays and paradings by men of effeminacy need not, of course, entail a loss of masculinity. We would suggest that the difference between straight and gay men who wear make-up, pastel colours, frilly shirts, etc. or who dress in full drag is a quantitative rather than a qualitative difference: gay men simply have a greater tendency to play in and out of the lure of femininity as display-as-availability.

Gender studies increasingly focus on the functionality of display. In *Epistemology of the Closet*, and borrowing J. L. Austin's terminology, Kosofsky Sedgwick gives a wittily multi-layered example: 'a T-shirt that ACT UP sells in New York bearing the text "I am out, therefore I am," is meant to do for the wearer, not the constative work of reporting that s/he *is* out, but the performative work of coming out in the first place' (p. 4). The T-shirt's slogan is a politically acute parody of Descartes's *Cogito*, but the wearing of such items is perhaps a little more than a performative act of self-outing: it proclaims that dress codes themselves need to be interrogated. Transvestism is gradually becoming more widely accepted, yet there continues to be an assumption that transvestites are gay, i.e. men who would like to be women, whereas surveys show that transvestism is at least as common among heterosexual men as among gays – and, of course, the myth that gays are would-be women is still all too prevalent. Paradoxically, in an era when sexuality is much more publicly debated, queer-bashing is on the increase, no doubt because men especially are frightened by the blurring of genders. The 1980s 'New Man' who featured largely in *Mothercare* catalogues and in articles in the press about sharing childcare, and therefore as a heterosexual and a father, was defined by his sensitivity (not unlike the eighteenth-century 'Man of Feeling'). He was a man committed to collaboration in domesticity, but he rapidly became a target for male mockery: 'manly' men thought that it was not enough to have proved his masculinity/ virility by siring children – he should also be seen to engage publicly, outside the home, in appropriate 'manly' activities, such as rugby or drinking in the pub. However, the demise of the 'New Man' owes less to such masculinist attitudes than to the response of women who pointed out that, in *material* ways, he was insufficiently different from the 'Old Man': he might take the children to the park at the weekend and pick up some groceries, but this was just another example of peacocking display, whereas the woman remained the custodian of the sink, the cooker and the washing-machine.

In *Armies of the Night*, Norman Mailer, one of the American proponents of the virility cult (who is probably unaware of the complexity and radicalism of Beauvoir's assertion on womanhood which underlines the importance of self-choosing), states baldly: 'Nobody was born a man; you earned manhood provided you were good enough, bold enough' (p. 25).[81] Yet we tend to forget that the Western ideology of manhood as proclaimed virility is a fairly recent phenomenon. In Victorian England, it was not until the 1880s that the 'stiff upper lip' became a defining feature of masculinity – and even Kipling's imperialist notions of how to be/become a Man were soon contested by First World War poets such as Brooke, Owen and Sassoon who chose to insist on the *pity* of war and, by extension, of men.

An extreme example of a transvestite is the seventeenth-century Abbé de Choisy, a close friend of Monsieur, the brother of Louis XIV, who participated actively in the French campaign against Holland (dressed as a man), became France's Ambassador to Siam and, after being ordained a priest, wrote an eleven-volume study of the history of the Church, but whose main fantasy was to dress as a woman. De Choisy's early career involved several months as an actress in Bordeaux playing *coquette* roles and when he returned to Paris he soon became a leader of female fashion. None the less he was – and, at least at Louis XIV's court, was known to be – a notorious hetero-sexual libertine whose conquests were as numerous as those of Don Juan. His choice to lead a man's life within and behind a mask of femininity may have been determined by the fact that, throughout his childhood, his mother dressed him as a girl, but the crucial point is that his transvestism was accepted, condoned and even (perhaps ironically) approved by a society which was dominated by concerns with power: as a supremely theatrical figure, de Choisy incarnated the Sun King's belief in, and dependence on, display as a strategy making possible the imposition of total authority.[82]

De Choisy's case teaches us much about the need to abandon the presupposition that we are ineluctably locked in an (ant)agonistic post-Victorian society wherein gender identities must be separated and identified as absolutes. As Foucault has consistently argued, we need to take account of gender and sexual practices in societies before the 'fall' (or the 'ascent') into the language of sexuality. Yet in order fully to interrogate the concept of masculinity and manhood, we must also be aware that most available cultural and historical studies are Eurocentric and that anthropological investigations of other societies offer insights which may aid us to understand, subvert and ultimately deconstruct Western categories of masculinity and femininity, and of sexual difference.

Hindu alternatives

In Hindu mythology, the gods are male, female and/or androgynous. Furthermore, as Wendy O'Flaherty has shown in *Women, Androgynes, and Other Mythical Beasts*, much Vedic iconography includes an imaging of the child as consort (see pp. 100–5). 'Absolute', 'virile' manliness is thus not encoded as a prerequisite for adult life; it is not imposed on boys and men as the necessary condition for societal success and acceptance. Indeed, as Sudhir Kakar points out in *The Inner World* (p. 110), Hindu cosmology includes an unusual degree of femininity: many of the most powerful gods are portrayed as female. These female gods (who, unlike their Greek and Roman analogues, cannot be hierarchised or demeaned by references to one overseeing, dictatorial male deity) function variously – and often simultaneously – as symbolic incarnations of what Kleinian theory would describe as 'the good breast' or 'the bad breast'. They permit and promote for men an attachment to the mother which leads to an acceptance of sexual ambiguity that might, in Western psychoanalytic terms, be seen as regressive (pre-Oedipal) rather than as Oedipal and dominated by castration anxiety. In Indocentric terms, however, the living-out of unresolved sex-identity conflicts can be a creatively mimetic enactment of episodes in founding texts such as the *Mahabharata* where kings may, when transformed into women, seek to remain women. Kakar and Ross have suggested in *Tales of Sex* that, for men, sex reversal with its concomitant abdication of phallic identity is an unconscious theme embedded in Indian culture (p. 99). While their argument is Indo-specific, they also propose that the fantasy of unity with the 'good mother', however bound up with fantasies of infan-tilisation it may be, is a fantasy shared by men in all other cultures.

This view is not as different from Western psychoanalytic thinking as might be thought. Freud suggests in 'The Transformations of Puberty' and, more powerfully, in *Beyond the Pleasure Principle* where regression is given the status of an ontological drive, that regression is functionally present in all formations of character-structuring and mental work. In *The Ego and the Mechanisms of Defense*, Anna Freud located regression as the primary defence mechanism and, in her much later essay, 'Regression as a Principle in Mental Development', argued that the child's desire to seek protection in the symbiotic and pre-Oedipal mother-relationship is always somehow present in, and underpinning, adult behaviour (pp. 138–9).

Irigaray's controversially feminist psychoanalysis, which insists on the role of the mother as the first, the last and even the permanent ego-model (though not ego-object), is also largely focused on regression, albeit with an understandable reluctance to use that term with its pejorative undertones.

Hindu culture is a useful (counter-)model for Westerners, because it simultaneously upholds notions of 'warrior' virility (with all the anxieties about potency that these entail) and offers psychologically determining texts and images which foreground ambivalence and gender ambiguity. Above all, by presenting gods and kings as polymorphous, it inscribes considerations of manhood and masculinity into a dialectic which can never be finally resolved – whereas in the West, the individual and collective operations of repression and suppression ensure that masculinity is rarely fully addressed as a multi-faceted problem. Hindu cosmology undoubtedly presents and permits androgyny as an acceptable male position, but this does not mean that it liberates women from oppression. The Hindu wife, mother, sister or daughter is expected to care for her menfolk and has no (or very few) social or textual models which might enable her to operate a process of individuation. So the Hindu psycho-sexual model is good for men, but it offers little hope or even exploratory space for women.

Androcentrism

Western languages are largely androcentric: 'man', 'l'homme', 'der Mensch' and so on are the terms used to designate the human being. Language is thus political, but it does not only oppress women, as Irigaray and her socio-linguist collaborators argue in *Sexes et genres*; it may well protect men who are anxious about their sexuality, yet it equally oppresses men who do not (want to) conform to the dominant ideology. Even Foucault's historical and sociological writings on sexuality tend to establish an essentially masculine model: in *Patterns of Dissonance*, Rosi Braidotti goes so far as to suggest that he 'forgets, following tradition, the factor of sexual difference' and that 'when Foucault speaks of the body, he is (almost always) speaking about the man's body' (p. 95). This tradition is not an unbroken continuum but it has acquired great force in the twentieth century. The contemporary West has elevated the *ideology* of masculinity as virility into a *myth* which allows little space for (anxious) speculation: as Barthes says, myth can 'reach everything, corrupt everything' (*Mythologies*, p. 144). We would argue that, while feminism has brought gender issues into the domain of the speakable, and while men are increasingly questioning how they may rewrite themselves and the language of masculinity, the problem of myth remains.

It is useful here to consider Barthes's elaboration of what myth is and does: 'Myth does not deny things, on the contrary, its function is to talk about them; simply, it purifies them, it makes them innocent, it gives them natural and eternal justification, it gives them clarity which is not that of explanation but that of a statement of fact' (*Mythologies*, p. 156). Whereas Foucault allows (partially and strategically) a place to silence and secrecy in the mechanisms of ideology and power within society, Barthes focuses on myth's ability to impose its authority by talking, by stating, by making public. In the context of men's studies, these apparently contradictory views are less opposed than might initially be thought. Both theorists perceive and present masculinity/male sexuality in terms of systems which are bound up with a concern with textuality – and yet, despite their 'committed' articulation of the problematics of individuation, they fall (to a certain extent) into the trap of naturalising and essentialising men – because men's studies has no real history, because 'man', unlike 'woman', has not yet become an object of multifarious discourses.

Peter Schwenger suggests in his study of modern 'masculine' writing that men are nervous about the 'effeminacy' of writing as a professional practice (although the established canon is largely made up of 'great' male writers!), and he concludes by stating that 'Fully to write one's manhood would be to write one's death' (*Phallic Critiques*, p. 153). This position is tenable only if one recognises its irony and its ambivalence. The symbolic death involved is not the death of oneself proposed by Christian theology but a swerve away from ideology into the uncharted, unscripted domains of masculinity as a separate territory which borders on, and, more importantly, overlaps with, that of femininity, a territory which is real rather than mythic.

Homosexuality and its discontents

One of the major advances in our understanding(s) of what a man is has been made by gay studies which, as a political and theorising practice, seeks to question and subvert the category of manliness. Aggressively attentive to the coercive force of historical presuppositions, many non-heterosexual men now seek to offer a new social presence (of ambivalence and uncertainty) – and a new textuality that will say and do different things, a textuality that will both contest the assumption that sexualisation is necessarily gender-specific and also foreground local, intra-sexual specificities.

In 'The Sexual Aberrations', Freud states explicitly that a homosexual orientation does not necessarily entail a loss of 'masculinity': 'In men the most complete mental masculinity can be combined with inversion' (*On Sexuality*, p. 53). The use of the term 'inversion' is undoubtedly problematic in that it rehearses, in psychoanalytic thinking, the vocabulary of medical and anatomical treatises from Galen until the Renaissance, most of which assert that the female genitals are an inverted form of the male genitals and/or that the clitoris is merely a dwarfed and concealed penis.[83] However, we should recognise that one of the main problems for homosexual men (and/or for those engaged in gay studies) is precisely the difficulty of finding appropriate terms.

In the modern world, terms have been *given* to gay men (sodomite, invert, pansy, poof, queer, faggot, etc.), and gay men have responded by inventing their own terms or reappropriating appellations from the dominant discourse (Uranian, gay, queen, friend of Dorothy's, golfer, faggot, queer, etc.). What is important for our purposes is that for homophobes the labels are interchangeable (although they may represent different class positions of the speaking subject), whereas for gays a taxonomic principle is usually at work, that is to say, even within systems which may be problematically coded, differences are made clear. Since homophobia is actively articulated and encouraged in the tabloid press and in supermarket magazines with their crude metaphorisations of homosexuality (of all forms) as 'deviant', gays and lesbians are beginning to realise that their sexuality is a linguistic issue as much as it is a political issue, hence their appropriation of previously pejorative terms such as 'faggot', 'dyke', and 'queer'. This last term is perhaps the most emblematic of the gay practice of re-coding language: for decades, gays resented it because it *says* that homosexuality is abnormal, yet the gay community has now chosen it as a kind of battle-cry, as a proclamation of difference and, more importantly, of presence. By deviating or re-routing a term which designates deviance, gays in the 1990s intend to combat not so much their political and social invisibility (that war has been – almost – won) as the apparent indifference of politicians to the pandemic problem of AIDS – and here it should be remembered that from the early nineteenth century onwards, 'pandemic' has been used to mean not only 'worldwide' but also 'relating to vulgar or sensual love'. Today's politicians often choose to use this latter sense in order to exculpate themselves from their 'sin of omission', that is to say the lack of public funding for AIDS research and AIDS education. However, the 'queer' or any other strategically homogenising label also poses problems within and for the gay community, precisely because it offers an umbrella term which unites gay men and lesbians of all sorts and thereby hinders public recognition of the differences that exist within homosexuality and lesbianism.

Language and its (re)codings are crucial agonistic operatives in the politics of homosexuality; they are also, as we shall show in greater detail later, means by which the gay community plays – in a seriously ludic way – on and with secrecy. It should be remembered, though, that the anxiety about language is a relatively modern phenomenon and that it was only in 1869 that the word 'homosexual' was coined – and, interestingly, its popular usage preceded that of 'heterosexual'. Sedgwick points out that it was initially 'a relatively gender-neutral term [...] though it has always seemed to have at least some male bias' (*Epistemology*, p. 17). This near-neutrality has been challenged by Irigaray who, in her sociological thinking, uses the neologism 'hom(m)osexuality' which parenthetically inscribes the male (the French 'homme') into the human being (the Latin 'homo') and which she uses to describe a society in which men exchange goods and women. While we prefer Sedgwick's term of homosociality with its emphasis on male bonding (which is not necessarily sexual and which men often effect exploitatively through the mediation of a woman), we also accept that Irigaray is justified in her conviction that male sexualities inform the political operations of Western societies.

Already in 1917, Hans Blüher argued that male homoeroticism was the force underlying the political state and that consequently homosexuality, especially that between men and boys, should be publicly reinstated as an integral aspect of masculine behaviour.

Modelled somewhat simplistically on the ideology of ancient Gre
city-states, his theory is, however, supported by the more historically
grounded work of Foucault, who, without seeking wholly to de-
sexualise pederastic relations, insists that they found a complex
(and ultimately desirable) societality: 'What is important to grasp
is not why the Greeks had a fondness for boys but why they had a
"pederasty", that is, why they elaborated a courtship, a moral reflection
and [. . .] a philosophical asceticism, around the fondness' (*History
of Sexuality*, II, p. 214).

One of the most important historians of sexuality, Foucault (like
Barthes) has a tendency to legitimise (to 'sanitise') sex through the
process of theorising: Greek homosexuality is presented as an essentially political practice and little attention is paid to the physicality of
pederastic relations and, in his considerations of modern homosexuality, he repeatedly insists that, before the nineteenth century
when the term was invented, there was no male homosexuality as
we understand and perceive it today. Recognising both that same-sex
practices and same-sex desire could – and can still – occur within
a range of public identities and that different historical periods assigned
different labels to homo/sexuality, Foucault makes a convincing
constructionist argument: the term 'homosexual' designates someone who adopts a homosexual identity, but this process of self-
identification can take place only when such an identity is available
in contemporaneous social discourses: 'Homosexuality appeared as
one of the forms of sexuality when it was transposed from a practice
of sodomy into a kind of interior androgyny, a hermaphrodism of
the soul. The sodomite had been a temporary aberration; the homosexual was now a species' (*History of Sexuality*, I, p. 43). Sodomy
has always been practised, but it was and is 'an utterly confused
category' (p. 101). The 'sodomite' was someone who performed
certain discrete acts but who was not defined by them – indeed,
as Jonathan Dollimore points out, 'before the nineteenth century,
the meanings of terms like sodomy and buggery might have been even
wider than is suggested by Foucault's argument' (*Sexual Dissidence*,
p. 238), and we would add that even today, in the legislation of some
states in the USA, the term 'sodomy' is used to designate a wide
variety of sexual practices. For Foucault, sodomy was a kind of
behaviour, whereas modern homosexuality is an identity – an identity
which is not necessarily associated with performance.

Foucault is now often criticised (especially by gay men), not for

ist stance which is valid and illuminating, but for
e uses in his argumentation. Many gay men resent
ogyny' and 'hermaphrodism', which they see as
the (biologising) 'Third Sex' theories of Krafft-Ebing
........., they also justifiably point out that Foucault pays
scanty attention to contemporary – and politically necessary –
definitions of the homosexual. However, we read his work differently:
given that his project is to adumbrate, or even to create, a history
of (homo)sexuality, it is crucial for him to employ/redeploy the very
terms that have historically marginalised gay men and practices.
We would thus argue that his discursive strategy is creatively ironic.
By re-inserting into contemporary discourses on homosexuality the
terms and concepts of the past, he challenges us to scrutinise all
terms that we might use, re-appropriate or invent to describe ourselves
or others.

In 'The Sexual Aberrations', Freud offers a psychoanalytic view
which usefully counterpoints Foucault's theory: 'In men, the most
complete mental masculinity can be combined with inversion' (*On
Sexuality*, p.53). Although we would reject the essentialism inherent
in Freud's position (is there really *one* masculinity?), we agree with
his distinction between what one does and how one perceives oneself,
and follow Foucault in believing that homosexuality is not a question
of acts, of preferences, even of the sex of one's partner, but of how
one identifies oneself – as an individual before even as a member of
a community.

However, the once criminalised and now still marginalised and
'minority' status of homosexuality has meant that, in order to be able
to express their acquired sense of identity, homosexuals have elaborated
coded languages, for instance, 'Polari', the secret language of gay men
in the London of the 1940s and 1950s. These languages serve as
bonding mechanisms, even if the practices and desires of the individuals differ widely. They are also proofs of the power relationship
between textuality and sexuality. One of the most celebrated articu-
lations of homosexual anxiety (which is often wrongly attributed to
Oscar Wilde) is Lord Alfred Douglas's statement in *Two Loves*: 'I am
the Love that dare not speak its name'. The point made here is central
to the politics of homosexuality, even now. Male heterosexual love/
desire *need* not speak its name because it is (presumed to be) the
norm; it undoubtedly speaks itself by saying itself, but it never names
itself, and so imposes its authority through the lacunary nature of

its discourse. Yet gay men, like women, are increasingly aware oι the constructing and determining power of language, hence the recent proliferation of linguistic and physical codes and of (wilful) manipulations of etymology.

In all societies, verbal and visual signals play an important role in courtship. The tapping of a fan, the dropping of a lace handkerchief, the lifting of a veil, the theft of a blanket, the acceptance to dance twice with the same man, the gift of one red rose (rather than a bouquet of red roses), the invitation to 'come back for coffee': all these are crucial markers of desire, albeit in different periods and cultures. The major point is that courtship is universally ritualised and that in each society the relevant codes are known to all – or, at least, to a numerically significant subgroup. (Societal specificity is, of course, problematic: for example, despite Ophelia's detailed, if delirious, cataloguing of flowers in *Hamlet*, a contemporary reader may not recognise the full symbolism of flowers in Shakespeare's plays or in Milton's poems, and a Japanese visitor to a French home may not comprehend the dismay of his hostess when he presents her with chrysanthemums – the flowers of life in Japan, they are the flowers of death in France.)

Codes are essential to the workings of society, but they also operate as defences against incomers. In this volume, Ross Chambers uses the concept of homosociality in his reading of Alan Hollinghurst's *The Swimming-Pool Library* in order to demonstrate the codedness of language. Precisely because of their marginal status, many homosexuals have elected to talk and write in code, so as to challenge the defining and 'fixing' function of social discourse. In their various prefaces to Renaud Camus's *Tricks* (an account of Camus's gay encounters), both Barthes and Camus insist on such terms as 'innocence', 'tranquillity' and 'objectivity'. While Barthes's desexualising of these erotic tales may be underpinned by his reluctance to appear publicly (i.e. in print) as gay,[84] Camus's position is characteristic of the recent trend of gay writers in France to legitimise their sexuality by denying that their (life and) works are titillating or pornographic. Jean-Louis Bory argues the case even more strongly: 'There is no need to *admit* that one is gay, because this is not a crime or a sin. There is no need to *proclaim* that one is gay, because there is nothing to be proud of. We must simply *say* we are gay, because that is what we are' (*Comment nous appelez-vous déjà?*, p. 14; our translation). Despite their willed neutrality and objectivity, these positions are

nsive, but they also focus us on the role language
y in the establishing of sexuality/sexualities.

lf is blind to the exclusionary nature of his use of
...t are specific to the gay community and, indeed, only to
a sophisticated metropolitan gay community (many provincial French
gays do not possess the Anglo-American vocabulary of sex that he
uses). This blindness is prevalent among many current gay writers
who assume that their lives and works are an open book to the gay
or even straight reader. However, they forget that any 'marginal'
sexual practice is invariably accompanied by a terminology known
to initiates but foreign to non-initiates. An excellent example is John
Preston who, in *I Once had a Master*, a collection of 'hard', pornographic S/M stories, refers to the colour of handkerchiefs worn in
either the right or left back pocket. Both the colour and the choice
of side are crucial for an understanding of the sexuality of the individual
characters, but Preston assumes that the knowledge is shared by all
his readers and so he gives no explanations. This assumption of
complicity thereby excludes readers who may wish to read the tales,
but who would have to spend hours tracking down a dictionary or
handbook of codes in a library, simply in order to be able to grasp
what was happening between X and Y. In other words, the concept (and
the potential reality) of a community are exploded by the exclusionary
textual mechanisms of complicity. In his 'Epilogue: On Writing
Pornography' where he both argues for the necessity of a recognition
that S/M men see and experience sex differently from other people
and asserts that 'the sex we have is precisely that which separates
us from the rest of society [... and makes us] alien' (p. 117), Preston
uses a 'we' which is undoubtedly as problematic for many gay men as
it is for women or straight men.

Our response here is anxiously complex: does one have to be a
woman to empathise with Madame Bovary or with Anna Karenina?
does one have to be a man to empathise with David Copperfield or
with Silas Marner? does one have to be straight to empathise with
Don Juan or gay to empathise with the Baron Charlus? The figures
chosen are all victims of their societies, albeit in different ways,
but our questions would seem to offer one common answer: reading
functions through and by projective imagination, literature is non-
didactic, non-proselytising, the sexual is textual as much as it is
gender-specific.

Contemporary gay men, like many feminists, are engaged in a

struggle to change the canon of texts that may be bought, read –
and studied in academic institutions. This endeavour is politically
important, but there is, especially for gays, the danger of what we
would call an appropriative desire to decode. A revelatory example
is that of Wilde's *The Importance of being Earnest*. Many attempts
have been made to homosexualise this play: E(a)rnest 'is' a code
for homosexual desire, Bunburying for sodomy or for gay cruising,
Miss Prism's Biblical quotation 'As a man sows, so let him reap'
a reference to the procreative barrenness of homosexuality, and
so on. Such interpretations can be virtuoso (if historically suspect)
pieces of hermeneutic reading, but they lose sight of 'the importance
of being ambiguous'. Wilde's play may just possibly be a homosexual
manifesto; it is, though, much more powerful in its exposure of
the hypocrisy and the courtship rites of Victorian England. After
all, Wilde's position as 'patron saint' of liberal and politically active
English homosexuality has less to do with what he may or may
not have done in (bed-)chambers or with the green carnations he
wore, or even with his outpourings in *De Profundis* than with his
manipulative commitment to textuality, to the ways in which the
'how?' and the 'what?' of (homo)sexuality can be made public and
can become itemised on the social agenda.

Our focus on homosexuality as a paradigm of contemporary maleness may itself seem manipulative. However, we would argue that
until the performative relationship between text(s) and sex is fully
accepted, men will be unable to individualise themselves – and
thus to (re-)enter society. Both homosexual theory and homosexual
fiction are increasingly tropological. For instance, Guy Hocquenghem's
concept of the 'superior' (i.e. promiscuous) homosexual who mech-
anically 'plugs in and out' of other men is predicated on the metaphor
of the *desiring machine* proposed by Deleuze and Guattari in *Anti-
Oedipus* – and Martin Dannecker, Hocquenghem's sternest critic,
takes issue less with his homosexualising socio-political position
than with the fact that his thinking and writing are overly figurative
and (perhaps?) determined by the pressure of contemporary meta-
phorisings.

Many gay writers of fiction inscribe a concern with writing and
metaphors/metaphorising into their works. In their respective col-
lections of 'hot' S/M stories, both John Preston and Bill Lee include
stories that present unnormative sexuality as fiction, as fantasy,
by referring to themselves or to the narrator as a writer. Writing

is thus a strategy for disculpation, for abdication of responsibility, at the same time as it is a means of promoting sexual identity.

Men and women must write themselves into presence as well as performing themselves into presence. The writerly obligation need not necessarily involve calligraphic scriptural activity, but signs have to be given and signs have to be read. In our deliberate lack of conclusion, we should like simply to present a wishful and complex maxim: we are all readers before we can become writers, therefore we are all 'feminised' before we can become 'masculinised'. This chronological hierarchy of textual activities is, of course, a fantasy ironically borrowed from history: we need constantly to refeminise, remasculinise, and *regender* ourselves. We are able to live and read differently.

Notes

1 All three published volumes of *The History of Sexuality* have been of enormous help in thinking through the questions underlying this Introduction – although we intend to approach some different issues from those privileged by Foucault, and shall adopt a more political and explicitly feminist stance.
2 Correspondence of Gerard Manley Hopkins and Richard Watson Dixon, Letter of 5 October 1878.
3 See Jean-François Lyotard, *The Postmodern Condition*, Section 3, for a brief account of his theory that 'the observable social bond is composed of language "moves"' (p. 11) and that 'to speak is to fight, in the sense of playing, and speech acts fall within the domain of a general agonistics' (p. 10).
4 See 'The Origin of the Work of Art', in *Poetry, Language, Thought*, p. 17.
5 See the Introduction to Worton and Still, ed., *Intertextuality*.
6 See Kristeva, 'Problèmes de la structuration du texte'.
7 The pupil and master relationship between Barthes and Kristeva is a fascinating one; two relevant texts are 'L'Etrangère' in which Barthes thanks his erstwhile pupil for teaching him (about intertextuality) and Kristeva's *Les Samouraïs*. *Les Samouraïs* is a *roman à clef* with autobiographical overtones, which clearly exists in an agonistic relationship with Simone de Beauvoir's *Les Mandarins*. In it a Barthes figure is represented in a most curious light during the *Tel Quel* trip to China. He refuses to get off the coach, and sits and dreams about making a homosexual advance to a young Chinese man for which he is (in his dream) dragged before an impromptu revolutionary court and chastised.
8 See 'Ideology and Ideological State Apparatuses'.
9 We would refer anyone who would deny the continuing importance of sex to Beauvoir's Introduction to *The Second Sex* in which she compares women who say they are just people to Sartre's Jews who want to be just people. Economic or other privilege may make it seem that you can escape sex or race identification in a given situation, but in a social context where others see through these lenses and indeed where there are material consequences to sex or race positions . . .

10 However, we need to be cogniscent of other philosophical and social systems, such as Zen Buddhism and Hinduism which *incorporate* – in a non-determining way – binary logic into beliefs and practices which may be more supple and fluid than their Judeo-Christian equivalents. We thus do not necessarily subscribe to the universalism of Lévi-Strauss's anthropology.

11 See Julia Epstein, 'Either/Or–Neither/Both; Sexual Ambiguity and the Ideology of Gender' for some detail on the question of hermaphrodites and on the social pressure for each human subject to be categorised as male or female. Judith Butler also tackles this question in *Gender Trouble*.

12 See Judith Still, 'Can Woman Ever Be Defined? A Question from French Feminism' for an earlier attempt to tackle this issue.

13 Our understanding of the state apparatus will influence our pragmatic stance on whether or not legislation should be sought or opposed in certain areas, for instance the question of censorship. A certain amount of feminist energy has been devoted to campaigns against pornography on account of a conviction that it encourages men to regard women as degraded, and even to commit acts of violence against them; see Andrea Dworkin, *Pornography: Men Possessing Women*. However, other feminists are convinced that, since the repressive state apparatus is in the hands of patriarchal forces, any legislation in this field will work first against the socially disempowered (for instance, lesbian or gay bookshops). The questions 'what is pornography?' and 'what effects does it have on the reader?' are textual questions about the relative importance of conditions of production, reception, context, content and form which we would have liked to address in greater detail in this Introduction.

14 For an analysis of 'The Girl with the Golden Eyes' (the text is in *History of the Thirteen*, pp. 307–91), see Shoshana Felman, 'Rereading Femininity'.

15 'Sarrasine' ends with the thoughtful Marquise de Rochefide deciding that she has nothing but contempt for life and passion, and so breaking her contract with the narrator that she would give him what he desired in exchange for the story. In 'The Girl with the Golden Eyes', the Marquise de San-Real decides to enter a convent because she has lost (in fact, killed) the eponymous heroine.

16 John R. Leo, 'The Familialism of "Man" in American Television Melodrama', in Butters, p. 32.

17 Interestingly, while several individual theorists of gay men's studies have examined 'high' culture in books, for example, Eve Kosofsky Sedgwick, Jeffrey Meyers, Wayne Koestenbaum, Jeffrey Weeks, Gregory Woods and David Bergman, much of the most interesting work on 'low' or popular gay culture is to be found in collective volumes, thereby testifying to the continuing importance of the socialist tradition in cultural studies, for example, Chapman and Rutherford or Segal and McIntosh. In this volume Ross Chambers presents an analysis of Alan Hollinghurst's *The Swimming-Pool Library*.

18 See Adrienne Rich, 'Compulsory Heterosexuality and Lesbian Existence'. Rich later felt that she had been somewhat harsh towards gay men.

19 See Delphy's 'Protofeminism and Antifeminism', a powerful critique of Annie Leclerc who appears to suggest in *Parole de Femme* that the priority should be changing attitudes to what has been negatively valorised, such as menstruation or housework.

20 See *Close to Home: A Materialist Analysis of Women's Oppression*, a collection of essays which represent various aspects of Delphy's work. Monique Wittig, whose work is very different from Delphy's but who equally considers herself to be a materialist feminist, also argues that women constitute a class.

21 See Spender, *Man Made Language* or Irigaray's work on linguistics in *Sexes et genres*. This can be juxtaposed with poetic/theoretical statements; Wittig's 'Author's Note' to the English edition of *The Lesbian Body* claims that language is masculine and

C

thus alien to women: 'If *I*[*J/e*] examine m/y specific situation as subject in the language, *I* [*J/e*] am physically incapable of writing 'I' [*Je*], I [*J/e*] have no desire to do so' (p. 11).

22 There are a number of works which attempt the difficult task of analysing the data on the difference between men and women's labour; for example Christine Greenhalgh's articles, 'Male–Female Wage Differentials in Great Britain: Is Marriage an Equal Opportunity?' or 'Participation and Hours of Work for Married Women in Great Britain', or P. J. Dolton and G. H. Makepeace, 'Marital Status, Child Rearing and Earnings Differentials in the Graduate Labour Market', or Heather Joshi, 'Gender Inequality in the Labour Market and the Domestic Division of Labour'.

23 Men's labour supply has stayed largely constant at 90 per cent or more participation for as long as *General Household Survey* data is available – but over the last couple of decades there has been a slight downward trend particularly for men under the age of eighteen or over the age of sixty.

24 Only extracts from *Parole de Femme* have ever been translated, and Leclerc's position can therefore seem more extreme than it does when her lyrical flights on the subject of women's pleasures are read in the general context of her critique of the cult of masculinity and her attempt to re-evaluate the female body – which is often regarded as dirty and therefore needing to be 'tampaxised'. Leclerc backs up her claim that masculinity is organised around death with a series of (of course highly selective) examples ranging from philosophers such as Georges Bataille (p. 127), Gilles Deleuze (p. 119) or Jean-Paul Sartre (pp. 123–5), to film stars such as Jean Gabin or Lino Ventura (p. 17) or aspects of everyday life such as the imperative to achieve erections (p. 109).

25 Domna C. Stanton attacks Kristeva, Irigaray and Cixous in 'Difference on Trial' in *The Poetics of Gender*, pp. 157–82.

26 'Writing a Letter with Vermeer', pp. 137–56. This virtuoso essay addresses general questions of the translation from French into English as well as from the literary-philosophical into the sexual-feminist which seem to have been one of the most significant shifts in the field of theory over the last couple of decades. Interestingly Gallop represents *écriture féminine* as 'a switch from the phallic to the oral sexual paradigm' (p. 140) – the metaphor of (French) kissing has often been overlooked in the attack on French feminists as obsessively vagino-centric or interested in labial lips alone.

27 Elizabeth Fallaize in *Contemporary French Women's Fiction* argues that Leclerc's letter is in fact addressed to her mother, a figure who finally merges with women in general. It certainly seems to us to be difficult to assert with certainty either that Leclerc writes as a lesbian (Gallop, p. 144) or even that she writes as if she had just passed a night of lesbian love-making (Gallop, p. 140) since she addresses the 'loving body' which gives birth to her in the morning as 'ma mère' (*La Venue à l'écriture*, p. 117).

28 See *Herculine Barbin*, the true story of a nineteenth-century hermaphrodite, with an Introduction by Michel Foucault, and Julia Epstein, 'Either/Or–Neither/Both: Sexual Ambiguity and the Ideology of Gender'.

29 Poststructuralist readings of Freud have often focused on the literariness of his writing, for example, the way that case-histories (and other works) are structured as narratives, and have analysed his deployment of certain key metaphors. See, for example, Malcolm Bowie, *Freud, Proust and Lacan*. We would note here also that Surrealism, one of the most influential aesthetico-political movements of the twentieth century, is largely based on an attempt to recode Freud's theorisings in poetic and painterly terms.

30 See, for example, the work of Juliet Mitchell and Jacqueline Rose.

31 Jacqueline Rose's Introduction to *Feminine Sexuality* is a good example. For a number of different perspectives on the current state of the debate between feminists and various kinds of psychoanalysis, see Elizabeth Wright, ed., *Feminism and Psychoanalysis: A Critical Dictionary*.

32 See, for example, David Macey, *Lacan in Contexts*, chapter 6.

33 Irigaray is a trained psychoanalyst who lost her post at the Department of Psychoanalysis at Vincennes because of her heretical work *Speculum*. (Lacanian psychoanalysis is notorious for such expulsions, and, the content of the theories aside, the practices of psychoanalysis as an institution may be regarded as antithetical to feminism.) The title refers to the medical instrument used for internal examinations.

34 See the Introduction to *The Second Sex*; Beauvoir also refers to Lévi-Strauss to support her argument that binary oppositions tend to structure our thinking. While she makes the analogy between the positioning of women and that of other disadvantaged groups such as black Americans, Beauvoir insists on the specificity of any given situation, for example the fact that women (particularly in the context of her time of writing) have no sense of unity as women because they are, for instance, spatially scattered amongst men.

35 See 'Signature Event Context' in *Margins of Philosophy* for a comment on the prevalence of binaries as hierarchical oppositions. Derrida's work is also relevant in that it seems to us to show up how close readings, how taking time over words and paying attention to the letter of the text, can be important politically.

36 See, for example, 'Woman Can Never Be Defined'.

37 One problem with Irigaray's agenda is that loving women may be no more than a route to heterosexual nuptials.

38 A number of contributors to this volume are working on this question of the gendering of style and content. Nancy K. Miller analyses the history of the division of eighteenth-century novels into male-authored libertine novels, canonised for their 'fine style', and women's novels of sensibility, which have generally fallen out of favour and are largely overlooked by the major (male) critics even in manuals purporting to give an overview of the century. Miller shows how close analysis of works by men and women of the period produces rather a different account from that suggested by the clichés of literary history. Jennifer Patterson argues that the work of André Breton does indeed have a masculine style, deploying metaphors of rape, for example, which can be disturbing for the contemporary female reader.

39 These are Foucault's three categories in the *History of Sexuality*, II and III.

40 See Clare Whatling's piece in this volume for an example of lesbian feminist reappropriation of S/M pornography in spite of vilification from anti-porn campaigners.

41 Margaret Whitford points out in her Introduction to the *Irigaray Reader* how few of Irigaray's philosophical texts have been translated; while most of Barthes's work is available in English translation, *Incidents* is not; see Judith Still, 'Can Woman Ever Be Defined?' for some examples of selective translations of Kristeva.

42 See *The Postmodern Condition* (pp. 79–81). The main text (published alone in French) deals with socio-economic questions, particularly that of the political economy of information in post-industrial societies. But a useful postscript is appended in the English translation which problematises any easy link between the historical conditions set out earlier and different cultural forms. The Foreword by Jameson highlights the polemical aspects of Lyotard's stand against that of Jürgen Habermas, for example. For a summary of Jameson's own position, which draws on Ernest Mandel to produce a general periodisation of base and superstructure, see 'Postmodernism or The Cultural Logic of Late Capitalism'.

43 Michèle Le Doeuff has written widely on Beauvoir pointing out both the problems of her adherence to existentialism (and the way it seems to position her as Sartre's

disciple) and, in 'Operative Philosophy' for example, on the positive aspects of her existentialist ethics.

44 These questions have been raised by Toril Moi in *Feminist Theory and Simone de Beauvoir* and by Elizabeth Fallaize in *The Novels of Simone de Beauvoir*. In *Simone de Beauvoir: A Feminist Mandarin*, Mary Evans argues that Beauvoir unwittingly accepts bourgeois possessive individualism rather than working-class interdependence – Moi reviews Evans's position in 'She Came to Stay'.

45 Sartre's *Being and Nothingness* is analysed in Collins and Pierce, 'Holes and Slime'; Moi relates this to Beauvoir in 'The Rhetoric of Biology in *The Second Sex*'.

46 It has been suggested that Beauvoir's adherence to the romance plot may, in fact, be more troubling; see Fallaize, 'Resisting Romance: Simone de Beauvoir, "The Woman Destroyed" and the Romance Script', in Attack and Powrie, ed., *Contemporary French Fiction by Women*, pp. 15–25.

47 See Cora Kaplan, 'Radical Feminism and Literature'. In *Sexual/Textual Politics*, Moi also points out the lack of gratitude Millett shows towards Mary Ellmann. Millett's privileging of Jean Genet (rather than a woman writer) as a counter-example to Mailer, Lawrence et al. has also been criticised although perhaps it could be seen as a point against the claim that she equates maleness and patriarchy.

48 Luce Irigaray argues, for instance in *Speculum* (p. 365), that, since women are placed outside systematic thinking or used as the silent ground which supports systems, there is no need to follow scholarly codes. Thus Irigaray integrates paraphrases, quotations and misquotations without acknowledgement. As a doctoral thesis, *Sexual Politics* is a rather different kind of animal and should perhaps be judged differently. Nevertheless we hope that the juxtaposition gives food for thought.

49 Barthes explains and analyses the figure of innoculation in *Mythologies*. Women's magazines are a good example of how a small dose of feminism can be injected without the disease proving fatal; Barthes shows in his piece on *Elle* in the 1950s how women are allowed to produce books as long as they produce babies as well. Rosalind Coward brings us more up to date in *Female Desire*; see also Judith Williamson, *Consuming Passions* and *Decoding Advertisements*.

50 Another worrying element in *The Female Eunuch* is the touch of homophobia which seems to be implicit in the references to 'faggots' or perhaps the designation of Wilde as irresponsible.

51 See 'The Mark of Gender' in *The Poetics of Gender*, pp. 63–73.

52 See Hélène Vivienne Wenzel, 'The Text as Body/Politics: An Appreciation of Monique Wittig's Writings in Context'.

53 See Martha Noel Evans, *Women and the Politics of Writing in Twentieth-Century France*, pp. 185–219.

54 Jennifer Waelti-Waters, *Fairy Tales and the Female Imagination*.

55 See Barbara Taylor, *Eve and the New Jerusalem*.

56 For example, Rousseau's famous 'dangerous supplement' is represented textually in his *Confessions* in a complex economy with the dangers of celibacy and those of commerce with women.

57 See Judith Still, 'A Feminine Economy' for a comparison of Cixous with other thinkers of the gift. These may be contrasted with Jean-François Lyotard, who emphasises the libidinal nature of capitalism (and the economic elements in the libido) in *Economie libidinale*. Lyotard controversially represents Marx as a 'lover' of capitalism, and the proletariat as a 'lover' of exploitation; his focus on the erotic charge in relationships which we may prefer to consider 'pure' for political reasons is a useful corrective.

58 See, for example, *On Feminine Writing: A Boundary 2 Symposium*.

63 From a different perspective, Gillian Beer argues, in this volume, for the crucial importance of the body for the writing subject in her analysis of a letter by Charles Darwin. Darwin is acutely aware of his own body as he writes, and his letter is also invaded by other bodies – that of 'natural' man, of woman as cultural artefact and, after these examples of racial and sexual difference, finally by that of an animal, the most explicitly objectified as available to be examined and consumed.

60 See, for example, Domna C. Stanton, 'Difference on Trial', in Nancy K. Miller, ed., *The Poetics of Gender*, pp. 157–82.

61 Many accounts of modernism, the kind of avant-garde writing beloved of French poststructuralists, disregard Virginia Woolf, Djuna Barnes or H. D. in their celebration of James Joyce, T. S. Eliot or Mallarmé. Kristeva, for example, chooses to work on Lautréamont. Similar processes of gendered canon formation can be observed in the case of postmodernism.

62 For instances of Cixous's reading practice see *Readings with Clarice Lispector*, or *Readings: The Poetics of Blanchot, Joyce, Kafka, Kleist, Lispector and Tsvetayeva*.

63 See Michel Foucault and Hélène Cixous, 'A propos de Marguerite Duras'.

64 Whitford, *Luce Irigaray: Philosophy in the Feminine*.

65 Janet Sayers claims that for Irigaray 'femininity [...] is essentially constituted by female biology, by the "two lips" of the female sex' (*Biological Politics*, p. 131); however, Jan Montefiore responds: 'This metaphor of "two lips" is *not* a definition of women's identity in biological terms: the statement that they are "continually interchanging" must make it clear that Irigaray is not talking about literal biology' (*Feminism and Poetry*). The best exploration of these positions is given in the writings of Margaret Whitford, of which the latest is *Luce Irigaray: Philosophy in the Feminine*. For Whitford the most important point about Irigaray is her desire to effect change in the Imaginary and Symbolic – and hence facilitate socio-political and economic change. The charge of biological essentialism is rendered less surprising by a possible confusion over genre; Irigaray does not embrace the absolute distinction between theory and poetry.

66 The importance of the pre-Oedipal moment is also emphasised by Kristeva, and her attendance to the semiotic. However, it would be a mistake to conflate these various complex analyses – beyond remarking a common desire to rectify a social and theoretical imbalance in the relative weight apportioned to maternal relations as opposed to paternal relations.

67 See, for example, 'Displacement and the Discourse of Woman'. Alice Jardine's *Gynesis* is an extended study of this feminisation of philosophy.

68 See 'French Feminism in an International Frame' reprinted in *In Other Worlds*. In *Breaking the Chain* Naomi Schor's clitoral hermeneutics shows how the clitoral detail is overlooked by a long chain of literary critics.

69 For further detail on this, see Whitford, op. cit.

70 'Geschlecht: Sexual Difference, Ontological Difference', p. 83.

71 For a lucid account of the major goals of gender theory, see Joan W. Scott, 'Gender: A Useful Category of Historical Analysis'.

72 Heath, 'Male Feminism', p. 1, and Showalter, 'Feminism and Literature', pp. 127–8, both in Jardine and Smith, ed., *Men in Feminism*.

73 The ambivalence of Camus's thinking and talking about men is evidenced throughout his work. Anxious to present accurate, objective images of the workings of society, he nonetheless frequently refers to icons of machismo and to European concepts of masculinity: in *The Outsider*, for instance, Meursault is 'saved' from passivity by knowing how to use a gun, and the 'sternness' of French judicial processes is set against the 'laxity' of the Arabs. Much irony is at play here, yet it is encoded in such a way that the text may be read as deeply conservative in its representations of sexual difference.

74 It is worth noting here that in 'In Memoriam', his great elegaic poem on the death of Arthur Hallam, Tennyson extensively uses the vocabulary of widowhood, feminising Hallam and occasionally himself.

75 See, for example, Ann Jefferson's coinage and usage of the term 'sister-text' in 'Autobiography as Intertext: Barthes, Sarraute, Robbe-Grillet', in Worton and Still, ed., *Intertextuality*, pp. 108–29.

76 It is not possible here to resume all Gilmore's arguments or to do justice to the breadth of his data, but we would like to acknowledge the influence his book has had on our own thinking.

77 On the social place of the *berdache* and other 'honorary women', such as the Tahitian *mahu* and the Omani *xanith*, see Gilmore, *Manhood in the Making*, passim.

78 'Who's that Man?', in Chapman and Rutherford, ed., *Male order*, p. 23. Analogous points are made in several of the essays in Gay Left Collective, ed., *Homosexuality: Power and Politics*.

79 For an extended analysis of this question, see Lawrence E. Klein, *Shaftesbury and the Culture of Politeness* (forthcoming).

80 In a paper on 'Queer Performativity' at the second annual 'Questions of Homosexuality' conference at the Institute of Romance Studies, University of London in June 1992, Eve Kosofsky Sedgwick defined gender as 'a form of performativity', as 'an act and a performance', and so as dramatic rather than referential. Sandy Petrey's analysis of *Indiana* in this volume highlights George Sand's representation of (heterosexual) manhood as social performance.

81 Mailer's desperate need to cling to an ideology of manhood as virile performance is revealed in *The Prisoner of Sex*. Everyone now laughs at Aristotle's gynaecology which proposed that the sex of a child was determined by external, contingent events (such as whether the wind was blowing from the north or the south), but Mailer's medical knowledge is equally suspect. His insistence that a child's character is determined by the quality of the act of its conception (the 'good fucks make good babies' myth) has, however, less to do with gynaecological accuracy than with his compulsive desire to promote virility.

82 For a detailed biographical and psychoanalytical study of this transvestite, see Geneviève Reynes, *L'Abbé de Choisy*.

83 On this subject, see, for example, Ian Maclean, *The Renaissance Notion of Woman*.

84 In this context, we would note that, although he was fascinated (theoretically and personally) by the multiplicity of contemporary sexual practices and notably S/M, Foucault chose to publish his essays and interviews on S/M only in specialist journals such as *The Advocate* and *Salmagundi*. These have yet to be collected in a volume.

Bibliography to Introduction

Foreign-language works to which we refer in the Introduction, with a few additions, are given here as English translations where these are available (otherwise translations are our own). For further references to works on (inter)textuality, see the bibliography to our Introduction to *Intertextuality: Theories and Practices*.

Althusser, Louis, 'Ideology and Ideological State Apparatuses', in *Lenin and Philosophy and Other Essays*, trans. Ben Brewster, London, 1971, pp. 121–73

Altman, Dennis et al., ed., *Which Homosexuality? Essays from the International Scientific Conference on Lesbian and Gay Studies*, London, 1989

Atack, Margaret, and Phil Powrie, ed., *Contemporary French Fiction by Women: Feminist Perspectives*, Manchester, 1990

Austin, J. L., *How to Do Things with Words*, London, 1962

Balzac, Honoré de, *History of the Thirteen*, trans. Herbert J. Hunt, Harmondsworth, 1974

Barthes, Roland, 'L'Etrangère', *La Quinzaine littéraire*, XCIV, 1970, pp. 19–20

—, *Mythologies*, trans. Annette Lavers, London, 1972

—, *The Pleasure of the Text*, trans. Richard Miller, London, 1976

—, *S/Z* trans. Richard Miller, London, 1975

Bartlett, Neil, *Who Was that Man? A Present for Mr Oscar Wilde*, London, 1988

Beauvoir, Simone de, *The Mandarins*, trans. Leonard M. Friedman, London, 1982

—, *The Second Sex*, trans. H. M. Parshley, London, 1988

Bergman, David, *Gaiety Transfigured: Gay Self-Representation in American Literature*, Madison, 1991

Bloom, Harold, *The Anxiety of Influence*, Oxford and New York, 1973

Blüher, Hans, *Die Rolle der Erotik in der männlichen Gesellschaft*, Jena, 1917

Bory, Jean-Louis, and Guy Hocquenghem, *Comment nous appelez-vous déjà? Ces hommes que l'on dit homosexuels*, Paris, 1977

Bowie, Malcolm, *Freud, Proust and Lacan: Theory as Fiction*, Cambridge, 1987

Braidotti, Rosi, *Patterns of Dissonance*, London, 1991

Butler, Judith, *Gender Trouble*, London, 1990

Butters, Ronald R., John M. Clum, and Michael Moon, ed., *Displacing Homophobia: Gay Male Perspectives in Literature and Culture*, Durham and London, 1989

Camus, Renaud, *Tricks*, Paris, 1988

Chapman, Rowena, and Jonathan Rutherford, ed., *Male Order: Unwrapping Masculinity*, London, 1988

Chasseguet-Smirgel, Janine, *Creativity and Perversion*, London, 1985

Cixous, Hélène, *Readings with Clarice Lispector*, trans. and ed. Verena Andermatt Conley, Minneapolis, 1990

—, *Readings: The Poetics of Blanchot, Joyce, Kafka, Kleist, Lispector and Tsvetayeva*, trans. and ed. Verena Andermatt Conley, Minneapolis, 1991

Cixous, Hélène, and Catherine Clément, *The Newly Born Woman*, trans. Betsy Wing, Introduction by Sandra M. Gilbert, Manchester, 1986

Collins, Margery, and Christine Pierce, 'Holes and Slime: Sexism in Sartre's Psychoanalysis', in Carol C. Gould and Max W. Wartofsky, ed., *Women and Philosophy: Toward a Theory of Liberation* New York, 1976, pp. 112–27

Coward, Rosalind, *Female Desire: Women's Sexuality Today*, London, 1984

Dannecker, Martin, *Theories of Homosexuality*, London, 1981

De Lauretis, Teresa, *Alice Doesn't: Feminism, Semiotics, Cinema*, Bloomington, 1984

Deleuze, Gilles, and Félix Guattari, *Anti-Oedipus: Capitalism and Schizophrenia*, trans. Robert Hurley et al., New York, 1977

Delphy, Christine, 'Protofeminism and Antifeminism', in T. Moi, ed., *French Feminist Thought: A Reader*, Oxford, 1987, pp. 80–109

—, *Close to Home: A Materialist Analysis of Women's Oppression*, trans. and ed. Diana Leonard, London, 1984

Derrida, Jacques, *Margins of Philosophy*, trans. Alan Bass, Brighton and Chicago, 1982

—, 'Geschlecht: Sexual Difference, Ontological Difference', trans. Reuben Berezdivin, *Research in Phenomenology*, XIII, 1983, pp. 65–83

—, *Spurs: Nietzsche's Styles*, trans. Barbara Harlow, Chicago, 1979

—, 'Choreographies', in Christie McDonald, ed., *The Ear of the Other*, trans. Peggy Kamuf, Lincoln and London, 1988

Dollimore, Jonathan, *Sexual Dissidence: Augustine to Wilde, Freud to Foucault*, Oxford, 1991

Dolton, P. J., and G. H. Makepeace, 'Marital Status, Child Rearing and Earnings Differentials in the Graduate Labour Market', *The Economic Journal*, XCVII, 1987, pp. 897–922

Duberman, Martin Bauml, Martha Vicinus and George Chauncey, Jr., ed., *Hidden from History: Reclaiming the Gay and Lesbian Past*, London, 1991

Duras, Marguerite, *The Vice-Consul*, trans. Eileen Ellenbogen, London, 1968

During, Simon, *Foucault and Literature: Towards a Genealogy of Writing*, London, 1992

Dworkin, Andrea, *Pornography: Men Possessing Women*, London, 1981

Elam, Diane, *Romancing the Postmodern*, London and New York, 1992

Epstein, Julia, 'Either/Or–Neither/Both: Sexual Ambiguity and the Ideology of Gender', *Genders*, VII, 1990, pp. 99–142

Evans, Martha Noel, *Women and the Politics of Writing in Twentieth-Century France*, Ithaca, 1987

Evans, Mary, *Simone de Beauvoir: A Feminist Mandarin*, London, 1985

Fallaize, Elizabeth, *The Novels of Simone de Beauvoir*, London, 1988

—, *Contemporary French Women's Fiction*, forthcoming, London, 1993

Felman, Shoshana, 'Rereading Femininity', *Yale French Studies*, LXII, 1981, pp. 19–44

Firestone, Shulamith, *The Dialectic of Sex: The Case for Feminist Revolution*, London, 1979

Foucault, Michel, 'What is an Author?', in Josué V. Harari, ed., *Textual Strategies: Perspectives in Post-Structuralist Criticism*, London, 1980, pp. 141–60

—, *The History of Sexuality*, vol. I: *An Introduction*, London, 1981; vol. II; *The Use of Pleasure*, London, 1987; vol. III: *The Care of the Self*, London, 1990 (all trans. Robert Hurley)

—, *Politics, Philosophy, Culture: Interviews and Other Writings 1977–84*, ed. Lawrence D. Kritzman, London, 1988

Foucault, Michel, and Hélène Cixous, 'A propos de Marguerite Duras', *Cahiers Renaud-Barrault*, LVXXXIX, 1975, pp. 8–22

Freud, Anna, *The Ego and the Mechanisms of Defense*, trans. Cecil Baines, London, 1936

—, 'Regression as a Principle in Mental Development', *Bulletin of the Menninger Clinic*, XXVII, pp. 126–39

Freud, Sigmund, *On Sexuality: Three Essays on the Theory of Sexuality and Other Works* (The Pelican Freud Library, vol. 7), Harmondsworth, 1977

—, 'Analysis Terminable and Interminable' (1937), in *Complete Psychological Works*, Standard Edition, ed. James Strachey, vol. 23, pp. 216–53, London, 1951

Gay Left Collective, ed., *Homosexuality: Power and Politics*, London, 1980

Gilbert, Sandra, and Susan Gubar, *The Madwoman in the Attic*, New Haven, 1979

Gilman, Charlotte Perkins, *Herland*, London, 1979

Gilmore, David D., *Manhood in the Making: Cultural Concepts of Masculinity*, New Haven and London, 1990

Greenhalgh, Christine, 'Male–Female Wage Differentials in Great Britain: Is Marriage an Equal Opportunity?', *The Economic Journal*, XC, 1980, pp. 751–75

—, 'Participation and Hours of Work for Married Women in Great Britain', *Oxford Economic Papers*, XXXII, 1980, pp. 296–318

Greer, Germaine, *The Female Eunuch*, London, 1971

Hanscombe, Gillian E., and Martin Humphries, ed., *Heterosexuality*, London, 1987

Hart, Jack, *Gay Sex: A Manual for Men who Love Men*, Boston, 1991

Heidegger, Martin. *Poetry, Language, Thought*, trans. Alfred Hofstadter, New York, 1971

Herculine Barbin Being the Recently Discovered Memoirs of a Nineteenth-Century French Hermaphrodite, trans. Richard McDougall with an Introduction by Michel Foucault, Brighton, 1980

Hocquenghem, Guy, *Homosexual Desire*, trans. Daniella Dangoor, London, 1978

Hopkins, Gerard Manley, *Correspondence of G. M. Hopkins and Richard Watson Dixon*, ed. C. C. Abbott, London, 1935

Irigaray, Luce, *Speculum of the Other Woman*, trans. Gillian C. Gill, Ithaca, 1985

—, *This Sex Which Is Not One*, trans. Catherine Porter, Ithaca, 1985

—, ed., *Sexes et genres à travers les langues: Eléments de communication sexuée*, Paris, 1990

—, *Elemental Passions*, trans. Joanne Collie and Judith Still, London, 1992

Jameson, Fredric, 'Postmodernism, or The Cultural Logic of Late Capitalism', *New Left Review*, CXLVI, 1984, pp. 53–92

Jardine, Alice, *Gynesis: Configurations of Woman and Modernity*, Ithaca and London, 1985

Jardine, Alice, and Paul Smith, ed., *Men in Feminism*, New York and London, 1987

Joshi, Heather, 'Gender Inequality in the Labour Market and the Domestic Division of Labour', in *Rethinking Socialist Economics*, ed. Nolan and Paine, 1986, pp. 258–69

Jung, C. G., *Aspects of the Masculine*, London, 1989

—, *Aspects of the Feminine*, London, 1989

Kakar, Sudhir, *The Inner World: A Psychoanalytic Study of Childhood*, Delhi, 1981

Kakar, Sudhir, and John Mundar Ross, *Tales of Sex, Love and Danger*, Oxford, 1987

Kaplan, Cora, 'Radical Feminism and Literature: Rethinking Millett's *Sexual Politics*', *Red Letters*, IX, 1978, pp. 4–16

Klein, Lawrence, E., *Shaftesbury and the Culture of Politeness*, Cambridge, forthcoming.

Koesterbaum, Wayne, *Double Talk: The Erotics of Male Literary Collaboration*, New York and London, 1989

Kristeva, Julia, 'Problèmes de la structuration du texte', in *Théorie d'Ensemble*, ed. *Tel Quel*, Paris, 1968, pp. 298–317

—, *La Révolution du langage poétique*, Paris, 1974

—, *About Chinese Women*, trans. Anita Barrows, New York and London, 1977

—, *Les Samourais*, Paris, 1990

—, 'Woman Can Never Be Defined' in E. Marks and I. De Courtivron, ed., *New French Feminisms*, New York, 1981, pp. 137–8

Lacan, Jacques, *Encore, Le Séminaire XX*, Paris, 1975

—, *Feminine Sexuality*, ed. Juliet Mitchell and Jacqueline Rose, trans. Jacqueline Rose, London and Basingstoke, 1982

Leclerc, Annie, *Parole de femme*, Paris, 1974

—, with Hélène Cixous and Madeleine Gagnon, *La Venue à l'écriture*, Paris, 1977

Le Doeuff, Michèle, 'Operative Philosophy', *Ideology and Consciousness*, 1979

Lee, Bill, *Leather Rogues*, San Francisco, 1991

Llewelyn-Davies, Melissa, 'Women, Warriors, and Patriarchs', in Sherry B. Ortner and Harriet Whitehead, ed., *Sexual Meanings*, Cambridge, 1981, pp. 330–58

Lyotard, Jean-François, *Economie libidinale*, Paris, 1974

—, *The Postmodern Condition: A Report on Knowledge*, trans. Geoff Bennington and Brian Massumi, Manchester, 1986

Macey, David, *Lacan in Contexts*, London and New York, 1988

Maclean, Ian, *The Renaissance Notion of Woman*, Cambridge, 1980

Mailer, Norman, *Armies of the Night*, New York, 1968

—, *The Prisoner of Sex*, Boston, 1971

Metcalf, Andy, and Martin Humphries, ed., *The Sexuality of Men*, London, 1985

Meyers, Jeffrey, *Homosexuality and Literature 1890–1930*, London, 1977

Miller, Nancy K., ed., *The Poetics of Gender*, New York, 1986

Millett, Kate, *Sexual Politics*, London, 1977

Mitchell, Juliet, *Feminism and Psychoanalysis*, London, 1974

Moi, Toril, *Feminist Theory and Simone de Beauvoir*, Oxford, 1990

—, 'The Rhetoric of Biology in *The Second Sex*', *The Oxford Literary Review*, VIII, 1986, pp. 88–95

—, *Sexual/Textual Politics*, London, 1985

—, 'She Came to Stay', *Paragraph*, VIII, 1986, pp. 110–20

Montefiore, Jan, *Feminism and Poetry*, London, 1987

Mulvey, Laura, 'Visual Pleasure and Narrative Cinema', *Screen*, XVI, 1975, pp. 6–18

Nestle, Joan, *A Restricted Country*, London, 1988

O'Flaherty, Wendy D., *Women, Androgynes, and Other Mythical Beasts*, Chicago, 1980

On Feminine Writing: A Boundary 2 Symposium ed. Verena Andermatt Conley and William V. Spanos, *Boundary 2*, XII, 1984

Pollock, Griselda, *Vision and Difference*, London and New York, 1988

Preston, John, *I Once Had a Master and Other Tales of Erotic Love*, Boston, 1984

Reynes, Geneviève, *L'Abbé de Choisy ou l'ingénu libertin*, Paris, 1983

Rich, Adrienne, 'Compulsory Heterosexuality and Lesbian Existence', in *Blood, Bread and Poetry. Selected Prose 1979–1985*, London, 1986

Rich, Ruby, 'In the Name of Feminist Film Criticism', *Heresies*, IX, 1980, pp. 74–81

Saitoti, Tepilit Oli, *The Worlds of a Masai Warrior: An Autobiography*, Berkeley, 1986

Sayers, Janet, *Biological Politics*, London, 1982

Schor, Naomi, *Breaking the Chain, Women, Theory and French Realist Fiction*, New York, 1985

Schwenger, Peter, *Phallic Critiques: Masculinity and Twentieth-Century Literature*, London, 1984

Scott, Joan W., 'Gender: A Useful Category of Historical Analysis', *American Historical Review*, XCI (December 1986), pp. 1053–75

Sedgwick, Eve Kosofsky, *Between Men: English Literature and Male Homosocial Desire*, New York, 1988

—, *Epistemology of the Closet*, Hemel Hempstead, 1991

Segal, Lynn, and Mary McIntosh, *Sex Exposed: Sexuality and the Pornography Debate*, London, 1992

Shiach, Morag, *Hélène Cixous: A Politics of Writing*, London, 1991

Sontag, Susan, *Illness as Metaphor*, London, 1979

—, *AIDS and its Metaphors*, London, 1989

Spender, Dale, *Man Made Language*, London, 1980

Spivak, Gayatri, 'Displacement and the Discourse of Woman', in Mark Krupnick, ed., *Displacement: Derrida and After*, Bloomington, 1983, pp. 169–95

—, *In Other Worlds: Essays in Cultural Politics*, New York, 1987

Still, Judith, 'A Feminine Economy: Some Preliminary Thoughts', in H. Wilcox et al., ed., *The Body and the Text: Hélène Cixous, Reading and Teaching*, Hemel Hempstead, 1990, pp. 49–60

—, 'Can Woman Ever Be Defined? A Question from French Feminism', in A. Cady, ed., *Women Teaching French: Five Papers on Language and Theory*, Studies in European Culture Paper 5, Loughborough, 1991, pp. 29–37

Taylor, Barbara, *Eve and the New Jerusalem: Socialism and Feminism in the Nineteenth Century*, London, 1983

Todd, Janet, *Feminist Literary History*, London, 1988

Waelti-Waters, Jennifer, *Fairy Tales and the Female Imagination*, Montreal, 1982

Wenzel, Hélène Vivienne, 'The Text as Body/Politics: An Appreciation of Monique Wittig's Writings in Context', *Feminist Studies*, VII, 1981, pp. 264–87

Whitford, Margaret, *Luce Irigaray: Philosophy in the Feminine*, London, 1991

—, ed., *The Irigaray Reader*, Oxford, 1991

Williamson, Judith, *Consuming Passions*, London, 1985

—, *Decoding Advertisements*, London, 1978

Wittig, Monique, *Les Guérrillères*, trans. D. LeVay, New York, 1973

—, *The Lesbian Body*, trans. D. LeVay, New York, 1976

—, 'The Straight Mind', *Feminist Issues*, I, 1980, pp. 103–11

Woods, Gregory, *Articulate Flesh: Male Homo-Eroticism and Modern Poetry*, New Haven and London, 1987

Worton, Michael, and Judith Still, ed., *Intertextuality: Theories and Practices*, Manchester and New York, 1990

Wright, Elizabeth, ed., *Feminism and Psychoanalysis: A Critical Dictionary*, Oxford, 1992

Sexual knowledge: the once and future texts of the *Romance of the Rose* [1]

Sarah Kay

In the retelling of our critical genealogy the Middle Ages are nearly always passed over in silence. The introduction by Judith Still and Michael Worton to *Intertextuality*, the progenitor of this present volume, leaps effortlessly from Aristotle to the Renaissance. So does Terence Cave's *Recognitions*. Andrew Martin's *The Knowledge of Ignorance* performs a yet more balletic feat, jumping from Genesis to Nicholas of Cusa. [2] Clearly this elision demonstrates in itself the vigour of an intertextual tradition: it is powerful enough to pass off as complete a history from which some 1600 years have simply been omitted. Now the contention of this present book is that the energy of intertextuality is in some sense libidinal. I should therefore like readers of this essay to ask themselves whether this contention throws any light on why the Middle Ages are passed over. Do the conventions of literary history succumb to the seduction of the Renaissance, as it points to the writers of Antiquity and says 'these are our fathers'? Do they turn their back on the medieval period as though it were faintly indecent, like the body of an ageing mother? Such oblivion isn't accidental, and is the more telling in view of the relevance to modern critical concerns of medieval textual practices.

The move of later 1960s cultural critique to undo the hegemony of the author was excitingly innovative, but it also entailed a return to the dissolution of authority in textuality which is characteristic of early medieval writing. The traditional character of medieval literature means that both 'authors' (for lack of a better word) and texts are subject to antecedent exemplars. Theories of intertextuality of one kind or another have dominated the critical scene in medieval French studies since at least the 1960s, the most influential theorist being Paul Zumthor whose 1972 *Essai de poétique médiévale* drew into its wake studies on all kinds of texts, and indeed eventually assumed a stranglehold on approaches to some of them. [3] In this essay, I shall start from the work of a more recent theorist, the Lacanian critic

Jean-Charles Huchet whose *Littérature médiévale et psychanalyse: Pour une clinique littéraire* was published in Paris in 1990.[4] Huchet reminds us that there are no autograph manuscripts before the end of the thirteenth century. Instead, we have a series of copies of copies, all different from each other, all made by scribes whose writing 'is only ever a reading, carried out with pen in hand' (p. 16). We do not have a single, determinate text of any work; instead, 'the text occupies quite specifically the place of the object of desire; it lies, withdrawn from, and beyond, the incarnations of itself; it is the lack in which the desire for/of literature [*le désir de la littérature*] originates' (p. 17). The same absence characterises the alleged sources of many medieval works, especially romances, the genre on which Huchet concentrates. As Sylvia Huot has put it, 'the conventional romance narrator of the twelfth and thirteenth centuries mediates between his audience and a real or posited pre-existent text or texts, usually identified as books and often in Latin'.[5] This stance parallels the way the audience will experience the work in performance, since 'the performer, reading to us out of the book held in his hands, is the extratextual manifestation of the narrator, reading to us out of his ancient books' (Huot, ibid.). There is, therefore, always a gap between the text and that which we read or hear; the text, in Huchet's words, is 'identified not with the product of writing, but with the summons [*l'appel*] which pre-exists it' (p. 17). The intractability of this absence is imaged, for Huchet, by the Grail, and thematised, throughout the corpus which he studies, by the unending desire of medieval lovers (*fin aman*).

For Huchet, then, the text is always an abstract construct, a present absence generated by intertextual processes, and infused with a libidinal energy which flows out into the 'content' of medieval works. I want both to use this idea and to qualify it, by looking at a poem which he considers only briefly, but which is the most powerful investigation of textuality and sexuality in the French Middle Ages: Jean de Meun's *Romance of the Rose*. Composed *circa* 1270, this vast poem is transmitted by some three hundred manuscripts, more than any other French vernacular text. It survived into the sixteenth century, slightly modernised linguistically, in printed editions, and was the first French medieval work to be the object of a scholarly edition (1735) when Enlightenment interest turned towards the Middle Ages.[6] Imitated and adapted by Chaucer and Dante, it is now the object of an intimidatingly ramifying critical literature. The *Rose* must rate, therefore, among the successes of world literature; yet its

procedures are typically medieval. In the first place, it is the continuation of an earlier narrative poem, apparently abandoned unfinished
some forty years earlier, and ascribed to Guillaume de Lorris. To the
4000 lines of Guillaume's dream vision of a lover's quest for a rose,
Jean added 17000 lines in which Guillaume's text is not only continued
but also cited, commentated, derided, and (in my view) ultimately
exploded. In the second place, approximately two-thirds of Jean's
continuation consists of quotations, in translation, of Latin texts.[7]
(This is not as mechanical as it sounds. In the Middle Ages, translation involves adaptation and commentary, often drawing on earlier
commentaries, i.e. it is itself a complex intertextual process.[8]) Chief
among the texts quoted are two philosophical dream visions: Boethius's
Consolation of Philosophy and Alan of Lille's *Plaint of Nature*. Jean
also draws substantially on a thirteenth-century academic polemic
by William of Saint-Amour, concerning Joachim of Fiore and his
prophetic mode of historiography. Translations and reworkings of
Ovid provide a further important ingredient.

In its dependence on anterior texts, Jean de Meun's *Rose* places in
relation with each other (at least) two very different discourses: one
of erotic quest, represented by Guillaume de Lorris, the broader
courtly tradition on which Guillaume's *Rose* depends, and which
includes the medieval reception of Ovid, and one of academic learning.
Formally, the two discourses intersect in their use of the dream-
vision framework: a first-person speaker records a dream in which
he is instructed by personified abstractions (principally Amor in
Guillaume de Lorris, Philosophy in Boethius, and Nature in Alan).
This conjunction has usually been taken as indicating that Jean is
philosophising the courtly *matière* of love. It could equally be read,
however, as an eroticisation of learning, and given that learning is
conducted through reading and writing, as an eroticisation of those
processes too. This confirms Huchet's account of medieval intertextuality as in some sense libidinal, but it also takes it further,
since it identifies an element in that desire as epistemephilia.

The argument of this paper is in three stages. First I consider how
Jean transforms Alan of Lille's writing metaphors into metaphors of
sexual difference. Next I examine a three-cornered interaction between
Jean, Guillaume de Lorris and Ovid, in which sex/gender roles are
problematised by competing oral discourses. Finally I consider the
implications of gender and sexual difference in the *Rose* for knowledge
and interpretation.

Nature and Genius: keeping a straight pen

A major source of Jean's *Rose* is Alan's *Plaint of Nature*, which may
have been composed *circa* 1160–5 (Sheridan, p. 35),[9] and most of
which apparently consists in a lengthy denunciation of male homosexuality by the goddess Nature. I shall contend that Alan's text is
itself homosexual, in the sense elaborated by Luce Irigaray,[10] and
that in rewriting it, Jean marks his own text as sexually different
from Alan's. The textual difference (or intertextual space) between
them is thus also a space of sexual difference.

Alan's Nature is God's vice-regent and substitute, but she irrespon-
sibly withdrew to 'the delightful palace of the ethereal region, where
the contending winds do not destroy the peace of unadulterated calm'
(VIII Prose 4; Sheridan, p. 146) and entrusted the day-to-day running
of the created world to Venus. Venus is a figure of sexual appetite in
men or women, and her task is to ensure that the earth's population
keeps reproducing. Nature's instructions to Venus use two images of
creativity, forging and writing:

> I assigned her [Venus] two approved hammers with which to nullify the
> snares of the Fates and also make a variety of things ready for existence.
> I also set aside outstanding workshops with anvils in which to do this
> work, giving instructions that she should apply these same hammers to
> these same anvils and faithfully devote herself to the production of things
> and not allow the hammers to stray away from their anvils in any form
> of deviation. I had also bestowed upon her an unusually powerful writing-
> pen for her work so that she might trace the classes of things, according to
> the rules of my orthography, on suitable pages which called for writing by
> this same pen and which through my kind gift she had in her possession,
> so that she might not suffer the same pen to wander in the smallest degree
> from the path of proper delineation into the byways of pseudography.
> (X Prose 5; Sheridan, p. 156)

The hammers–anvil image is an image of heterosexual intercourse
which emphatically polarises the active, male hammers (containing
the generative force to defeat death) and the passive female anvils.[11]
The picture of male genitalia is somewhat grotesquely completed by
the addition of a large pen to the two hammers. The 'pages which
called for writing' occupy with respect to the pen the same passive
role as the anvil did to the hammers. Yet on them, 'the classes of
things' (*all* things?) are to be written. The page metaphor seems to
back away here from the evocation of female genitals, suggesting

instead the 'text' of all existence, penned by Nature's writerly skill. The image of writing, that is, evokes the replenishment of creation rather than the more specific activity of sexual reproduction. It is less sexual, and correspondingly less clearly gendered, than the image of the forge.

This difference is confirmed when, in Nature's absence, things go wrong. Some young men, 'intoxicated with thirst for money, converted Venus' hammers to the function of anvils' (VIII Prose 4; Sheridan, p. 136); and some hammers make use of these 'counterfeit' anvils, leaving the real ones 'bewailing the loss of their own hammers and begging for them with tears' (!) (X Prose 5; Sheridan, p. 164). The grotesqueness of these passages suggests a distaste for sexual activity generally (a dirty, laborious, low-class occupation, even when you get your hammers and anvils the right way round) as much as a condemnation of homosexuality. Alan is far more at ease with the metaphor of writing:

> For the human race, fallen from its high estate, adopts a highly irregular [grammatical] change when it inverts the rules of Venus by introducing the use of barbarisms in its arrangements of genders. Thus man, his sex changed by a ruleless Venus, in defiance of due order, by his arrangement changes what is a straightforward attribute of his [i.e. his gender]. Abandoning in his deviation the true script of Venus, he is proved to be a sophistic pseudographer. (VIII Prose IV; Sheridan, p. 134)

Writing, in this passage, means writing grammatically accurate Latin. Virtually all of Nature's homophobic diatribe expands on this image, denouncing the faults of the 'text' of human behaviour, and stressing the need for correctness in grammar (i.e. Latin composition), rhetoric and dialectic. Alan's whole work, in highly intricate Latin, exhibits the arts that Nature (!) prescribes.[12]

Grammar, rhetoric and dialectic are the three essential skills of medieval clerical education. Only males have access to this education, so when he urges the correct practice of these disciplines, Alan must have male readers in mind. However, the term that he uses is *homo*, 'human being', rather than *vir*, 'adult male'. Thus, whereas the image of the hammer and anvils is explicit about (but perhaps uncomfortable with) sexual difference, the image of writing and the text is more evasive: it affirms masculinity, but draws back from confronting sexual difference; it implies the male penis, but subsumes it into a creative phallus which is the poet's pen and Nature's plan rolled into one.

This conflation of gender, art and neo-platonic revelation is confirmed by the last instance of the theme of writing in the *Plaint*. The work concludes with Nature's priest, Genius, anathematising all those who are guilty of the faults Nature has condemned. A complex figure with a long history in literature, Genius in twelfth-century writing is a figure both of physical regeneration and of priestly power.[13] These two forces, physical and spiritual, intersect in the imagination (*genius* is related to *ingenium*, 'imagination'), making Genius also a figure of the poet, who works with both concrete images and 'higher' truth.[14] Genius is described as wearing clothes on which 'the images of objects, lasting but for a moment, faded so quickly that they eluded the pursuit of our minds' (XVIII Prose 9; Sheridan, p. 215). He constantly draws 'images of things that kept changing from the shadowly outline of a picture to the realism of their actual being' (ibid; Sheridan, p. 216). So long as he writes with his right hand, he produces models of excellence (Helen for Beauty, Hercules for Strength, etc.). When that tires and he resorts to his left hand, imperfect images result. Intriguingly lovely though this description is, it reveals the obfuscation of sexual difference in twelfth-century (and later?) humanism: for although unambiguously masculine, and the figure of a male poet, Genius is also envisaged as representing the reproduction of forms for *all* humanity. Alan's constant suppression of the female or the feminine means that his image of writing is both sexed and a denial of sexual difference. It is 'homosexual' in the sense that it allows for the existence of only *one* sexuality.

Jean de Meun takes from Alan the Nature–Genius partnership. Jean's Nature, like Alan's, laments human sexual deficiency – insufficient commitment to reproduction is the target here, however, homosexuality being barely mentioned – and calls on Genius to anathematise those who fail to further her work. In an outrageous sermon, Genius tells Amor's supporters that they won't have eternal life unless they have frequent intercourse. In this way, Nature and Genius throw their weight in favour of the forces trying to win the rose. The imagery of sex as writing diffused through the *Plaint of Nature* is concentrated by Jean de Meun in this sermon. In this new, burlesque context, the engagement of textuality with sexuality is heightened and transformed.

In advocating sexual activity, Genius uses three metaphors: ploughing, forging and writing. The ploughing image is a bit ambiguous, since ploughing is one of the results of the decline from the Golden

Age after the castration of Saturn, a myth Genius comments on at some length, (20032–211; Dahlberg, pp. 329–31);[15] whilst Genius is in favour of metaphorical 'ploughing', he is apparently against the real thing. The forging image obviously recalls the laments of Alan's Nature. In Jean, Nature herself is presented as working at a forge; if men keep at it with their hammers on the anvils provided, they will be continuing her work. As in Alan, it is, however, the image of writing which is predominant. Man should reproduce himself by writing with his 'pen' on the 'tablets' provided by Nature (see 19545, 19629–36, 19672–6, etc.; Dahlberg, pp. 322ff.). Genius himself is a writer. He reads from a written script, dictated to him by Nature; his job, as well as being her priest, is to work as Nature's scribe, reciting to her the tally he has made at her instruction of all her creatures (16278–84; Dahlberg, p. 275).

Whereas in Alan the image of writing manages at once to be sexual and to fight shy of sexual difference, in Jean it is clearly sexed. Genius addresses a male audience (Amor's army of barons, the supporters of the dreamer) and represents *male* sexuality, not reproduction in general; he is complemented by Venus, who figures *female* sexuality in the *Rose*, and so also becomes gender-specific by contrast with her role in Alan. The images of sexual activity are all clearly expressive of anatomical difference. The female component is regularly evoked (in Alan the 'pages' metaphor occurs only in the one passage quoted above) and Genius identifies throughout with the masculine side of the polarity. Here he is, for example, expanding on his anathema:

But those who do not use the pens, by means of which the mortal live for ever, on the beautiful and valuable tablets which Nature certainly didn't prepare for them in order that they should lie idle, on the contrary she lent them in order that all [men] should be writers upon them, so that all men and women might live; those who receive the two hammers and do not work straight at forging on the right anvil with them as they should; those whose sin blinds them through their pride that leads them astray, so that they break up the straight path in the rich and fertile field and go like wretches to plough in the fallowland where their seed is lost ...; those who despise such a mistress [as Nature] and read the text askew, and refuse to set about correctly understanding the right meaning, but rather pervert the text when they come to read it: may all these, along with the excommunication which damns them, since they are resolved to go that way, lose, before they die, the purse and the testicles which are the sign that they are male! May they lose the pendants on which the purse hangs! May the hammers fixed inside them be torn out! May the pens be taken from them, since they haven't wished to write on the precious tablets that were so suited to them! And may they have their bones broken so that they never mend if they don't plough straight with their ploughs and ploughshares! (19629–80; Dahlberg, pp. 323–4)

Genius's attentions to male genitals remind us that another meaning of the word 'genius' in twelfth-century poetry is a life force inhabiting each testicle,[16] a meaning only latent in Alan's text.

In superimposing his Genius's exhortation to reproductive sex on Nature's attack on non-heterosexual sex in the *Plaint*, therefore, Jean marks the cultural importance of sexual difference which Alan's text seeks to evade. His speakers locate themselves in a world which is no longer homogeneous, and the words they utter have no pretentions to being addressed to all, or on behalf of all. The pen may still be phallic, potent and creative, but it is no longer all-subsuming: something different from it is acknowledged as existing. Jean's text, in accepting sexual difference, is itself sexually different from the text it rewrites.

Venus and Adonis: mixing voices

I now turn to a part of the *Rose* whose intertexts belong not in academic writing but in the Ovidian–courtly tradition, in order to see how the writerly introduction of sexual difference is qualified by oral discourse about gender.

The story of Venus and Adonis is set into the plot of the *Rose* at a point where Amor has realised that he will be unable to break down Jalousie's castle and gain entrance to the rose garden without calling on the help of his mother Venus. Messengers despatched to fetch her find her warning Adonis against the dangers of hunting fierce animals. He later died, the narrative continues, gored by a wild boar, and because Venus was away, she did not help him. The story concludes with the following moral:

Fair sirs, whatever happens to you, remember this exemplary tale [*exemple*]. Those of you who do not obey your *amie* must know you are being extremely foolish. You should believe them all, for their words are as true as history. If they swear, 'We are yours entirely', believe them as though it were the Lord's prayer. Never give up believing them. If Reason comes, don't believe her; even if she were carrying a crucifix, don't believe her any more than I did. If Adonis had believed his *amie*, his life would have been a lot longer. (15751–64; Dahlberg, p. 267)

Jean's ninety-line narrative is a drastic abbreviation of Ovid's *Metamorphoses*, X 515–739.[17] The moral, however, is an addition. It appears to be a *réplique* to the moral drawn at the end of another adaptation in the *Rose* of the *Metamorphoses*: the Narcissus story, told by Guillaume de Lorris in the first part of the poem, and which somewhat surprisingly concludes, 'Ladies, learn this *exemple*, you who misbehave towards your lovers [*amis*]; for if you let them perish, God will know how to reward you' (1507–10; Dahlberg, p. 51).

This instance of intertextuality differs markedly from the Jean–Alan interaction. Although quoting Ovid could be seen as a learned allusion, the imagery of writing is not invoked to signal clerical achievement. The whole dynamic of the Adonis story is rather that of oral literature: Venus warns, Adonis ought to listen. The verb repeatedly used for her warning (*chastier*, 15727, 15728, 15729) is one often used in performed lyric, and forms the basis of a literary genre of instruction, the *chastiement*. Indeed, the morals quoted above could be read as mini-*chastiements*, in which noblemen and noblewomen are apostrophised with (pseudo-)advice on 'courtly' behaviour: 'Sirs, treat your *amies* thus', 'Ladies, this is how not to treat your *amis*'. In both the Adonis and Narcissus stories, however, the speaker goes unheeded: Adonis takes no notice of Venus; Echo's courtship of Narcissus meets with his indifference, and she is reduced to an empty voice. It is, I think, no coincidence that both these ignored speakers are female. If Genius's sermon has provided a strong model of sexual difference, it has left a lot of problems unaddressed. Many readers may feel no happier with his confident summons to phallic activity than they were with Alan's neurotic homophobia. The Adonis nexus considers textuality beyond the pen, and explores the confusion of discourses which complicate the social experience of sexual difference. Just as the space marked out between Genius's sermon and Nature's plaint comes to signify the sexual difference between the two texts, so the ironies and overlaps of the various texts in the Adonis passage mark the shifts and contradictions of gender identity, particularly for women.

The morals, absent from Ovid, are a good starting point for analysis. That of Guillaume de Lorris has attracted much attention because it seems so inconsequent.[18] His retelling of the Narcissus story stresses the equivalence between the destinies of Narcissus and Echo. Her unrequited love for him, her curse and her death occupy lines 1444–68 (Dahlberg, p. 50), only slightly less than the lines 1469–1506

(Dahlberg, pp. 50–1) narrating Narcissus' love for his reflection and death at its indifference to him. Each of these two halves ends with a commentary which appears to take Echo's side. Her curse, that Narcissus should suffer a joyless passion, is pronounced in order that 'he might know and understand what pain loyal lovers suffer who are so vilely rejected' (1463–6), and is upheld by God as 'reasonable' (1467); Narcissus' fate meets with the comment, 'thus he had his reward and his deserts from the girl whose love he had refused' (1504–6). The narrative, then, appears to back the girl against the unresponsive male. Why then does the concluding moral sound a warning to unresponsive women? Because it is typically women who cause men to suffer? Because it was Echo's fault all along for chasing after Narcissus? Whatever the reason, and even if there is no reason apart from demonstrating the fatuity of moralising, the passage neatly illustrates the imbrication of the courtly with the misogynistic. Intense emotion (of men) goes hand in hand with severe policing (of women).

Irony on this score is more apparent in the Adonis moral, which consciously presents itself as the other half of this 'his' and 'hers' diptych. The speaker here is, in a sense, the same 'person' as the speaker of the Narcissus moral, since this is still 'his' dream, although his character has gone downhill rather since Jean took over. In a 3000-line harrangue, Reason has tried to dissuade him from the pursuit of the rose but he persists in blind allegiance to Amor (4229–7229; Dahlberg, pp. 93–137). That he has turned his back on Reason is evident, since he argues here that because one woman was right once (had Adonis obeyed Venus, he wouldn't have died), all women should be believed at all times. His very stupidity, however, places his utterance on an interesting border between 'courtliness' (assigning authority to women's decrees in matters of love) and misogyny (denying them validity); their words are as true as both history and the words of Christ when they pronounce that most unconvincing of clichés 'We are all yours'. (The expectation that declarations of fidelity are either deliberate lies or else incapable of fulfilment has already been firmly established in readers' minds by the cynical advice on courtship and deception given by Ami to the dreamer, 7236–9999; Dahlberg, pp. 138–78.) Women must be believed, then, regardless of whether what they say is credible.

This self-undermining *chastiement* resumes, with an amusing swagger, the ironies already present in the story that precedes it.

Adonis appears to accept Venus' authority, acquiescing to all her requests; but he does so in a spirit of indifference to what she says ('whether it were true or false', 15733) in order to 'get some peace' (15734). The courtly term *amie* resonates oddly with this explicit contempt ('he set little store by what his *amie* told him', 15731–2). Like the moral, this is a departure from Ovid's text which merely says 'the boy's manly courage [*virtus*] would not brook her advice' (709, p. 115).

Both these passages continue and enlarge upon a confusion of discourses which is already discernible in Venus' words. Broadly, Venus advises Adonis to avoid dangerous animals while hunting, advice which could be passed off as sensible, if scarcely glamorous. In the *Metamorphoses*, she tells at length the story of how she transformed Atalanta and her lover into lions as punishment for their ingratitude and sacrilege towards her, and thus provides a rationale for her fear that lions, at least, may threaten her happiness with Adonis. In the *Rose*, however, this narrative is omitted and Venus' words focus anxiety about competing sex/gender roles. She addresses Adonis with the courtly apostrophe *ami*, and some of the animals she exhorts him to hunt are linked to the love chase in courtly literature (stags, does, deer). Others, however, are more explicitly associated with sex (*connins*, 'little rabbits/cunts') or lust (goats). And the 'unmanliness' of her advice is implicit in her anti-heroic vocabulary: '*Ami*, when your pack of dogs is ready, and you go in search of quarry, if you find one that runs away, chase it once it is in flight: run after it boldly, but never let your step be turned against those that fiercely defend themselves. Be cowardly and lazy against the bold, for against those with bold hearts no boldness can be secure; it is dangerous to fight against the bold-hearted. (15699–15712; Dahlberg, p. 266). Her own phraseology makes Venus' advice unfollowable. The 'courtly' chase, reduced to a cowardly coney hunt, is the scene not of virility but of abjection.

Here, too, the *Rose* does not correspond with Ovid's text. It is, however, in the tradition of medieval allegoresis of Ovid, as transmitted by the early fourteenth-century *Ovide Moralisé*.[19] In this massive compilation, the Adonis narrative is followed by three 'moralisations', the first of which uses an ethical vocabulary close to that of Jean de Meun. Venus is glossed as a figure of lust and Adonis as a figure of pleasure, who is hunting his own downfall. When Venus counsels him not to hunt dangerous beasts, this is because 'lust wishes to be idle and has no thought of work or effort, rather wishes to lead an idle life, for idleness leads to lust' (X 3728–32). The *Ovide Moralisé* had, however, taken a distinctly more 'courtly' tone when first describing the value of Venus' injunctions: '[Adonis] never listened to the advice [*chastoi*] that his *amie* had given him. It was foolish and criminal to disobey his *amie*'s commands. Ill will come to him of it, I don't doubt' (X 2455–9). The moralised Ovid has thus kept separate positive and negative readings of Venus' role which jostle together in the *Rose*.

The problem with Venus' speech in the *Rose*, then, is that it is right overall (it *is* dangerous to hunt fierce animals and Adonis *does* die) but unacceptable in detail. She is both possessed of authority as a courtly lady (and a goddess to boot), and deprived of it by the tradition of anti-feminism. The responses of her two male listeners bring out the paradox: Adonis doesn't believe her (even though he should); the dreamer recommends believing all sweethearts (even though one shouldn't).

Thus while, as I said, this narrative recalls the oral genre of the *chastiement*, its intertext extends beyond that, to the indefinite oral texts of cliché and prejudice. The lack of a determinate boundary between oral literature and social discourses has major implications for readers/hearers of the story, caught up in the same sex/gender ideologies as the text. Jean's narrative points up the stupidity and banality of these stereotypes without attempting to resolve their contradictions; there is, after all, no 'outside' of social discourses, only the irony 'between' them. Indeed, the narrator's imposition of an anti-feminist position ('lust saps manhood') on a female speaker (Venus) underlines how inescapable such cultural positions are. It is difficult for the reader to avoid complicity with them, since the very fact of recognising a discourse implies some degree of collaboration with it: in picking up the different threads that are interwoven in the Adonis narrative and sorting them into discrete, named discourses, I am to some degree acknowledging their cultural dominance and paying tribute to their power. Misogynist texts in particular rely heavily on a social intertext, summoning their readers to supply an all-too-familiar context in which to read anti-feminist *topoi*.[20]

Whereas written textuality is a masculine prerogative, the oral belongs to women as well. Women's words tend to go unheeded, but any speech may be infiltrated by a social *doxa* which is beyond individual control. The stupid dreamer, who recommends unquestioning belief in women, is in some ways an ideal reader, since the power of these social codes places textual reliability, truth and falsehood out of reach of all of us.

Knowing textuality

I have argued that Jean's Genius narrows the significance of the corresponding figure in Alan's *Plaint*. I want now to look at the ways this relativisation affects the text as a source of knowledge. Our attempts at constructing meanings for Genius's sermon, and for the *Rose* as a whole, can be informed by the way Genius himself reads the works that preceded him, and what he learned (or failed to learn) from them.

Genius's sermon is based on large sections of the *Plaint* in which Nature reveals to the dreamer the shortcomings of the created world. Alan's metaphors are opaque, and the *Plaint* is diversely interpreted by modern critics. But the role of the sex–writing metaphor seems to be to link man's bodily behaviour with his 'true' spiritual meaning, just as the fabulations of allegory link the letter and the spirit of the text. Improper use of the body, like corrupt linguistic usage, leads man away from the life which Nature intended him for, and makes him falsify the true text of creation.

Jean de Meun uses the dream-vision framework to spark an interaction between erotic and philosophical discourses, and his figure of Genius contributes to both: the dreamer is encouraged along the path to consummation, and visions of heavenly reward are offered to the sexually productive. Genius propounds this revelation in a way which keeps the metaphor of writing to the fore. He comments lengthily on the text of Guillaume de Lorris's description of the rose garden and the spring of Narcissus, and then jettisons it in favour of a text of his own, describing a paradise park where the saved will follow the Lamb (20279–636; Dahlberg, pp. 332–7). This is the bliss to which those who copulate will have access: the more they 'write', the closer they will get to the ideal text. I cited earlier a passage where Genius emphasises the importance of reading, as well as writing, correctly: lovers/hearers should not read askew (19657–62; Dahlberg, p. 324). He himself may seem to have read and understood Alan of Lille, since his message implies a homology between the bodily and the spiritual: 'proper' sexuality and the joys of eternity are united in a 'proper' textuality.

I think, however, that the eroticism of Genius's sermon short-circuits the philosophical orientation of Alan's text. The libidinal impulse in Alan is often experienced as a desire to get off the topic of sex. The sexual metaphor, in his text, is highly 'metaphoric' in that it carries the reader through, 'translates' or 'transfers' quickly to other terms (writing, grammar, discipline, Nature, truth ...). By contrast, Genius's sermon, though reliant on the tropes of the twelfth-century tradition, is extraordinarily literal-minded. Alan's Genius had preached that homosexual activity denied entry to heaven. Jean's Genius reads this as a claim that heterosexual activity guarantees you a place there! He laments the Fall of man, imaged by the castration of Saturn which put an end to the Golden Age; but his recipe for salvation is to put castration into reverse by a wholehearted return to the sexual function! Alan's metaphors may be opaque, but they seem always to drift away from the body. Genius's terms, by contrast, are retained there. Sexual activity (in the lower body) becomes ploughing, forging or writing (in the upper body), but that seems to be the end of the road; there is no admittance to the metaphysical. It is true that Genius's message overall is that the sexual body gives eternal life to the spirit. But the very outrageousness of this contention draws attention to the gap between bodily and metaphysical discourses, more than it asserts continuity between them. The homologous hierarchies of body and soul, letter and spirit, on which neo-platonist allegory depends, are invoked by Genius, but they are ironised, relativised and parodied.

In putting forward his ideal text, Genius criticises the part of Guillaume de Lorris's *Rose* where the rose garden was first described.[21] The dreamer saw it reflected in Amor's spring, the very spring where Narcissus met his end, and the occasion for the retelling of his story. The Narcissus story is pre-eminently a fable about the problems of recognition and reading – another instance of interaction between the erotic and the epistemic strands in the *Rose*. Genius foregrounds this interaction by criticising Narcissus' failure of perception, and contending that the water of life in his own text is a much surer guide to truth. In citing passages from the description by Guillaume de Lorris of Amor's paradise garden, and glossing them as indicative of limitation, suffering and damnation, Genius offers a 'strong' model of a reader's freedom to bestow 'meaning' on a text. Here, for example, is his commentary on Amor's spring (the words in italics are quotations from Guillaume's text):

And then he says that it is endless, *that it is brighter than refined silver*. You see what nonsense he is serving up! On the contrary, it is so black, turbid and foul that anyone who sticks their head there to gaze into it [or: to see himself reflected in it] cannot see a thing. [...] At the bottom, he says, there are two crystals which the sun, which is never dark, *causes to shine so brightly with its beams* that anyone who watches them can always see half of the things enclosed within the garden, *and he can see the remainder* if he decides to sit at the other side, the crystals are so clear and powerful. Indeed, they are murky and harmful. Why, when the sun beams its rays at them, can they not show everything at once? Because, by faith, they are unable to, on account of the darkness that obscures them. They are so murky and dark [...] that they have no power to reveal anything. (20431–60; Dahlberg, p. 335)

If this is how Genius treats the work in whose continuation he figures, we may feel licensed to treat *his* text in an equally inventive fashion.

I suggested earlier that the Adonis story figures dilemmas in the reception and understanding of spoken discourse. If Adonis and Narcissus are in some ways parallel figures, so are Genius and Venus: both want their own text to be taken as authoritative, but with little likelihood of success. Both of them are compromised, in different ways, by sexual difference, Genius because his partiality restricts him, Venus because she is overdetermined by anti-feminist as well as courtly stereotypes.

The gender hierarchy, created by sexual difference, is homologous with the other hierarchies in play in the *Rose*: body and soul, letter and spirit, and, we might add, sex and philosophy, reading and writing, oral discourse and written text, continuation and model. Any of these hierarchical relations is worth analysing. I think, however, that the sex–gender hierarchy occupies a position of particular privilege amongst them, because as we have seen it pervades the discourses of philosophy and textuality in the *Rose* as well as the love quest. And the impetus which sexual difference imparts to the text is deconstructive: it both presents a model of hierarchised difference and undoes it. The ambiguity of Venus, which I have examined in detail in the Adonis story, characterises her role throughout.[22] Whereas the *Plaint* concludes with Genius's anathema, giving the male poet-figure the last word, in the *Rose* Genius's sermon is ineffective; Venus' torch alone brings down the walls of Jalousie's castle, and the lover gets the rose. But the question whether this makes Venus 'authoritative' or not remains unresolved.

The prominence, in the *Rose*, of sexual difference as an agent of textual instability recalls the writings of Barthes and Derrida in the late 1960s and early 1970s. It is particularly reminiscent of Derrida's *Spurs*, in which Nietzsche's comments on sexual difference, combined with his stylistic evasiveness, appear a privileged means of figuring pressure upon the conceptual hierarchies of his philosophical predecessors.[23] Because 'woman is a name of the untruth of truth' (p. 51), she does not simply reverse existing oppositions, she suspends them, allowing the lower of two hierarchised terms to invade the one we have been led to think of as secure in its superiority, and transforming metaphysics into writing:

> The question of the woman suspends the decidable opposition of true and non-true and inaugurates the epochal regime of quotation marks which is to be enforced for every concept belonging to the system of philosophical decidability. The hermeneutic project which postulates a true sense of the text is disqualified under this regime. Reading is freed from the horizon of the meaning or truth of being, liberated from the values of the product's production or the present's presence. Whereupon the question of style is immediately unloosed as a question of writing. (p. 107)

Likewise in Genius's sermon, the letter encroaches on the spirit and the body, striving for salvation, assumes the role of the soul; the continuation insinuates itself 'above' that which it continues, and the reader dictates to the writer. All these processes of instability are figured by the Adonis story, where the feminine is both inferior and superior, both compelling of belief and unbelievable, both true and untrue.

I started my reading of the *Rose* with the account of textuality outlined by Jean-Charles Huchet. For Huchet, medieval texts are desirous of other texts, and the *Rose*, with its vast array of intertextual reference, its extraordinary proliferation of manuscripts, and the enormous weight of critical literature (not to mention the medieval imitations and adaptations) exhibits an apparently inexhaustible libidinal energy. But it further qualifies the nature of this desire as a desire to read and to understand – a desire that can never be other than frustrated since the more Genius comments on Alan of Lille or Narcissus, the further he moves away from them; and as a desire to be read, and to be understood – a desire which is equally doomed to disappointment, since the more Venus talks to Adonis, the less he wants to hear, and the longer Genius preaches, the less we believe his priestly credentials. Jean's dream vision has as its protagonist a lover so stupid and so deaf to all the learning showered on him by other speakers that the whole process of listening and understanding is placed in doubt. And the status of 'sources' and of 'imitations', not to mention 'interpretations' and critical readings (such as this one) is in doubt too. The *Rose* both stages and inspires a massive programme of re-reading *and* questions our capacity to understand and learn from prior texts.

Why then, to return to my very first question, do the Middle Ages get forgotten? What desire is satisfied by ignoring texts like the *Romance of the Rose*? Perhaps this neglect is propelled less by a preference on the part of modernity for different parents than by a demand for infancy: a desire to postulate a time before the complexities of language, a space 'outside' modern conceptions of textuality, a state before the Fall. Yet I doubt if any period is as conscious as the medieval one of the effects on language of the Fall. The word for the male genitals – *coilles* – is used only twice in the 21000 lines of the *Rose*, in both cases in the context of castration.[24] The loss of potency and plenitude is the condition in which the dreamer, in his dream world, lives out his obsession with sex and language. What separates modern textuality from that of the *Rose* is not alterity so much as a disconcerting similarity.

Notes

1 My title is inspired by a recent book by Donald Maddox, *The Arthurian Romances of Chrétien de Troyes: Once and Future Fictions*, Cambridge, 1990, itself an allusion to the Latin tag designating Arthur as *rex quondam futurusque*, 'the once and future king'.
2 Michael Worton and Judith Still, ed. *Intertextuality: Theories and Practices*, Manchester, 1990; Terence Cave, *Recognitions: A Study in Poetics*, Oxford, 1988, justifies the lacuna on the grounds that Aristotle's *Poetics* were unknown in the Middle Ages; Andrew Martin, *The Knowledge of Ignorance: From Genesis to Jules Verne*, Cambridge, 1985.
3 *Essai de poétique médiévale*, Paris, 1972. An important concept elaborated in this book is that of *mouvance*, the propensity of medieval vernacular works to undergo alteration as a result either of oral transmission or of scribal/editorial intervention. A consequence of *mouvance* is that the 'work' is itself characteristically an intertext. Also influential was Zumthor's concept of 'register': an intertextual key, or map, underlying manifestations of a particular kind of text (e.g. the love lyric), and furnishing their entire semiotic, thereby making redundant concepts such as authorship, subjectivity, or reference to historical reality.
4 The translations are mine.
5 Sylvia Huot, *From Song to Book: The Poetics of Writing in Old French Lyric and Lyrical Narrative Poetry*, Ithaca and London, 1987, p. 84.
6 The *Rose* was also the object of a major literary-critical debate, the so-called *querelle de la Rose* of the early fifteenth century, in which Christine de Pisan and others were involved.

7 See Karl August Ott, 'Jean de Meun und Boethius', in Ute Schwab and Elfriede Stutz, ed., *Philologische Studien: Gedenkenschrifte für Richard Kienast*, Heidelberg, 1978, pp. 193–227.

8 See most recently Rita Copeland, *Rhetoric, Hermeneutics, and Translation in the Middle Ages: Academic Traditions and Vernacular Texts*, Cambridge, 1991.

9 *De Planctu Naturae*, ed. T. Wright in *Satirical Poets of the Twelfth Century*, London, 1872. I cite it by section, and by page reference in the English translation by James J. Sheridan, *Alan of Lille: The Plaint of Nature, Translation and Commentary*, Toronto, 1980.

10 Notably in *Speculum de l'autre femme*, Paris, 1974.

11 The active–passive distinction reflects one tradition in ancient physiology according to which the male provides the form, the female merely the matter and the mould for the offspring.

12 Cf. Sheridan's comment, 'Nevertheless one cannot escape the conclusion that it may be a display piece. The author revels in every device of Rhetoric' (p. 33).

13 Jane Chance Nitzche, *The Genius Figure in Antiquity and the Middle Ages*, New York, 1975.

14 Winthrop Wetherbee, 'The Theme of Imagination in Medieval Poetry and the Allegorical Figure "Genius"', *Medievalia et Humanistica*, VII, 1976, pp. 45–64, and *Platonism and Poetry in the Twelfth Century: The Literary Influence of the School of Chartres*, Princeton, 1972, pp. 93–5.

15 Citations from the *Romance of the Rose* are by line number in the edition by Daniel Poirion, *Guillaume de Lorris et Jean de Meun: Le Roman de la Rose*, Paris, 1974, and by page number in the English translation by Charles Dahlberg, *The Romance of the Rose: Guillaume de Lorris and Jean de Meun*, 2nd edition, Hanover and London, 1983. Since Dahlberg's translation is rather stuffy (he belongs to a school of *Rose* criticism which views the whole poem as an orthodox Catholic polemic), I have supplied my own.

16 See Nitzche, *Genius*, p. 90, and Wetherbee, *Platonism*, pp. 182–4.

17 Ovid, *Metamorphoses*, trans. Frank Justus Miller, London and Cambridge, Mass., 1956.

18 David Hult, *Self-fulfilling Prophecies: Readership and Authority in the First 'Roman de la Rose'*, Cambridge, 1986, pp. 273–5.

19 *Ovide Moralisé: Poème du commencement du quatorzième siècle*, ed. C. de Boer, in *Verhandelingen der Koninklijke Akademie van Wetenschappen te Amsterdam*, XV, 1915; XXI, 1920; XXX, 1931–2; XXXVII, 1936 and XLIII, 1938. Books X–XIII are in vol. XXXVII. There being no English translation of this text, I have supplied my own.

20 See Jill Mann, *Geoffrey Chaucer: Feminist Readings*, Hemel Hempstead 1991, pp. 48–86, especially p. 62; and R. Howard Bloch, 'Medieval Misogyny', *Representations*, XX, 1987, pp. 1–24.

21 On this much-discussed passage, see in particular Kevin Brownlee, 'Jean de Meun and the Limits of Romance: Genius as Rewriter of Guillaume de Lorris', in Kevin Brownlee and Marina Scordilis Brownlee, ed., *Romance: Generic Transformation from Chrétien de Troyes to Cervantes*, Hanover and London, 1985, pp. 114–34.

22 Created from Saturn's severed genitals, Venus, while female and a force of feminine desire, is also a transform of the phallus. See my 'The Birth of Venus', in Kevin Brownlee and Marina Scordilis Brownlee, ed., *Boundaries and Transgressions in Medieval Culture* (forthcoming).

23 Jacques Derrida, *Eperons: Les Styles de Nietzsche / Spurs: Nietszche's Styles*, trans. Barbara Harlow, Chicago, 1979.

24 See Daniel Poirion, 'Les Mots et les choses', *Information Littéraire*, XXVI, 1974, pp. 7–11 (p. 8).

Cultural memory and the art of the novel: gender and narrative in eighteenth-century France

Nancy K. Miller

> What configuration of power constructs the subject and
> the Other, that binary relation between 'men' and
> 'women', and the internal stability of those terms?
> Judith Butler, *Gender Trouble*

The history of authorship in France is a narrative constructed by
gender. For the eighteenth century, this construction can be read
quite clearly in the accounts describing the various modes of the novel,
the genre in which women's participation was from the beginning
both foundational and acknowledged. My general argument is that by
their social and cultural assumptions about gender and writing, the
literary categories that have served retrospectively to organise the
variety of prose fiction within the novel as genre in the eighteenth
century have effectively excluded the works of women writers from
their historical relationship to the production of literature.[1] Specifically, to designate all women's texts as belonging to the domain of
the *roman sentimental* (the novel of feeling) displaces that writing
into the margins of the cultural record. What is *le roman sentimental*?
Henri Coulet, in his classic study, *Le Roman jusqu'à la révolution*,
puts the matter succinctly: 'Under this heading are included, somewhat
arbitrarily, novels that have different subjects and forms, but whose
purpose is to depict and analyse feelings rather than to describe
manners' (p. 378).[2] Because the history of the novel is typically seen
as an evolution toward the realism of the nineteenth century, which
is to say the novel of manners (*moeurs*), and because the novels of the
eighteenth century are typically seen through that paradigm, to
classify women's novels as *romans pour coeurs sensibles*, novels for
the 'feeling heart', is both to separate their works from the dominant
tradition and to refuse their powers to read the world, their powers
to know and describe the real.

If all women's writing tends to be included in the category of *le roman sentimental*, what of men's writing? Here, to be sure, there is greater range, but the mode that dominates – whatever the sub-genre – is that of *libertinage*. As Coulet argues with respect to the novel before 1760 (while acknowledging the arbitrariness of the date):

> Libertine style is perhaps more a question of technique than of perspective; its prevalence in the eighteenth century demonstrates its importance as a method of expression, but also its inconsistencies as a system of thought. There is libertinism in thinkers as different as Prévost, Marivaux, Montesquieu, Diderot and Voltaire, and one doesn't have to look far to find it in Rousseau as well. The eighteenth century as a whole recognised and proclaimed the role of the senses, and the way in which the moral is determined by the physical, and looked for a seemly language to expound this role in the feeling that was most often idealised: love. (p. 386)

The quickest way to think about what the term *libertine* has signified historically for the novel is to note the extraordinary appeal – fascination might be a better word – today in France, England and the United States of Laclos's *Liaisons dangereuses*, the masterpiece of the genre, we might say, in the theatre and as a film. It is not difficult to grasp why the term *libertine* should apply to the *Liaisons*. But it is important to understand what else this term means for the eighteenth-century novel: the dominant mode of fiction described as libertine, which is to say, in the most general (generic) possible terms, the plot of serial heterosexual engagement seen from a male-authored and male-narrated perspective, in practice comes to include all works to which critics and literary historians *also* assign the two prime values of mimetic representation essential to the genre of the novel: the portrayal of *moeurs* and psychological analysis; a vision of social life, subjected to some form of moral judgement. These terms are not especially precise, of course, but that is exactly why they are effective. What concerns us here is the fact that for the uses of literary history, the label *libertine* rather than limiting a work's attractiveness by its thematics of sexual power games, finally relocates the work within the mainstream of what is today in France regularly and quite unself-consciously called 'the national patrimony'.[3]

Since, as this essay will show, men's writing which describes 'manners' (social behaviour) in a libertine style also analyses the feelings seemingly assigned to the *roman sentimental*, we might ask whether it is possible that in this gendered division of authorial labour the women's writing of *le roman sentimental* portrays not only feelings but also manners? Women's writing in the *ancien régime*, I will argue, does represent the manners of social life and to miss this is to miss a crucial account of women's relations both to the powers that construct their identity as social subjects and to the power of representation. In the pages that follow, by bringing together texts that are normally kept apart, I hope to contribute to a revisionary account of the genre's development as a contested and contestatory cultural performance in which women's voices play a crucial dialogic role. In a word: sentimental texts by women writers produce a critique not only of the world and manners of libertine texts but also of the categories of heterosexual power relations that construct them.

I'm going to take the case of two novels written within the same decade to consider both what sentimental and libertine fictions have in common and the grounds of their differences. The texts I have chosen are Charles Pinot-Duclos's 1751 *Mémoires pour servir à l'histoire des moeurs du XVIIIe siècle*, a memoir-novel, and Marie-Jeanne Riccoboni's 1759 epistolary fiction, *Lettres de Milady Juliette Catesby à Milady Henriette Campley, son amie*.[4] Duclos's *Mémoires* and Ricoboni's *Juliette Catesby*, like many eighteenth-century novels, represent the vicissitudes of a heterosexual plot within an aristocratic setting in which the protagonists spend most of their waking hours dealing with the hermeneutic perplexities posed by the opposite sex; despite the difference of genre, they both tell the story of a sentimental education that ends with marriage. More specifically, however, I have chosen to pair the two novels because by virtue of their insistence on gendered valences of memory, notably the remembering and forgetting of sexual event, they illuminate the fundamental ambiguity of the famous 'reign of women' said to characterise eighteenth-century social life. If Ricoboni's novel, which, one could argue, is engendered by the various meanings of the verb to 'forget' (meanings activated by a young man's sexual oversight), it also provides a reflection on what women's memory remembers for the culture.

At stake for us then in this paired reading will be a tiered reflection: what can these narratives of gender and memory, memory and sexual experience tell us about so-called sentimental and libertine modes of fiction?[5] What does sentimental or libertine memory tell us not only about the politics of literary traditions but about what might be entailed in changing them? Finally, what does the gendering of memory have to do with the differential relation of men and women to the representation of *moeurs*, to what we might call fictional reality?

I begin with the Duclos because the novel's structure clearly shows the generic constraints it embodies. For me this is the main interest of the text. I could equally well have chosen his better known *Confessions du Comte de* ∗∗∗ (1741) or Crébillon's 'masterpiece' in the genre, *Les Egarements du coeur et de l'esprit* (*The Wayward Head and Heart*) (1735–6) as instances of the social construction of masculinity under the *ancien régime*. These texts all begin with a young man's entrance into the world, his sexual initiation and social education at the hands of a variety of women.⁶ Duclos details twenty-three in the 'roman-liste' of the *Confessions*; here, he's down to nine. After running through the list, the hero finally settles on a virtuous woman who is truly worthy of him, with whom he can live happily ever after.

The relationship between memoirs, the libertine and the representation of *moeurs* is articulated explicitly in the *avertissement* to the reader that frames Duclos's novel: 'Love, amorous intrigues, and even libertinage have always played such a large role in most men's lives, and especially those in high society [*le monde*], that a nation's customs [*moeurs*] would be hard to understand if such important subjects were left out.' And the narrator explains that, 'Since I intend to focus on the errors of my youth, it should not be surprising that love will play a large part' (pp. 10–11). To say love, of course, is to mean women; indeed as Henri Coulet puts it in the preface to Duclos's novel, women 'are the most important thing in the Mémoires' (p. ii). Interestingly, then, in these three versions of the book's focus, what matters is women; unnamed, they nonetheless inhere in the authorial project – in libertinage, in love, in 'the customs of a nation'. For the narrator, the errors of his youth are essentially the time spent with the wrong women; women, who will all ultimately be erased from memory by the perfection of the one who is chosen at the end to end the memoirs.

The purpose of this young man's recollection, and its relation to the genre of the text itself is articulated explicitly in terms of memory and sexual experience, or rather in terms of the women with whom the man has had affairs. 'It's not my intention to recall here all the women I've known; most of them seemed to forget our liaisons, and sometimes I myself barely remember them. I want to include only those relationships which had something singular about them, and I shall not forget one particular woman whom I especially liked, but our liaison was so stormy that it was unbearable' (p. 104). Missing from the list are those women who lacked the singularity to imprint forcefully on his memory, those women who like him forgot to notice what they were doing. As it turns out, the liaison with the 'one particular woman' will be the last before the change of heart that brings about the end of the novel: the penultimate *égarement* (straying) before leaving his dissolute life.

This summary is meant to provide a flavour of the tone and structure of this novel, in which through the reconstruction of his sexual life a man negotiates his social and moral identity. What remains to consider is the manner in which this trajectory of self-fashioning based on the movement through women gets fixed and becomes the emblem of heterosexual union; but I want to defer consideration of the marriage trope until we get to the end of our discussion of Riccoboni's text.

If Duclos's narrator cannot remember all the women he had affairs with, Riccoboni's Juliette Catesby cannot forget the man of her life. Indeed she cannot forget the man whose 'oubli' as it will be ambiguously named – whose forgetting – shattered her happiness. The novel opens with Juliette's separation from the friend Henriette to whom the letters of the novel are addressed; she is leaving in order to avoid meeting again this man who, as she puts it, 'for two years was always on my mind, and nothing has been able to make me forget him' (p. 8). Henriette, whose letters we as readers don't see, has written to offer a way out of the situation:

> You tell me to *forgive Milord Ossery*, or *not to think about him anymore*. Forgive him! Ah, never! ... Not think about him? ...
> I can avoid this man, renounce him, hate him, loathe him; but forget ... Oh, I cannot! (pp. 20–1)

What has Ossery done that leads him to ask the woman he loves to forget all about him: 'Must I be reduced to wanting you to forget me? Ah, I shall never forget you, I shall always adore you; I shall always think about you!' (p. 67)? When Ossery's letter comes to announce his departure and the rupture of their engagement, he alludes to a 'horrible secret' that he cannot reveal because it involves another person, calls himself an ingrate and disappears.

The reader doesn't discover the explanation for Ossery's behaviour until the last quarter of the novel when Ossery reappears on the scene and begs for permission to see Juliette. He finally writes to give an account of his behaviour. The passages below are excerpts from a long

self-narrative – a male memoir-novel *en abyme* – which includes a
brief account of his general social behaviour. In all respects, he is
the antithesis of Duclos's narrator: embarrassingly well-behaved.
It is against this self-portrait, and the earlier representation Juliette
had made of his charm, that the story of the *oubli* unfolds.

Ossery explains that he was on his way home when he encountered,
on their return from a hunting party, some old acquaintances from
his university days; one of them, Montfort, was a good friend and
presses Ossery to join the group for a dinner at his country estate. It is
an all-male dinner and the conversation turns to women: their beauty,
their soul, their taste and so on. The host, Montfort, claims that the
most attractive of women is the least sophisticated, and to prove his
point produces his young sister, Miss Jenny, a portrait of modesty.

The sister is rapidly ill at ease in this bachelor setting and asks
permission to withdraw. A few moments later, Ossery feels uncomfortable and goes to get some fresh air. Looking for his way out he finds
himself instead alone in a small room with Miss Jenny. He asks her to
show him to the garden, but since the only candle has just gone out, and
Miss Jenny can't find the bell to ring for help, the two of them start
stumbling about in the dark, looking for the door, bumping into each
other, and tripping over the furniture. Jenny falls down. The description
of what then happens is the crux of the novel:

> Her fall caused mine; soon great peals of laughter showed me that she was
> not hurt. Her immoderate playfulness made an extraordinary impression
> on me; it emboldened me: the disorder of my mind went straight to my
> heart. Overcome by sensual desires, I forgot my love, my integrity, laws
> that I had always held sacred, my friend's sister. A respectable girl appeared
> to me at that moment as nothing but a woman offered up for my desires,
> for that crude passion that instinct alone inflames. An impetuous impulse
> overtook me; I dared all, I cruelly abused the confusion and innocence
> of an incautious young girl, whose innocence caused her downfall. (p. 150)

> [. . .] I was beginning to think of my unfortunate adventure as a weakness
> that would soon be lost to memory, when the catastrophic consequences
> brought it forcefully back to me and obliged me to suffer the penalty of
> my lack of caution. (p. 151)

As a result of Ossery's 'weakness' Miss Jenny gets pregnant; because
of what he owes the brother, Ossery feels obliged to marry her; they
have a daughter, and then the young wife dies. It is as a widower that
Ossery returns to beg Juliette's forgiveness.

Juliette has to determine how to interpret Ossery's story before the novel can reach closure. And what follows is her *explication de texte*:

> ... an unfortunate adventure! this *small room* ... this *darkness* ... his boldness ... he calls this *an unhappy accident* ... *I forgot my love*, he says ... Yes, men have *this way of forgetting*; their heart and their senses can act independently; at least, that is what they claim, and by making these distinctions that they consider excuses, they reserve for themselves the option to be aroused by love, seduced by pleasure, or carried away by *instinct*. How can we disentangle the genuine feeling that motivates them? (pp. 167–8)

In her protest against the inequities that structure these arrangements between the sexes, Juliette underlines two important problems familiar to feminist theorists today: what to call what has happened, and what to do about it: 'Les hommes ont de ces *oublis*.' Men have this way of forgetting.' In his preface to the novel, Sylvain Menant describes Ossery's action as 'un moment d'égarement' ('a momentary lapse') – thus remaining within Ossery's own vocabulary and the lexicon of libertinage made famous by Crébillon; in a recent full-scale study of Riccoboni's work, Joan Stewart calls it 'a passing infidelity' (p. 82). Most recently, a feminist critic of the novel, Susan Lanser, calls it rape.[7]

The letter in which Juliette rereads Ossery's words with Henriette insists specifically on the implications of its language: 'His *confused* mind ... his *disordered* judgement ... ah, what a disorder! It has certainly cost me some tears! Must I forgive him?' (p. 168), and the letter ends on her indecision: 'Oh, I don't know what to decide!' (p. 169). Yet the very next letter announces, 'Ah, all is forgiven, all is forgotten' (p. 170); and the novel ends in a flurry of events a few pages later, with marriage. Does it condone a rape? or forgive a libertine lapse? For Lanser the abruptness with which the marriage is brought off and the jubilation of the husband's marital discourse – 'Milady Catesby is no more; she is my wife, my friend, my mistress, the good spirit who gives me back all the blessings of which I was deprived' (p. 173) – undermine a straight reading of closure. Can Riccoboni's heroine by a remarkable display of 'noblesse de sentiment' really have forgiven the libertine?[8]

Let us return to our paired reading to help us evaluate the marriage strategy. In his desire to reform, Duclos's narrator returns to the woman to whom he tried to make love at the very beginning of his career, Mme de Canaples. Then married, and unlike most of the women in the libertine world, although attracted to her suitor, even more

attached to her 'devoir' (p. 21), Mme de Canaples now is widowed
and in theory, like the Princesse de Clèves after her husband's death,
free to marry. But she hesitates, and her tone, the narrator explains,
is that of a person not wanting to appear to 'have forgotten her principles
so quickly and who would like to be talked out of them' (p. 136)
but who is not saying no, only deferring (p. 136). As if to prove the
Princesse right almost seventy-five years later, the narrator discovers
that in the interim he has also fallen in love with a poor relation of
her late husband's whom Mme de Canaples has decided to take under
her wing. Before he can confess his dilemma, Canaples shows him
she has deciphered the state of his heart and arranged a marriage for
him and the charming orphan: 'So our marriage took place, and from
that day on my wife has devoted her time to pleasing me; Madame de
Canaples seemed to take her pleasure from ours, and it increased our
joy to owe it to her, and to find in her a benefactor, a mother, a friend,
a guide, and a model of virtue. The calm and happy state of affairs
I am revelling in has convinced me that true happiness exists only
in uniting pleasure and duty' (p. 148).

Libertine or sentimental? Feelings or social analysis? Do these
novels describe two different worlds? In both, the male protagonist
splits sexuality from feeling and forgets about its consequences; in
both, marriage comes to put an end to such libertine exploits; in both,
the representation of the 'customs of a nation' depends on the social
relations between the sexes and is submitted to the moral judgement
of authorial voice.[9] Written in the decade that precedes the publication of Rousseau's *La Nouvelle Héloïse*, the novel of feeling that in
literary history marks at once the highpoint of the novel's feminisation
and the erasure of women writers from its history, the two texts point
to an emergent bourgeois desire for a model of union between the
sexes that would escape the contamination of the aristocratic model
of masculine privilege and abuse. In this sense sentimental and
libertine are but two sides of the same coin: Riccoboni's fictions are
novels for the 'feeling heart', if we include in the domain of the heart
a social critique of libertine paradigms of sexual relation in which
feeling is women's only power, a power that is also their weakness.
Duclos's are libertine, if we understand by this that the libertine
paradigm of multiple pleasure makes sense only against its sentimental
belief in women's singular and redemptive virtue: Mme de Canaples's
self-abnegation.

And yet, if the novels explore the same territory – the stakes of gendered relations in a world of leisure and privilege – the standpoint from which this social interaction is narrated and judged produces different reading effects; point of view, we might say, ultimately constructs different readers. The construction of this differentiated readership is at the heart of canon-formation and its history is typically evaluated in the language of memory: thus, Voltaire recalling Duclos's commercial success, *Les Confessions du Comte de* ∗∗∗, remarks: 'This isn't a book that will be handed down to posterity; it is only a chronicle of good luck, a story that goes nowhere, a novel without a plot, a work that leaves nothing to think about, and that one forgets as the hero forgets his mistresses. However, I imagine that the natural-ness and liveliness of the style, and especially the subject matter, have entertained young men and old ladies' (Etiemble, ed., p.xvii). The only full-scale study of Riccoboni's work until recently was called *Une Romancière oubliée* ('A forgotten lady novelist'). But that is another story.[10] For now we will deal with what the female novelist remembers.

In counterpoint to Duclos's worldly voice of masculine forgetful-ness, in which, as Voltaire points out, women are re-collected in order for the man to recollect himself, Riccoboni's novel produces a female voice that throughout the space of the novel *remembers*. This voice attached to her past interrogates – sometimes anxiously, sometimes angrily – the *consequences* of being forgotten. Through the letters of one woman to another, Riccoboni tracks the move-ments of a female subjectivity that oscillates between forgetting and remembering, forgetting and forgiving. And in the end she turns the question of forgetting's aftertext over to a community of women readers – Riccoboni's female plural 'nous' – for their response: 'How can we disentangle the genuine feeling that motivates them?' (pp. 167–8).

Juliette Catesby, finally, like many novels in this tradition, also inscribes the signature of the woman writer whose material, like Riccoboni's, is precisely the story that Ossery's narrative of Miss Jenny tells. In the reading Juliette provides of his self-forgetting, Riccoboni suggests another way for the story to turn out: if Ossery had told Juliette the truth, the two women might have become friends. As it stands, because Ossery's silence followed his forgetting, a dead woman lies between them. From a feminist perspective on gender and narrative, this sketch of another kind of plot can also be read as moral discourse on *moeurs*.[11]

These problems of genre and the gendering of memory's narratives are inseparable from the relations of gender and power. In its etymology *libertine* includes the root of freedom: an exercise of mind played out in the body most often enjoyed by men, men free to forget. This freedom for women is often imagined in the eighteenth century by male libertine novelists: Laclos's creation of Merteuil is the most famous example. But as even the recent representations of that fiction show, this experiment is finally intolerable, insupportable in women. This for some is seen as a feminist point on Laclos's part. Riccoboni famously objected to his representation of Merteuil, not as an author, she said, but as a woman. And he answered by saying he was just being a 'realist': showing the way things were; that she, like other women writers, was gifted for embellishing reality: showing how things should be.

Rereading Riccoboni's novel paired with Duclos's, or indeed with Laclos's, suggests that what her acts of embellishment prove to be are a powerful critique of social life in eighteenth-century France: of a libertine sociality that depends, as we have seen, on a separation of sexuality from feeling; a split, most importantly, that allows the one to forget the other. From the realm of feeling in which women are meant to live, the libertine view of the world is of a world without memory – except, we might say, as a track record: a world of sequences cut off from meaning, from the 'meaningful bodies' that women inhabit in the sentimental universe.[12] To forget these texts, by calling them sentimental, to remember only the stories they comment on, respond to and rewrite, is not only to miss half of history but to repress half the fictions of its cultural memory and their refusal to forget.

Notes

1 An earlier version of this essay appeared in French under the title 'La Mémoire, l'oubli et l'art du roman: textes libertins, textes sentimentaux' in the collection *Femmes et pouvoirs sous l'ancien régime*, ed. Danielle Haase-Dubosc and Eliane Viennot, Paris, 1991, pp. 238–58. I would like to thank Sally O'Driscoll for translating the primary and critical material from the French; page numbers refer to the French originals.

2 Paris, 1967, p. 378. Coulet is the clearest about the category. The adjective *sentimental* entered the French language only with the translation in 1769 of Sterne's 1768 *A Sentimental Journey*. The editors of the Arthaud manuals (*Littérature française 5: De Fénelon à Voltaire*, ed. René Pomeau and Jean Ehrard, and *Littérature française 6:*

De L'Encyclopédie aux Méditations, ed. Michel Delon et al., Paris, 1984) use variants of sensibility, the language of the period, to describe the works of women writers: 'romans pour coeurs sensibles' (novels for those with feeling). In the 1988 edition of Hachette's manual for secondary school teaching, the editors of the volume for the eighteenth century, Xavier Darcos and Bernard Tartayre, combine women and sensibility by devoting part of a chapter on the novel to 'Women's writing'. In it they include excerpts from Riccoboni, Tencin, Graffigny and Deffand. What is interesting, and even surprising, is the characterisation of this writing as having a 'feminist character', which is described as 'a very conscious determination to give a voice to woman, to her particular sensibility and to her demands, in a society called upon to evolve' (p. 223). To my knowledge, this is the first inclusion of women writers in manuals at this level; it is also the first general description of women's writing in the eighteenth century as feminist, rather than the usual clichés of sentimental. The writing, moreover, through the internal apparatus of the manual, is specifically contrasted to excerpts of men's writing – Prévost, Rousseau, Diderot, etc. – within the volume. Despite the marginalising gesture of the women's chapter – as opposed to an account of named authorship ('The libertine novel', with Crébillon and Duclos, for instance), recognition by the signature – this represents significant progress and compares favourably to manuals designed for university students and the general public like the Arthaud volumes.

3 Thus, in the introduction to his critical edition of Duclos's *Les Confessions du Comte de* ***, Paris, 1967, Laurent Versini, categorising the book both as a 'roman de moeurs' (novel of manners) and a 'roman de moraliste' (*moraliste*'s novel), describes Duclos's writing as that of an 'elegant libertinage, learnt from Crébillon', and links him to the 'tradition of the classical *moraliste*' (p. xxxviii). At the same time, however, the 'rehabilitation' of libertine writers often includes a gesture of distancing from the implications of the label. In the 1977 edition of Crébillon's *Les Egarements du coeur et de l'esprit*, Etiemble first tries to lift Crébillon out of the category 'licentious', or worse 'coarse', to make him into a writer to be taken seriously: 'Every writer is of his time, and that is how it should be – so long as he escapes by wanting to be universal. Crébillon is definitely universal in the *Egarements*, because of his subject' (p. 28). In the 1985 re-edition, Jean Dagen, in his introduction, argues along similar lines: 'It is highly problematic to define Crébillon as a libertine novelist. The 'libertine novel' is an invention of historians who, whatever they may say, take too literally a certain moralism that it would be unjust to impute only to Rousseau. Crébillon was, quite simply, what he wanted to be: a novelist' (p. 57).

4 Both of these novels, which had been out of print since the nineteenth century, appeared in the 1980s in a Desjonquères edition: Riccoboni in 1983, Duclos in 1986. These facts, however, give them a false symmetry. On the one hand, Riccoboni's novel was extremely popular at the time of publication; there were twenty editions by 1800, several translations and more printings of any novel before *La Nouvelle Héloïse*. The blurb on the back jacket includes Diderot's praise. But then Riccoboni becomes, we might say, a woman author. Consequently, she is most generally referred to as having written the sequel to Marivaux's *La Vie de Marianne* and as having had a correspondence with Laclos that is published with his novel in the Pléiade edition; also as the wife and daughter-in-law of famous actors of the Comédie Italienne.

The *Mémoires*, unlike Duclos's other works, were not successful, but Duclos remains in the tradition, most famously by anthologisation in the Pléiade *Romanciers du XVIIIe siècle*, ed. Etiemble, Paris, 1966. Secretary of the Académie française, admired by Stendhal, Duclos is remembered for his *style* and through it has become part of the French cultural mainstream. Thus Versini maintains that we should see in Duclos 'a witness to his time and an indispensable link in the chain between the 17th century *moralistes* and a Laclos or a Stendhal' (*Les Confessions du Comte* ***, p. liv). Neither of these texts belongs to the 'masterpiece theatre' model of literary history; they do not bear the famous signatures of the most celebrated Enlightenment figures. Duclos is referred to as one of the *minores*, or in the category of books described by Emile Henriot – in the title of the classic *Les Livres du second rayon: Irréguliers et libertins*, Paris, 1948 – as on the second shelf down. I make use of these categories only as a familiar shorthand because it isn't my purpose here to show all the ways in which canon-formation is dependent on a politics of taste.

5   I develop the notion of reading in pairs in *Subject to Change: Reading Feminist Writing*, New York, 1988, pp. 129–31.

6   This is in some sense a double education. As Geoffrey Bennington argues, in *Sententiousness and the Novel: Laying down the Law in 18th-century Fiction*, Cambridge, 1985, naming what he calls the 'pré-monde': what goes on before high society . . . is also a scene of education' (p. 67).

7   *The Novels of Madame Riccoboni*, Chapel Hill, 1977. Susan Sniader Lanser's *Fictions of Authority: Women Writers and Narrative Voice*, Ithaca, 1992, by its brilliant readings of ideology in women's narratives, has greatly influenced my understanding of this problematic text.

8   It is difficult to come down firmly on one side or another. Like *Catesby*, Riccoboni's first two immensely successful novels participate equally in the indictment of masculine privilege and its abuse, but end instead with female defiance and rage, including a sublimely staged suicide. The novel itself includes a great deal of internal feminist commentary on men and marriage itself that runs against the grain of any reading of the ending as complacent heterosexual plot.

9   In fact, one could argue that all libertine texts are also sentimental. It would also be interesting to think about what Duclos's echo of Lafayette can tell us about male writers' appropriation of earlier feminist traditions. (Here, Duclos takes the Princesse's self-possession and transforms it into a support for male satisfaction.) The language Henri Coulet uses in his preface to the Duclos is in this sense perhaps symptomatic when he describes the narrator as 'a libertine by imitation and a sentimentalist caught between *Tendre-sur-estime* (love-respect) and *Tendre-sur-reconnaissance* (love-gratitude)' (p. ix). (On the feminist implications of Scudéry's fictions see Joan DeJean's *Tender Geographies*, New York, 1991.)

10 Emily Crosby, *Une Romancière oubliée, Madame Riccoboni*, Paris, 1924. (The title may have been an echo of a study devoted to another neglected woman writer: *Une 'Primitive' oubliée de l'école des coeurs sensibles: Mme Graffigny*, Paris, 1913.)

I think it can be argued that the combination of the sexual material in which a male subject produces himself through women, with what are seen to be these qualities of style and representation, has proved irresistible to a great many male critics, who, like Etiemble, through their own conscious or unconscious identification with the heroes of these adventures, have kept these texts alive in cultural memory (despite, of course, a certain waxing and waning of critical fortunes that characterises all literary works). Thus, in the introduction to the *Egarements* (1985): 'The abbé Sabatier de Castres, who was never considered prophetic, writes in *Trois siècles de la littérature française* (1775) . . . Most of his works are hardly read today except by young officers in the garrisons. Now we know a certain young officer who . . .' and we rejoin memory with Laclos.

The shaping of literary traditions has largely been managed by male readers, who build on a male tradition of poeticians, critics and grammarians (not to mention military officers!) of the period. It will become possible to offer alternative readings of these texts and of sentimental ones once feminist critics have had an opportunity to reread – what I call overread – both the texts and their critical contexts. See *Subject to Change*, pp. 83–90.

11 Once again, the question of point of view is crucial. Riccoboni, for instance, describes another of her novels precisely as a novel of manners: 'The manners of our aristocracy (that is, our polite [*honnête*] aristocracy), the tone of our court, easy to overdo and seldom caught exactly – that is the whole merit of the *Lettres de Madame de Sancerre*' (in Stewart, p. 86).

  In a recent commentary on the publication in a Pléiade edition of Rétif de La Bretonne's memoirs, Michel Braudeau questions, much in the spirit of my remarks on Duclos, the relation between memory, sexuality, and the representation of a world that calls itself *moeurs*: 'In his *Calendrier*, published together with *Monsieur Niclolas*, he gives a list of the women who meant the most to him, putting one on each day of the year, a little like an almanac; he admits to fathering about a hundred and fifteen children. How much truth, how much fantasy is there in a list of this type? There is no way to know exactly, and anyway, does it matter? Rétif's work has been praised for its description of the manners of his time. It is true that there are many juicy or realistic details in his innumerable adventures and one can stumble upon the price of a furnished room in Revolutionary Paris. But we must not delude ourselves about the realism of this document, which is greatly influenced by an imaginary strongly directed by the "grand narrator", as Nicolas calls himself' (*Le Monde*, 22 December 1989, p. 14).

12 The expression is Janet Todd's, whose book *Sensibility*, London, 1986, interestingly analyses many of these issues in relation to the English novel.

Gender, conversation and the public sphere in early eighteenth-century England

Lawrence E. Klein

In a mid-seventeenth-century setting that discouraged women from serious intellectual engagements, Margaret Cavendish was a learned *femme forte*. In Londa Schiebinger's recent account of how women were excluded from the practice of science just as they were written out of its history, Cavendish symbolises the road not taken.[1] Even so, Cavendish wrote twenty-one books. She was, as she announced in one of her volumes, a woman of ambition,[2] and, though excluded from traditional all-male educational institutions, she pursued learning since 'Thoughts are free, nor can ever be enslaved: and we are not hindered from studying [...] but may be as well read in our Closets, as Men in their Colleges'.[3] If for men of a certain social elevation the university was the locale for intellectual development, women of the same social elevation, Cavendish suggests, could resort only to the solitude of a domestic enclosure for the same thing.

An important measure of the perception of social change over the next half-century is found when one turns to one of the statements of intention with which the *Spectator* opens. In an early number (this was Addison writing), the Spectator announced: 'It was said of *Socrates*, that he brought Philosophy down from Heaven, to inhabit among Men; and I shall be ambitious to have it said of me, that I have brought Philosophy out of Closets and Libraries, Schools and Colleges, to dwell in Clubs and Assemblies, at Tea-Tables, and in Coffee-Houses'.[4] In this passage, Addison allies himself with an effort to resituate learning, suggesting, among other things, that both 'college' and 'closet', the locales mentioned by Cavendish, have been superseded by new ones. Indeed, this often cited passage is indicative of wider changes both in the available maps of discourse and in the actual landscapes which such maps attempted to interpret. Obviously, these changes had implications for the gendering of discursive practices and for women's relation to discourse in society. This essay concerns those implications.

Addison's insistence that learning should be sociable was an attempt to envision and create a public discourse conducive to the improvement of society. His statement is therefore representative of a development, of European significance, which England pioneered – namely, the creation of a public sphere (a term now associated with Jürgen Habermas, to whom I shall turn shortly). England pioneered, first, in the development of those institutions of intellectual and discursive sociability which constituted the public sphere and, second, in the creation of an ideology of the public sphere.

We are used to thinking of public and private as separate spheres that have been gendered throughout the history of Western political and social thought. Feminist historical accounts stress the persistent re-enactment of the exclusion of women from public roles, power and citizenship.[5] In studies of the eighteenth century, this pattern takes the specific form of the construction of the 'domestic woman', whose enclosure reached a peak in the nineteenth century.[6] However, in the face of these commonplaces, some scepticism is in order. As Amanda Vickery has argued in a survey of interpretive trends in women's history:

> At bottom, the separation of the home and work-place, the rise of the new domestic woman, the separation of the spheres, and the construction of the public and private all describe the same phenomenon in different words. Accordingly, like the insidious rise of capitalism, the collapse of community, the nascent consumer society and the ever-emergent middle class, *the* definitive separation of sexual spheres can be found in almost any century we care to look at.[7]

It is clear that, in some ways, women had a higher public profile in eighteenth-century England than they had had earlier. It is usually admitted that there were more women writing and publishing. The audience of women readers expanded, with an accompanying re-direction of reading matter for a female audience. Concomitantly, the representation of women was more common in the culture of print. However, our ignorance about the public roles of women in the eighteenth century is still great: though literary historians have done much to recover the identities of women writers, a cultural history delineating women's roles not just as writers but as brokers, net-workers, patrons and consumers has yet to be written.[8]

One study that grapples with the apparent contrast between greater female publicity and the dominant models of feminist history (separate spheres, the domestic woman) is Kathryn Shevelow's study of early eighteenth-century periodicals. She writes that, 'during the eighteenth century, as upper- and middle-class Englishwomen increasingly began to participate in the public realm of print culture, the representational practices of that culture were steadily enclosing them within the private sphere of the home'.[9] Her study is an admonition against the glib or naive association of participation in print culture with the metaphors of emancipation and empowerment. As she shows, print culture was quite capable of allowing women to participate while simultaneously representing women as most fit for the domestic life. Inclusion and containment, thus, proceeded together.

However, Shevelow's account is persuasive only to a point. For one thing, it is highly teleological, directed at finding those elements of the early eighteenth century that look forward to and prepare for the nineteenth century. The importance of domestic ideology in the periodicals does not obviate other ideological elements within them. Attending only to domestic ideology simply assimilates the eighteenth century to the nineteenth, eliminating the possibility that women might have enjoyed certain opportunities and encouragements that were subsequently cut off. In addition, Shevelow's account fails to explain the ideological grounds for women's greater participation in print culture. What arguments made it possible for women to appear as participants in print culture? When later in the century women engaged conspicuously in intellectual sociability (the bluestockings) or forthrightly in political discourse, whether as feminists (Wollstonecraft) or not (Catherine Macaulay), on what basis did they operate?

I mean to suggest that the public and private realms are less well segregated from one another and less exclusively gendered than they are sometimes represented to be. One model that is suggestive in this regard is Jürgen Habermas's interpretation of the eighteenth century in terms of the development of a public sphere. Habermas identifies the 'public sphere' with the practice of rational critical discussion: it is private persons coming together to discuss matters of public import or, in his words, 'a forum in which the private people, come together to form a public, readied themselves to compel public authority to legitimate itself before public opinion'.[10] Working in a Marxist tradition, Habermas calls the personnel of the public sphere a bourgeoisie, but more important is his association of the public sphere with certain institutions, such as coffee-houses, clubs and salons, as well as with print media (see *Structural Transformation*, pp. 31–43).

One virtue of Habermas's historical model is that the eighteenth century exists not just as the prologue to the nineteenth but as a moment with its own distinctive patterns and possibilities that were disrupted by later developments (such as the rise of a culture of expertise and the commodification of the media). Even more important is the fact that Habermas's public sphere is not in a simple dichotomous relation to the private sphere. Rather, Habermas is concerned to delineate an intermediary zone between the intimate sphere of the family and the official sphere of the state. His public sphere is public in that it is defined by open discussion of matters of collective import; but it is also defined by the activities of private individuals outside the official zone of the state (see *Structural Transformation*, pp. 27–31).[11]

The fact that the public sphere intermediates between state and family – zones usually gendered as male and female – suggests that there may be a parallel accommodation in the matter of gender, that the eighteenth century offered ways to validate a female role in public discourse. Salons are obviously a suggestive venue for considering women and the public sphere, and, indeed, Habermas identifies them as one institutional expression of the public sphere. Though (male) *philosophes* sometimes caricatured salons as shallow and inconsequential, recent work suggests that we ought to take eighteenth-century salons seriously as elements in pre-revolutionary French political culture and as venues in which women played a significant part. The work of Dena Goodman[12] makes a series of related points: that the salon was the institutional centre of the Enlightenment; that the salon as an actual venue of intellectual practice enacted a significant political practice (the 'republic of letters' in which the salon was situated is a rubric to be taken seriously); and that women were central in this polity as discursive mediators. This analysis accords with recent attempts to supplant the model of 'absolutism' in pre-revolutionary France with an alternative picture of a complex political culture in which cultural and discursive politics loomed large.[13] This analysis also provides an account of the salon as an important institutional locus for the political identity of women.

The Parisian salon does not seem to have been imitated in London until after 1750 (though it is unclear whether that impression reflects historical actuality or simply our historical ignorance), and even then salons functioned differently in the two capitals.[14] Nonetheless, the French salon tradition made an important contribution to the construction of the public sphere in eighteenth-century England. For the

ideology of the public sphere in early eighteenth-century England
was principally built on traditions of civility and civil conversation,
which had been nurtured in seventeenth-century French salons.
Such traditions were channelled into the construction of a notion of
the public sphere in the early eighteenth century. The values of
equality, reciprocity and freedom, which, according to Habermas,
were constitutive of the eighteenth-century public sphere, were
available to early eighteenth-century writers in the idiom they called
politeness.[15]

My argument will be that gendered notions of conversation and
discourse played a positive role in defining the character of the public
sphere in the eighteenth century and also in endorsing the female
voice. The development I am interested in provided a legitimation of
female publicity.

Patriarchalism, whether considered as a set of presuppositions or as an
array of practices, was rampant in the Renaissance and early modern
periods.[16] However, within the overall framework of male dominance,
ideas and practices of gender varied. Though the Renaissance saw
little basic change in the notional status of women, the revival of
stoic and Platonic ideas required shifts within the discourse of gender
in which female capacities and roles were re-evaluated.[17] Humanism
itself may have offered little to female humans, but both Protestant
and Catholic religious initiatives transformed women into Bible
readers. In social practice, a monolithic patriarchal model was defied
at many points by actualities, from the power of female rulers and
the lives of court women down to the working lives of ordinary
women.[18]

Of specific interest here is life at court and, by extension, among
aristocratic and other elites, which yielded models of womanhood
running athwart patriarchal presuppositions. In these milieux, women
were co-creators of the polished and pleasurable life at which the
court aimed. They therefore required mental and social capacities
and accomplishments beyond physical and sartorial attractiveness.
In particular, the exigencies of the court necessitated a revaluation
of female discursive capacities. In the patriarchal paradigm, women
were to be silent. Aristotle said so in the *Politics*, and Renaissance
and early modern writers repeated the invocation: 'Maids must be
seen, not heard ...'[19] Classical authority was backed by Christian
authority, which traced the Fall to the defects of female garrulity

(see *Renaissance Notion*, pp. 16, 54 and *Doctrine for the Lady*, pp. 48–51, 100–1).[20] However, the taciturn woman was clearly out of place in the Renaissance court: this venue endorsed the participation of female voices in courtly discussion.

Though Italians pioneered this theme in the sixteenth century, it was taken up and broadened in seventeenth-century France, where the discursively empowered female shifted locale beyond the limits of the court to the aristocratic *hôtel*. There the discursive practice we know as the salon arose, initially in the bedroom alcove. The *ruelle*, as it was called, was devoted to intimate conversation between guests and the host. Since the function of this space was sociability, it became an intersection between the household domain, to which women were largely confined, and the wider world of society, knowledge, culture and politics. However, because it was a part of the household, it was a space in which women could set the tone, and they did (see *Paradis des Femmes*, pp. 5–6. 113ff.).

Of course, this sort of situation was susceptible to patriarchal critique, but what is important was the development of a response: in the salon milieu, arguments were produced endorsing feminine capacity and hailing functions at which women were peculiarly apt. In brief, women were represented as agents of civilisation, setting standards in a wide range of matters. This view of women built on patriarchalist suppositions associating women with feeling (as distinct from reason), with vanity and cosmetic surfaces (rather than depth), with the pleasures of sociability (as opposed to the rigours of solitude), with dependence (as opposed to autonomy), with practice (rather than theory and contemplation). However, some French writers of the seventeenth century transvaluated these associations: in Carolyn Lougee's formulation, liabilities were turned into assets.[21]

This rehabilitation of women redeployed standard distinctions between genders. For instance, in one discussion of conversation noted by Ian Maclean, the female concern with ornament disciplined conversation. It was argued that, while the discussion among women on their own was too shallow, the discussion among men on their own was too unsociable, whether because it wound down into pedantic concern with detail or because it exploded into an uncontrolled storm of controversy. The presence of both sexes was required to nurture a conversation that was both substantive and sociable – polite conversation, in short (see *Woman Triumphant*, p. 146).

This paradigm of polite conversation became available in England through the reading of French texts and their translations. One author who bridged the worlds of French and English conversation was Charles de Marguetel de Saint Denis, sieur de Saint-Evremond (1613–1703), who, after an early career as soldier and courtier, fell from royal favour in France, taking up permanent residence in London in 1670. He wrote in French but his essays were translated repeatedly during the Restoration period and into the eighteenth century. His writings helped shaped the polite culture of gentlemanly amateurism that prevailed among the eighteenth-century English elite. This culture revolved around conversation about literature, ethics and politics. As Saint-Evremond wrote: 'The most essential Point is to acquire a true Judgment, and a pure Understanding. Nature prepares us for it, but Experience and Conversation with polite Persons, brings it to Perfection'.[22]

The pressures within the discourse of politeness to transvalute gender assessments are very evident in 'The Character of a Woman that is Not to be Found'. Here Saint-Evremond described an ideal woman. The perfect complicity of 'the Air of the Face, the Qualities of the Mind, and those of the Soul' made her a paragon of *honnêteté*. She turned out to be a consummate conversationalist, combining a strictly rigorous mind and a thoroughly sociable style. While repeatedly praising her reason and wit for their comprehensiveness and acuity, Saint-Evremond indicated that her special attribute was the sociable standard to which she submitted reason and wit. While 'nothing escapes her Penetration' and 'her Judgment leaves nothing unknown', still 'her serious Moments don't make you purchase a solid Conversation at the loss of her Gaiety: Her Reason pleases, and her Judgment is agreeable ...' (*Works*, I, pp. 208, 212).

But 'the woman that is not to be found' was not simply an ideal woman, since, it turns out, ''tis rather the Idea of an accomplished Person'. Saint-Evremond wrote: 'I would not look for it amongst the Men, because there is always wanting in their Commerce, something of that Sweetness which we meet in that of Woman; and I thought it less impossible to find in a Woman the strongest and soundest Reason of Men, than in a Man those Charms and Agreements that are so natural to Women' (*Works*, I, pp. 213–14). As discursive agents, men were likely to sacrifice agreeableness and sociability: while others might disregard this propensity, Saint-Evremond regarded it as a liability. Meanwhile, his ascription of 'sweetness' to women was not just a paternalist gesture since the polite culture which Saint-Evremond was engaged in constructing assigned central importance to sociability. Thus, when projecting an ideal of accomplishment that synthesised the intellectual and the social, Saint-Evremond fixed on women to embody it. His polite ideal was best figured in the woman and so was necessarily feminised.

Thus, the enhanced stature of sociability and politeness involved a normative enhancement of the feminine. An English feminist text of the late seventeenth century took advantage of these associations, unpacking at length the implications of Saint-Evremond's short essay. The female author of *An Essay in Defence of the Female Sex* of 1696 gave a gendered cast to the entire discourse of politeness: politeness, she argued, was absolutely crucial for conversation, and women were crucial in the rise of politeness.[23]

Her theme was the dependence of conversation and, more generally, human society on such values as complaisance and civility, without which human interaction must fail. She indicated the traps of an insufficiently socialised discourse through a series of 'characters' embodying, among other kinds of conversational failure, bluff solitude and philistinism, learned inconsequence and pedantry, vain imposture of many kinds and uncontrolled contentiousness. By contrast to these dysfunctional modes of interaction, politeness constituted a discursive discipline, making virtues visible, accessible and beneficial to others and also assuring that virtues did not degenerate into vices. She wrote:

> 'Tis true a Man may be an Honest and Understanding Man, without any of these Qualifications; but he can hardly be a Polite, a Well Bred, an Agreable, Taking Man, without all, or most of these. Without 'em, *Honesty*, *Courage*, or *Wit*, are like Rough *Diamonds*, or *Gold* in the *Ore*, they have their intrinsick Value, and Worth, before, but they are doubtful and obscure, till they are polish'd, refin'd, and receive *Lustre*, and *Esteem* from these. (*Essay in Defence of the Female Sex*, pp. 135–6)

The notion, rehearsed here, that politeness complemented virtue was a commonplace of the discourse of politeness.[24] The point of the *Essay* was precisely to gender this complementarity, making women the agents of politeness. She wrote: 'there are other Quallifications, which are as indispensably necessary to a Gentleman, or any Man that wou'd appear to Advantage in the World, which are attainable only by Company and Conversation, and chiefly by ours' (*Essay in Defence of the Female Sex*, p. 23).

How, according to the author of the *Essay*, did women function to enhance civility? While presupposing complete female equality with men (she ascribed all their pretended incapacities to education and social conditions imposed on them), she grounded women's civilising function in the disadvantages they suffered. According to the author, men brought different expectations (from the masculine standpoint, lower expectations) to conversation with women than they brought to conversation with other men. Thus, male condescension itself helped to civilise since it forced men to abandon qualities they reserved for discourse among themselves: aggression and contentiousness, obsessiveness, gravity and self-solemnity – all of which were destructive to polite conversation. To talk to women, men had to embrace a different set of qualities: the pursuit of pleasure, ease and liberty, a sense of humour, the constant framing of learning by the standard of sociability. If traditional all-male discussion suffered, polite conversation benefited. In a parallel way, female disabilities became polite advantages. For instance, that women were sequestered from a classical education helped them to restrict their subjects of interest and concern to precisely those zones that were most apt for polite conversation (*Essay in Defence of the Female Sex*, pp. 9ff., 36–8, 57–8, 136–43).

Thus, English writers of the early eighteenth century inherited ideas from the early modern civility tradition that gave women a significant place in conversation and the larger processes of civility. Such insights informed the construction of the public sphere as a polite zone in the early eighteenth century.

The Whig cultural ideologists of the early eighteenth century used politeness to construct a notion of the public sphere. Their public sphere was a public discourse suitable as a vehicle for the clarification of public matters and the advancement of public morals as expressed in economic and political life, in religion and in arts and letters. Politeness was relevant to this undertaking as both end and means. First, politeness was the term that described the outcome of public discourse, the gradual refinement and improvement of society. Second, politeness was the term that described the disciplines requisite for public discourse, a set of discursive norms for the operation of discourse.[25]

To an extent, this was a straightforwardly political and ideological project. Addison, Steele and the third Earl of Shaftesbury, to mention its most influential proponents, were all Whigs whose efforts on behalf of the post-1688 regime involved redefining the public and private manifestations of virtue in new ways, appropriate to the complexities of eighteenth-century commercial society and remote from earlier religious and civic versions of the concept. For them, publicity was a new kind of authority in discourse, inquiry and culture. It opposed older, more traditional forms of authority that the Whigs associated with the pre-1688 regime and with the aspirations of the present Tories – most important, the court and the Church with the various agencies they both sponsored (including the universities).[26]

However, the early eighteenth-century emphases on sociability and politeness were also rooted in more general changes in the social environment. Shaftesbury, rather abstractly, and Addison and Steele, much more concretely, produced cultural ideology in the face of a new sort of urban environment that appeared first in London in the later seventeenth and early eighteenth century and, then, throughout the eighteenth century, was imitated elsewhere.[27] While premised on the growing commercialisation of English society, this 'urban renaissance', as it has been called, was the product of the participation of a wide range of people from throughout the upper and middling levels of society with a wide range of motives. The remapping of discourse and culture by the Whig cultural ideologists was an effort to get an intellectual grasp on this new urban phenomenon and to shape it in terms of a social and political vision.

The Spectator's intention, cited at the beginning of this essay, to resituate learning from closets, libraries, schools and colleges to clubs, assemblies, 'tea-tables' and coffee-houses exemplified this larger process. Insisting that learning be sociable meant that it should be incorporated into public discourse, directed at moral and civic concerns and expressed in an accessible idiom. This initiative criticised traditional educational institutions for their pedantry, unsociability and lack of civic relevance. The *Spectator* passage also captured the partisan motivation for removing 'learning' from the universities, which had proved themselves bastions of Toryism.[28]

It is, of course, relevant that, as Margaret Cavendish knew so well, the older institutions of learning were all-male, while the newer ones included women. If 'clubs' were male institutions, 'assemblies' were mixed; if early eighteenth-century coffee-houses were places for men, 'tea-tables' referred to places dominated, if not monopolised, by women.[29] Though Shaftesbury's vision of polite discourse was strongly homosocial, Addison and Steele's was not. For the latter, favourable speech conditions obtained among 'Assemblies of People of the highest Merit; where there is Conversation without Mention of the Faults of the Absent, Benevolence between Men and Women without Passion, and the highest Subjects of Morality treated of as natural and accidental Discourse' (*Spectator* no. 449, IV, p. 80). In addition to amalgamating good breeding and philosophy, good conversation was premised on the co-operation of the sexes. Even women by themselves could be represented as alert to discursive concerns of society. The women conversants of *Tatler* no. 157 spent several hours in discussion of the Sacheverell trial and the opera.[30] Thus, they were represented as consumers and discussants of theatre, both political and conventional.

This is not to deny that the periodicals endorsed the domestic virtues for women, in the manner made clear by Kathryn Shevelow. Nor is it to deny that the periodicals constantly relied on traditional patriarchal stereotypes. As represented in the periodicals, women needed to be saved from their obsession with fashion and ornament, 'this unaccountable Humour in Woman-kind, of being smitten with every thing that is showy and superficial' (*Spectator* no. 15, I, p. 66). However, according to the periodicals, this was a problem not just for women but for an entire society caught in the undertow of fashion. Fear of fashion was a central thematic of the periodicals; the taxonomy of fashion victims, one of their leitmotifs. The aim, however, was not to suppress but rather to discipline the yearning for form and to define the limits of the ornamental life. The very centrality of the concept of politeness in the periodicals indicates that ornament and fashion – good form, in short – were being recuperated as necessary accompaniments of virtue. When the Spectator wrote that the gentleman should situate himself between the sloven and the fop (*Spectator* no. 150, II, p. 91) or that moral discourse must be simultaneously serious and entertaining (*Spectator* no. 179, II, pp. 204–6) or that every form of excellence is accompanied by a particular grace and manner (*Spectator* no. 292, III, pp. 38–9), the periodical was echoing the commonplaces of the civility tradition.

It is not surprising then that, if women were criticised in the periodicals for their weakness for ornament (a weakness, it is emphasised, shared by men), they were also praised for their civilising capacities. Echoing the *Essay in Defence of the Female Sex*, the *Tatler* said not only that good form was needed to actualise virtues, but also that women were the eminent vehicle for this process. *Tatler* no. 30 (I, pp. 223–6) discussed three brothers, one apt at learning and bound for the university, another apt at domestic relations and bound for a family, and the third made for social success. While the first two enter the relatively unsociable realms of learned solitude or private domesticity, the third, by contrast, enters the sociable world of politeness. In consequence, his training in the 'graceful Manner' is as 'a Page to a great Lady of my Acquaintance', by which he

> will be well skill'd in the common Modes of Life, and make a greater Progress in the World by that Knowledge, than with the greatest Qualities without it. A good Mien in a Court will carry a Man greater Lengths than a good Understanding in any other Place. We see, a World of Pains taken, and the best Years of Life spent, in collecting a Set of Thoughts in a College for the Conduct of Life; and after all, the Man so qualified shall hesitate in his Speech to a good Suit of Clothes, and want common Sense before an agreeable Woman. Hence it is, that Wisdom, Valour, Justice, and Learning, can't keep a Man in Countenance that is possess'd with these Excellencies, if he wants that inferior Art of Life and Behaviour, call'd Good Breeding.

Here again was the commonplace about virtues requiring polish to come fully into their own. Again, from the standpoint of politeness, the conventional homosocial educational institution was stigmatised. The appropriate venue for the synthesis of 'Wisdom, Valour, Justice, and Learning' with 'Good Breeding' was a social world in which women were the agents of politeness and refinement.

Thus, in a world that was being constructed around the touchstone of refined sociability or politeness, women had an assured place. Of course, it might be argued that the role assigned to women in a passage such as this was quite ancillary, serving as a catalyst to male self-actualisation. However, the emphasis on the complementarity of the sexes suggests, first, that the relation of men and women was mutually beneficial and, second, that the ultimate beneficiary of complementary male/female relations was the public sphere itself.

Spectator no. 128 (II, p. 8) echoed the sort of complementarity already seen in Saint-Evremond between female sociability and male seriousness. According to the Spectator, vivacity was the particular gift of women while gravity typified men. Each sex had to police its natural bias to prevent it from withdrawing from the highway of reason to the paths of extremity. Thus, men and women were seen as counterparts. The mutuality of the sexes was also a point made in *Spectator* no. 433 (IV, p. 21), where the mutual regard of the sexes was said to lead to the improvement of each. Life, it was said, would be very different without gender difference: it was only male endeavours to please the opposite sex that polished and refined them out of those manners that were most natural to them.

The complementarity of the sexes is a signal instance of a larger pattern in the Whig periodicals, the effort to take account of and interpret diversity in society. The papers situated themselves in a diverse material, social and moral world and engaged enthusiastically in the tasks of representing multiplicity in any number of domains. They pictured the manifold world of fashions, produced prodigious numbers of social groups and categories, sketched a wide range of individual characters and multiplied moral cases.[31] In presenting a gallery of social types, the periodicals offered a moral sociology in which the major predicament was moral incompleteness and partiality. However, the periodicals also offered a solution to this problem in the possibility of an inclusive public discourse guided by the norms of politeness. In a way consistent with the liberal tradition, the periodicals sketched the possibility of arriving at truth and virtue through a discursive integration of individuals.[32]

This way of representing gender relations was not simply the assignment of men to the public sphere and women to the private. Eighteenth-century politeness did not only limit women's civilising role to the reproductive and nurturing functions of the household. Politeness was a way of construing a public sphere which, as Habermas asserts, was a zone between the intimately private and the officially public. In this zone, communicative interactions of men and women were regarded as significant not just for the moral development of members of each sex but for the public sphere as such and its goal of advancing society.

It is true that, in the eighteenth century as in the seventeenth and the nineteenth, the vast weight of ideological assertion and social practice contributed to the limitation of women's freedom and the subordination of women to men. However, the history of gender relations, in ideology and in practice, has not been monolithic. In particular, the dichotomy of public and private and its usual gendering is too blunt an instrument for understanding the changing character of those relations. In this essay, I have tried to show that the domestication of women itself cannot fully explain the subordination of women, because there was a space in the public sphere for them. This may not have liberated women in any transcendent sense but it did create spaces for women in the representation and the practice of public discourse.

Notes

The author thanks Dena Goodman and Amanda Vickery for helpful suggestions on this essay. Spellings and punctuation follow the originals except in a few cases where silent changes have been made for the sake of clarity.

1 Londa Schiebinger, *The Mind Has No Sex? Women in the Origins of Modern Science*, Cambridge, Mass., 1989, pp. 25–6, 32–4, 47–59.

2 Margaret Cavendish, *Natures Pictures*, London, 1656, preface.

3 Margaret Cavendish, *The Worlds Olio*, second edition, London, 1671, preface.

4 *Spectator* no. 10, in Donald F. Bond, ed., *The Spectator* (5 volumes), Oxford, 1965, I, p. 44. All subsequent references to the *Spectator* are to this edition and are given in the text.

5 For a summary of relevant views, see Carole Pateman, 'Feminist Critiques of the Public/Private Dichotomy', in *The Disorder of Women: Democracy, Feminism and Political Theory*, Cambridge, 1989, pp. 118–40. On the gender politics of the civic tradition, see Nancy C. M. Hartsock, *Money, Sex and Power: Toward a Feminist Historical Materialism*, Boston, 1985, pp. 186–230.

6 This paradigm is the controlling notion in such works as: Ruth Perry, *Women, Letters, and the Novel*, New York, 1980, pp. 27–62; Bridget Hill, *Eighteenth-Century Women: An Anthology*, London, 1984, pp. 3–12; and Vivien Jones, *Women in the Eighteenth Century: Constructions of Femininity*, London and New York, 1990. A more complex version of the relation of gender to the public/private distinction, with which this essay is in sympathy, appears in Terry Lovell, *Consuming Fiction*, London, 1987, pp. 10–17, 27–31, 36–43.

7 Amanda Vickrey, 'Golden Age to Separate Spheres? A Review of the Categories and Chronology of English Women's History', presented at the William Andrews Clark Memorial Library, 1 June 1991. Another challenge to the tropes of women's history is Sylvana Tomaselli's 'The Enlightenment Debate on Women', *History Workshop*, XX, 1985, pp. 101–24.

8 See Alison Adburgham, *Women in Print*, London, 1972. The literary recovery goes on in works such as: Alice Browne, *The Eighteenth-Century Feminist Mind*, Brighton, 1987; Mary R. Mahl and Helene Koon, ed., *The Female Spectator: English Women Writers before 1800*, Bloomington and London, 1977; Charlotte F. Otten, *English Women's Voices*, Miami, 1992; Katharine Rogers, *Feminism in Eighteenth-Century England*, Brighton, 1982; and Hilda L. Smith, *Reason's Disciples: Seventeenth-Century English Feminists*, Urbana, 1982. There is also the older, encyclopaedic but hardly analytic work: Myra Reynolds, *The Learned Lady in England, 1650–1760*, Boston and New York, 1920. For women's history in general, one had to turn, until recently, to old works such as Alice Clark's *Working Life of Women in the Seventeenth Century*, 1919, and Ivy Pinchbeck's *Women Workers and the Industrial Revolution*, 1930. A new social history of eighteenth-century women is now becoming available in research by Amanda Vickery, 'Women of the Local Elite in Lancashire, 1750–c.1825', unpublished Ph.D. thesis, London University, 1991. For some suggestive evidence about women in relation to cultural patronage, see Carole Taylor, 'From Losses to Lawsuit: Patronage of the Italian Opera in London by Lord Middlesex, 1739–45', *Music & Letters*, LXVIII, 1987, pp. 1–25.

9 Kathryn Shevelow, *Women and Print Culture: The Construction of Femininity in the Early Periodical*, London, 1989, p. 1. She admits that the period does involve an opening as well as closing of opportunity: see pp. 23–4, 65–6, 193.

10 Jürgen Habermas, *The Structural Transformation of the Public Sphere*, trans. Thomas Burger with Frederick Lawrence, Cambridge, 1989, pp. 24–5. The book first appeared in German in 1962.

11 An excellent analysis appears in Dena Goodman, 'Public Sphere and Private Life: Toward a Synthesis of Current Historiographical Approaches to the Old Regime', *History and Theory*, XXXI, 1992, pp. 1–20.

12 Dena Goodman, 'Enlightened Salons: The Convergence of Female and Philosophic Ambitions', *Eighteenth-Century Studies*, XXII, 1988–9, pp. 329–50; 'Seriousness of Purpose: Salonnières, Philosophes, and the Shaping of the Eighteenth-century Salon', *Proceedings of the Annual Meeting of the Western Society for French History*, XV, 1988, pp. 111–18; and 'Governing the Republic of Letters: The Politics of Culture in the French Enlightenment', *History of European Ideas*, XIII, 1991, pp. 183–99.

13 See the discussion of this issue in the introduction to Jack R. Censer and Jeremy D. Popkin, ed., *Press and Politics in Pre-Revolutionary France*, Berkeley, 1987, pp. vii–ix. Also, Keith Michael Baker, 'Public Opinion as Political Invention', in *Inventing the French Revolution*, Cambridge, 1990, pp. 167–71, and Roger Chartier, 'The Public Sphere and Public Opinion', in *The Cultural Origins of the French Revolution*, trans. Lydia Cochrane, Durham, NC, 1991, pp. 20–37.

14 Evelyn Gordon Bodek, 'Salonières and Bluestockings: Educated Obsolescence and Germinating Feminism', *Feminist Studies*, III, 1975–6, pp. 185–99. Sylvia H. Myers, *The Bluestocking Circle*, Oxford, 1990, is very informative about the intellectual engagements of the bluestockings but not about their salon practices.

15 It is worth noting that the source of this ideology was neither Locke, whose importance in eighteenth-century political discourse is usually overestimated, nor the civic humanist tradition, which is usually offered as the chief alternative to Lockean ideas in the eighteenth century.

16 In general: Margaret Ferguson, Maureen Quilligan and Nancy J. Vickers, ed., *Rewriting the Renaissance: The Discourses of Sexual Difference in Early Modern Europe*, Chicago and London, 1986, pp. xv–xxiv; Suzanne W. Hull, *Chaste, Silent and Obedient: English Books for Women 1475–1640*, San Marino, 1982; Ruth Kelso, *Doctrine for the Lady of the Renaissance*, Urbana, 1956; Ian Maclean, *The Renaissance Notion of Woman*, Cambridge, 1980.

17 Carolyn C. Lougee, *Le Paradis des Femmes: Women, Salons, and Social Stratification in Seventeenth-Century France*, Princeton, 1976, pp. 34–40; Maclean, *Renaissance Notion of Woman*, pp. 20, 56–7, 85–7.

18 The classic feminist critique of humanism is Joan Kelly-Gadol, 'Did Women have a Renaissance?', *Women, History and Theory*, Chicago and London, 1984. See the critique of Kelly-Gadol in Judith Brown, 'A Woman's Place was in the Home: Women's Work in Renaissance Tuscany', in Ferguson et al., *Rewriting the Renaissance*, pp. 206–24. Also, Maclean, *Renaissance Notion of Woman*, pp. 66, 85–9.

19 Quoted in Peter Stallybrass, 'Patriarchal Territories: The Body Enclosed', in Ferguson et al., *Rewriting the Renaissance*, p. 126.

20 Maclean, *Renaissance Notion*, pp. 16, 54; Kelso, *Doctrine for the Lady*, pp. 48–51, 100–1.

21 See Lougee, *Paradis des Femmes*, pp. 21–33, and Ian Maclean, *Woman Triumphant: Feminism in French Literature 1610–1652*, Oxford, 1977, pp. 119–52.

22 Charles de Marguetel de Saint Denis, sieur de Saint-Evremond, *The Works of Mr. de St. Evremont*, London, 1700, I, p. 170.

23 *An Essay in Defence of the Female Sex*, London, 1696. I follow Hilda Smith (*Reason's Disciples*, pp. 144, 150n.) in calling the book anonymous, though it has been attributed to Judith Drake and Mary Astell, among others.

24 See for instance: S. C. *The Art of Complaisance*, London, 1677, p. 1; Pierre d'Ortigue, sieur de Vaumorière, *The Art of Pleasing in Conversation*, London, 1691, p. 5; John Hughes, 'Of Style' (written 1697), in *Poems on Several Occasions: With Some Select Essays in Prose*, London, 1735, pp. 247–8; Abel Boyer, *The English*

Theophrastus, London, 1702, pp. 50, 104, 108; *The Management of the Tongue*, London, 1706, pp. 2–3; Henry Felton, *A Dissertation on Reading the Classics*, London, 1713, pp. xiii–xv.

25 For a general account of the language of politeness, see Lawrence E. Klein, 'The Third Earl of Shaftesbury and the Progress of Politeness', *Eighteenth-Century Studies*, XVIII, 1984–5, pp. 186–214.

26 See Lawrence E. Klein, 'Liberty, Manners and Politeness in Early Eighteenth-century England', *The Historical Journal*, XXXII, 1989, pp. 583–605, and 'Shaftesbury, Politeness and Religion', in Nicholas Phillipson and Quentin Skinner ed., *Political Discourse in Early Modern Britain*, Cambridge, forthcoming.

27 An excellent survey of this development across England is Peter Borsay, *The English Urban Renaissance*, Oxford, 1989.

28 One challenge of post-1688 Whiggism was purging the universities of Toryism: see John Gascoigne, *Cambridge in the Age of the Enlightenment*, Cambridge, 1989, pp. 71–114.

29 It should be noted that women were proprietors of coffee-houses (Pinchbeck, *Women Workers and the Industrial Revolution*, pp. 296–7), and manuscript references indicate that women were to be found in them as customers (e.g., Anthony Hewiston, ed., *The Diary of Thomas Bellingham*, Preston, 1908, p. 44).

30 In Donald F. Bond, ed., *The Tatler* (3 volumes), Oxford, 1987, II, pp. 378–83. All subsequent references to the *Tatler* are to this edition and are given in the text.

31 See the remarkable *Spectator* no. 442, IV, pp. 52–4, in which the Spectator requested submissions from readers. The Spectator produces a catalogue of types by extending his invitation to 'all manner of Persons, whether Scholars, Citizens, Courtiers, Gentlemen of the Town or Country, and all Beaux, Rakes, Smarts, Prudes, Coquets, Housewives, and all sorts of Wits, whether Male or Female ...'. I develop this aspect of the periodicals in 'Property and Politeness in the Early Eighteenth-century Whig Moralists: The case of *The Spectator*', in Susan Staves and John Brewer, ed., *Early Modern Conceptions of Property*, London, forthcoming.

32 On the continuity of eighteenth- and nineteenth-century themes in social and political thought, see John Burrow, *Whigs and Liberals*, Oxford, 1988.

Four bodies on the *Beagle*: touch, sight and writing in a Darwin letter

Gillian Beer

> Fanatics have their dreams, wherewith they weave
> A paradise for a sect, the savage too
> From forth the loftiest fashion of his sleep
> Guesses at Heaven; pity these have not
> Traced upon vellum or wild Indian leaf
> The shadows of melodious utterance ...
> Whether the dream now purposed to rehearse
> Be poet's or fanatic's will be known
> When this warm scribe my hand is in the grave.
>
> John Keats, 'The Fall of Hyperion'[1]

> While some scientists see their endeavour in predominantly adversarial terms, as contests, battles, exercises in domination, others see it as a primarily erotic activity.
>
> Evelyn Fox Keller, *Reflections on Gender and Science*[2]

The 'warm scribe', in Keats's compelling description of the writer's hand, cancels the distance between cold print and body. A hand reaches out from the text, is occupied in the text; brushing aside the print on the page, it makes the reader conscious of the hand's activity in reading as well as writing. We smooth the page, we turn it, each alone. The past body of the writer is here insurgent, meeting the reader's hand, matching it, touching it. The effect is rare, and daring. It relies upon Keats abandoning the dualistic hierarchies of mind and body, having available to him without favour all his five senses. Writing his experiences on the voyage of the *Beagle* some ten years after Keats composed 'The Fall of Hyperion', Darwin shares the problematic of empathy that Keats explored: impressions are a ferment, sharing the body, keeping the mind agog, multiplying positions. Yet to survive they must be set down, impacted as ideas, authenticated by alien readers.

In this passage Keats insists that *only* the written gives any hope of survival. The unrecorded lofty dreams with which the savage 'guesses at Heaven' remain incommunicable to those outside the tribe, those born in another time. The writer dead, the hand may survive as idea – but only if that idea holds (and continues to hold) the imagination of many. The arcane world of fanatical belief gives way to time; the circle of disciples dies out. Darwin, energetically observing and writing before the establishment of genetic theory, had to have the patience of the pioneer – the patience not to know for sure within his lifetime 'Whether the dream now purposed to rehearse / Be poet's or fanatic's', whether it would prove to be authentic or delusive.

Like Keats, Darwin started on a medical career and left it part-way through his studies. For both, the problem of pain was a factor in the decision to quit. Before anaesthesia or the practice of hypnosis, before disinfectants, the sights and sounds connected with surgery were terrible indeed. And for the practising doctor not only sight and sound were involved, but touch. The doctor must implicate himself, must use his hands to cause suffering, however much the outcome of that suffering was planned as recovery. The hand is the most conscious, and at the same time the most intimate, point of contact between the individual and the surrounding world. Bodies may be jostled in a crowd, helplessly, but the hand's activities are always in some measure knowing. To reach out; to strike; to stroke; to incise; to inscribe: such are typical activities. And, for the anatomist, to dissect *and* to describe: the hand as scalpel and as pen. Darwin's hand is active in all these ways. He early loved shooting, with its acute eye–hand coordination, but he renounced it. His own 'hand' in communication is extraordinarily resistant to interpretation. He writes in a close exquisite calligraphy that appears instantly decipherable at a distance and proves inscrutable close to.

In *Realism, Writing, Disfiguration: On Thomas Eakins and Stephen Crane*, Michael Fried has insisted on the fraught relations between the surgeon's and the painter's and writer's crafts in the activity of representation. In his example, Eakins the painter and Crane the writer work with effects of perspective, of violence to the body, and of prone and upright positions as implicit commentary on the activity of production. The viewer finds it painful either to look at or *'to look away from'* the operation pictured in Eakins's *The Gross Clinic*: 'so keen is our craving for precisely that confirmation of our own bodily reality'.[3]

That confirmation, Fried suggests, is always conflicted and is put under pressure particularly by the thematisation in writing and painting of horizontal and upright: 'an implicit contrast between the "spaces" of reality and of literary representation – of writing (and in a sense ... of writing/drawing) – required that a human character, ordinarily upright and so to speak forward-looking, be rendered horizontal and upward-facing so as to match the horizontality and upward-facingness of the blank page on which the action of inscription was taking place' (*Realism*, pp. 99–100). For Darwin on the *Beagle*, I shall argue, *prone* and *upright* held particular intensities of meaning. Fried's emphasis on the power-relations of hand, eye and subject is valuable particularly for its recognition that the *subject* (in both senses) is not only the figure painted or described. It is also the subjectivity and subjection of the viewer or reader experiencing empathetic desire – and the interpellated subjectivities of the writer too. The activity of writing or drawing is figured in that which is described, even while it figures it. As Lacan remarks:

> With a two body psychology, we come upon the famous problem, which is unresolved in physics, of two bodies.
>   In fact, if you restrict yourselves to the level of two bodies, there is no satisfactory symbolisation available.[4]

In this essay I shall place at the centre of my argument a quite short passage from a particular letter from among the many that Darwin wrote while on the five-year voyage of the *Beagle*. By doing so, I hope to raise to the surface profound concerns that Darwin can, textually, only glance towards. These concerns are at once sensual, theoretical, political and sexual.[5] Darwin's difficulty in delimiting any one of these domains is fundamental to his creativity. His extreme openness to sense-experience produces also in his writing a form of nostalgia so intense that it may be called mourning – a nostalgia that acts perhaps as the screen for more enduring grief.

In the letter, three particularly strong and sequent images of naked bodies emerge. The fourth body of my title is Darwin's own. But the number four is here not so much a limit as a multiplier. The bodies Darwin sees in his mind's eye *stand in for*, and symbolically subvert, a range of categories.

The period of his life-writing that I concentrate on here is that of the early 1830s, and the date of the letter I shall cite is 23 July 1834, when the *Beagle* docked at Valparaiso in Chile after a difficult passage more than two years into the voyage and having already visited (among places that disagreeably fascinated and impressed Darwin) Tierra del Fuego and the Falkland Islands. But in order to frame my argument within this time-focus, it is necessary first to set the letter within Darwin's intellectual and emotional experience at that period, and then to look forward to the accomplished form of evolutionary theory that Darwin finally publishes in *The Origin* twenty-five years later.

When Darwin set out on the voyage of the *Beagle*, he was still 22 and not yet a Victorian. This was the period of the Bridgewater treatises in which God's providence was demonstrated through the natural world and the eye was still held to be the perfect instrument of discernment. Helmholtz's demonstration of the eye's imperfections was still twenty years in the future and first embraced by Darwin twenty years after that, in the last edition of *The Origin*, as evidence for the uncertain processes of natural selection against the model of absolute design. It's as well to register these controlling absences. But, for the later phase of my argument, it is important also to note at the start the surgeon and art-theorist Charles Bell's Bridgewater essay on *The Hand* which first appeared while Darwin was on the *Beagle* and which he read on his return.[6] Darwin already admired Bell's work on the fine arts, on anatomy and on the expression of emotion (a topic that Darwin would much later make his own).[7]

Bell insisted on touch rather than on sight as the 'common sensibility': 'the most necessary of the senses, it is enjoyed by all animals from the lowest to the highest in the chain of existence' (p. 214).[8] Towards the end of the treatise, indeed, Bell compares the excellences of eye and hand and emphasises that the eye depends on the balance of the whole body. The eye, he argues, is the symbolising summary sign of that which is already experienced by the hand; the eye therefore relies upon correspondence with the hand. In a sinewy and complex syntax, he places at the climactic point of an extended sentence, the eye's pulse of delay, a moment behind the hand's immediacy: 'the sign in the eye of what is known to the hand' (p. 349).

In Bell's analysis, the image of the eye as camera is jettisoned. In its stead the eye is experienced *from within the body*, as part of a set of muscular rhythms. The efficacy of these rhythms relies upon the body's balance and the equable distribution of our consciousness of the body held in ambient space. The swivelling eye strokes the outer world with the sway of the whole body. The eye's motions become a meta-form of touch, minutely sensible to the 'place, form, and distance of objects':

When, instead of looking upon the eye as a mere camera, or show-box, with the picture inverted at the bottom, we determine the value of muscular activity; mark the sensations attending the balancing of the body; that fine property which we possess of adjusting the muscular frame to its various inclinations; how it is acquired in the child; how it is lost in the paralytic and drunkard; how motion and sensation are combined in the exercise of the hand; how the hand, by means of this sensibility, guides the finest instruments: when we consider how the eye and hand correspond; how the motions of the eye, combining with the impression on the retina, becomes the place, form, and distance of objects – the sign in the eye of what is known to the hand: finally, when, by attention to the motions of the eye, we are aware of their extreme minuteness, and how we are sensible to them in the finest degree – the conviction irresistibly follows, that without the power of directing the eye, (a motion holding relation to the action of the whole body) our finest organ of sense, which so largely contributes to the development of the powers of the mind, would lie unexercised. (p. 349)

The hand, touching, caressing, dissecting, *writing*, is as necessary to Darwin as is the eye for his theoretical purposes and for his life aboard ship. In the particular lettter that I examine, the *mind's eye* of memory plays across a repertoire of allusion between the senses, and in particular those of touch and sight.

A good deal of the meaning of the voyage came to Darwin through a polymorphously intense response to sensuous stimuli, and through seasickness. On the voyage of the *Beagle*, even the smallest island gave promise of relief to the endlessly seasick landsman and he seized every opportunity to undertake land journeys. Visiting the almost entirely male community of Ascension Island towards the end of his circumnavigation he commented that 'Many of the marines appeared well-contented with their situation; they think it better to serve their one-and-twenty years on shore, let it be what it may, than in a ship; in which choice, if I were a marine, I would most heartily agree'.[9] Confinement in an island is, in his view, infinitely preferable to confinement in a ship: celibacy there at least does not include seasickness.

For long-distance travellers by ship, the shipboard life becomes a travelling homeland from which to survey the changing world. But as Darwin continued queasy throughout his five years, it was a shifty homeland. The foreign at least offered terra firma. The British ship, the *Beagle*, offered no island of stability. The emotional stresses of life on board, in particular his frequently stormy relations with Captain

Fitzroy, made disembarking at a succession of islands and territories the more pleasurable. Though five years may now sound like a leisurely pace around the world, to Darwin the recurrent impression was of haste, prematurity, incomplete encounter. The ship exacted departure, or demanded urgent and anxious land-voyages to catch up at the next port of call.

Darwin was on this five-year journey throughout the period of his young manhood and was, very likely, celibate during that entire time. In Darwin, as in Keats his near contemporary, we meet the kind of mind and body on whom nothing is lost, and to whom everything is simultaneously available: sounds, smells, domestic life, the vegetation of remote landfalls, the heat of the day, companionship and cooking, beetles in ditches, the writing of earlier travellers such as Humboldt, the manifold flora and fauna, the luscious single flower, the variety of humankind, the particular encounter. For both of them, sexual congress is absent. On his long land journeys from the *Beagle* this passion of curiosity and response sometimes made progress difficult. The effect as it is described is at once erotic and infantile: 'In England any person fond of natural history enjoys in his walks a great advantage, by always having something to attract his attention; but in these fertile climates, teeming with life, the attractions are so numerous, that he is scarcely able to walk at all' (p. 29).

Like a young child, impressions crowd in so thick that the idea of 'going for a walk' is lost in the immediacy of sensation. Darwin left at home a widowed father and maternal older sisters. His mother had died when he was 8 years old and he retained – remarkably – only one sharp memory of her. When Fox's child later died, Darwin wrote to him that he had not yet himself suffered the loss of a close relative. The degree of denial, repression or displacement this suggests is indeed remarkable. An unfocused nostalgia for an experience without boundaries, for exploration, even infiltration, may be a response to loss. (Though it is timely to recall that the maternal functions were probably more widely distributed in the kind of household in which he grew up than would be familiar today. Nurses, sisters, servants and – most strikingly – his father all composed a maternal resting place.)

On the voyage of the *Beagle*, Darwin found it hard to do without his family; he suffered homesickness, exacerbated by (and perhaps helping to explain) his persistent seasickness. His balance never made the adaptation to seaboard life. Babies in the womb are held and rocked at ease in amniotic fluid without suffering problems of balance or seasickness. But in that captain's cabin Darwin felt himself reduced at intervals to infantile dependency without comfort. No wonder that he spent as long as possible on shore, seizing every opportunity to have his senses restored to him. Those senses blazed the stronger on land for their recovery. His position on board ship as part naturalist, part gentleman companion to the captain, did not in itself require of him so indefatigable an exploration of the territories and peoples the ship's course touched upon. He chose it.

But his alternating experiences of prone and upright, sickness and equilibrium, made him very aware that observing is never neutral. Darwin knew that observing depends as much upon the body as on the reason, that ear, eye and balance are closely implicated. Like Keats again, he had spent time as a medical student and knew his anatomy. And both these early-bereaved men responded to touch, taste, hearing, smell, as strongly as to sight. The work of mourning can take the form of celebration. Darwin's polymorphous responsiveness to territory (earth, insects, peoples, plants, trees and pools) serves him for comfort and excitement. Nature for him is 'She' in a more than formal usage. Yet he does not insist on this she-ness as difference.

Darwin's curiosity was intensely libidinous. The two energies – to merge and to classify (loosing the borders of the body into oneness with its environment or eagerly articulating and naming) – are both present to a high degree in his descriptions. He as often describes himself seated or prone as mounted or walking. He places his body in a variety of relations to the physical world. Lying prone is both the naturalist's professional position for observation and, for Darwin, a pleasurable declension into the sensory world. His strong intellectual desire to make links and to discover kinship brings the counter-impulses of merging and of naming into a controllable relationship. His language in the *Voyage of the Beagle* and in the letters of the time often shows the yearning and the embarrassment of categories that he was struggling with.

Darwin was an active letter writer throughout his five years' travel, as the first volumes of his Correspondence show. He also kept a journal which was later to form the basis of the *Voyage*. Moreover, he had field notes to maintain and specimens to bottle and dispatch with accompanying notes. When he was not travelling, a quite large part of his day, particularly on board ship, was taken up with writing.

His most frequent correspondents were his sisters, but he also maintained a lively exchange with a number of co-workers and friends. Letters went and arrived in clumps, sometimes delayed for weeks on either side by the exigencies of transport. One only of these many letters was addressed to his school and college friend Charles Whitley. It is that letter that I dwell on now.

Whitley, much more conservative in opinion than Darwin, had been a crony at college. They both belonged, for example, to the Gourmet or 'Glutton' Club which specialised in eating strange meat: 'the name arose because the members were given to making experiments on "birds and beasts which were before unknown to human palate" ... hawk and bittern were tried, and their zeal broke down over an old brown owl "which was indescribable"'.[10] Like Darwin at that time Whitley was destined for the Church. The letter under discussion has a certain immediate interest in being his sole communication to Whitley while away (a couple of letters passed between them shortly before he set out on the *Beagle*). The letter proves also to be the repository of much repressed emotional disturbance. Perhaps Darwin was moved to write by a passage in a letter from Catherine Darwin (27 November 1833) which may – like letters from Henslow – have reached him only on arriving at Valparaiso many months later. The letter reminded him of Whitley's active existence and told him of his quite poignantly avid concern for news of Darwin:

> I can't conceive how Mr. Whitley knows all about your plans, movements, discoveries &c, for I don't think you correspond with him. Whitley says that two letters of your's have passed though his hands, to other people (not to himself) and that he perfectly longed to break the seal of them, but of course did not. (*Correspondence*, I, p. 357)

The long silence between them and its sudden breaking seems linked to a crisis of *Heimweh* for Darwin – a crisis which involves not only nostalgia for past scenes but for past selves. Darwin fears that both his youthful self and the imagined future self of his younger years is now irretrievable. Past and future alike are altered beyond recall by the experiences of his protracted journey. 'Body and mind' are in a state disjunct from his settled and carefree past (or a past now imagined to have been settled and carefree). Landing at Valparaiso, the stylish capital of Chile, after a perilous sea-passage after their stay in Tierra del Fuego puts him back in touch with a society more like that from which he came originally, and during his stay there he 'had the good fortune to find living here Mr. Richard Corfield, an old schoolfellow and friend, to whose hospitality and kindness I was greatly indebted'.[11]

But arriving there also marks for him the distance he has travelled from such societies: he is stranded between two – or more – worlds. When in this letter he imagines sexual love and procreation, he turns humorously to the language of Jane Austen. He has no other tongue in which to communicate to his past peers, but that language will not do to represent all that he now needs, knows and fears to be debarred from.

As he writes, he veers between humour, yearning, amazement and a curious sequence of images whose juxtapositions tell almost as much as the vignettes themselves. He begins by reminding Whitley 'that there is a certain hunter of beetles & pounder of rocks, still in existence'. Covering his own forgetfulness of Whitley, he remarks that 'it will serve me right, if you have quite forgotten me. – ' (*Correspondence*, I, p. 396).

I do hope you will write to me. ('H.M.S. Beagle, S. American Station' will find me); I should much like to hear in what state you are, both in body and mind. – ¿Quien sabe? as the people here say (& God knows they well may, for they do know little enough) if you are not a married man, & may be nursing, as Miss Austen says, little olive branches, little pledges of mutual affection. – Eheu Eheu, this puts me in mind, of former visions, of glimpses into futurity, where I fancied I saw, retirement, green cottages & white petticoats. – What will become of me hereafter, I know not; but I feel, like a ruined man, who does not see or care how to extricate himself. – That this voyage must come to a conclusion, my reason tells me, but otherwise I see no end to it. – It is impossible not bitterly to regret the friends & other sources of pleasure, one leaves behind in England ... We have seen much fine scenery, that of the Tropics in its glory & luxuriance, exceeds even the language of Humboldt to describe. A Persian writer could alone do justice to it, & if he succeeded he would in England, be called the 'grandfather of all liars'. –

But, I have seen nothing, which more completely astonished me, than the first sight of a Savage; It was a naked Fuegian his long hair blowing about, his face besmeared with paint. There is in their countenances, an expression, which I believe to those who have not seen it, must be inconcevably wild. Standing on a rock he uttered tones & made gesticulations than which, the crys of domestic animals are far more intelligible.

When I return to England you must take me in hand with respect to the fine arts. I yet recollect there was a man called Raffaelle Sanctus. How delightful it will be once again to see in the FitzWilliam, Titian's Venus;

how much more than delightful to go to some good concert or fine opera. These recollections will not do. I shall not be able tomorrow to pick out the entrails of some small animal, with half my usual gusto.[12]

And then he turns to request news of friends in common, ending 'Often & often do I think over those past hours so many of which have been passed in your company. Such can never return; but their recollection shall never die away. – '. The intensity of valediction here, the sense of being like 'a ruined man', affirms that Whitley can act only as a mirror self for a past that Darwin no longer shares, a future that sets off in a different direction. Darwin needs a different pen, now, which will outgo the culture he has left and which that culture could not credit: 'he would in England be called the "grandfather of all liars"'. So his state of unknowing about his old friend, though wryly humorous, also bids farewell to his own past identity. Instead he turns to a different double: the Fuegian seen standing on a rock.

In my discussion I shall concentrate on the three bodies conjured in this passage: the Fuegian, Titian's Venus, and 'some small animal'. They are all, as he writes, absent: fantasies of Darwin's own inscribing eye, hand and brain. So the fourth body (Darwin's) is/was the only present body. This shifts the question of 'the gaze' into a different dimension. Darwin 'sees' the projected figures as he writes; perhaps his correspondent will see them too – as may that trail of illicit after-readers among whom we must, in this instance, number ourselves, reading a letter addressed to quite another person one hundred and fifty-odd years ago, yet startled into constructing and construing a symbolic sequence of images again in the mind's eye.

Lacan summarises Sartre's discussion of the gaze in terms of its humanistic premisses:

> The author's entire demonstration turns around the fundamental phenomenon which he calls the gaze. The human object is originally distinguished, *ab initio*, in the field of my experience, and cannot be assimilated to any other perceptible object by virtue of being an object which is looking at me. From the moment this gaze exists, I am already something other, in that I feel my self becoming an object for the gaze of others. (*Seminar*, I, p.215)

Among these three mental images only the Fuegian looks back at Darwin; Titian's Venus gazes out of the frame of the picture into a sideways distance that the viewer cannot share; the small animal is already dead, about to be pickled. The three figures are across a spectrum in more than one way: they move from active to passive, from upright to prone, from an interactive gaze to dead upturned eyes, from male to female to unsexed. The Fuegian is animated; the Venus half-reclining; the animal upturned. The Venus is in each of these sequences the hinge category, ambiguously sited: private and communal; womanly and cultural; self-possessed art object; a body never to be touched, paint become flesh in recollection.

In writing the recollected image of his first sight of a savage, Darwin suggests indirectly that the man was far away from him, perhaps seen from ship to shore. The straining of the eye to grip and interpret this figure becomes also a representation that confirms his assumption of extreme cultural distance between them. It also figures the man's resistance to authoritative interpretation. (For nineteenth-century readers the scope of a term like 'savage' was larger than it can now be for us: it includes distance and superiority but need not imply repudiation.) The 'savage' man on his mountainside is represented as 'wild' somewhat in the manner of Thomas Gray's late eighteenth-century poem 'The Bard' about the last prophetic Celts: a member of an earlier and vanishing race whose visions are incommunicable now. This figure cannot be held within even the possibility of Western translation.

The trope of race theory at the time was of other races as children beside the adult Caucasian. But this is a man, aloof, and Darwin is the baffled pupil unable to tap his lore, as well as being the inhibited adult rendered uneasy by the man's 'smeared' surface. Darwin is 'astonished', a word which always includes a strong physical input, a clonk or freezing of the perceiver's bodily frame. Such heartfelt difficulties in tracking kinship, it seems to me, must go to fuel Darwin's much later work *The Expression of the Emotions in Man and Animals*,[13] where he restoratively includes images of animals and of sane and mad people, of young and of old, to affirm the continuities of emotional gesture across species.

In this letter and elsewhere (for this is a scene he returns to), Darwin communicates a sense of fascinated helplessness at finding himself unable to interpret the profound difference of the other man. Gesture is a kinship experienced in the body. Yet it is also a kind of writing, an interchange of meaning stabilised between actor and viewer. Here no *relation*, in the sense of message or narrative, can be established. The other is 'inconceivably wild'. But that which is inconceivable is also here a mirror-image. On his hillside the naked man looks and cries out to the young Darwin. As Darwin recollects it here, they seem to be alone together. Revealingly, closer to the event, he writes of a *group* of men on the mountain.[14] In this dream-like and desolated scanning for meaning, an intimate, alienated pair of men emerges: Darwin and the naked Fuegian. And Darwin writes his account with naked hand – had seen his opposite and double with the naked eye.

The topographical and cultural distance Darwin supposes between himself and the Fuegians (though disagreeable to us now) is valuable to him in reaching towards a new theoretical position. It allows Darwin to extend the spectrum of humankind to such an extent that it begins to overlap the distance between humankind and other animals: instead of the severe disjunction between the human and other species enjoined by creationist theory the whole measure can be encompassed, 'we are all netted together'.

Yet the dismay of seeing his own male body figured in so dissimilar a guise, given back to him through observation, estranged, immediately produces in the letter a counter-image of the naked body. This time it is one from Western culture. And it is that of a woman. Again the constraint of the visual distance, the embargo on touching, dominates.

Now he recalls the large and sensuous picture of *Venus and Cupid with a Lute-player* by Titian (Fig. 1), then, as now, centrally placed in a gallery of the Fitzwilliam Museum in Cambridge. The naked Venus faces the viewer but her gaze is dreamily off out of the picture to our right and she has just ceased to play the recorder whose music lies in front of her beside a half-seen viol. Her naked feet rest against the velvet cloak of the lute player, his back to us, his gaze on her. The suggestion is of a body at ease in an ambient atmosphere that sustains and gently warms. Behind the couch a landscape of increasing wildness is in view: near to, a park with Petrarchan deer beneath the trees, a little further off the rough groves of a rising land, and behind them blue and rugged mountains, a savage landscape held in retreat behind the sumptuous presence of the woman's body. Textures and sounds are invoked as part of visual experience.

In the museum – as in watching the man on the rock – distance is insisted upon. But the tactile is aroused. Touching is embargoed and experienced at once. From the distanced voluptuousness of the picture Darwin catches up its references to music (lute, viol, flute) and imagines the more complete satisfactions of the ear engrossed by voice and instruments. *Hearing* will produce a resolution of bodily

experience and culture 'much more than delightful'.[15] The 'uttered tones' of the Fuegian, less intelligible than those of domestic animals, are here assuaged in the hoped for music of his own society – a music that affected him with profound physicality. The first two bodies of the letter also bring to the surface a trouble about the cross-over of fundamental categories: the human and the animal, the sentient and the art object. And the categories of self, kin, and stranger.

In the letter Darwin turns restlessly from the first two bodies to a third. Both these images have proved inscrutable, or at least impenetrable. The figures of the man – here – as Nature, the woman as Culture, produce both yearning and impasse. They remain untouchable. But in his practice as a zoologist Darwin does touch. He also unveils, invades, lays bare the interiority of small creatures: he is all at once dismayed by a sense of intimate contiguity with that body also. Preserving specimens involves disembowelling.

All the bodies he has conjured in this meditation, including his own, seem suddenly present in the 'small animal'. Disturbingly, the Venus in the Titian portrait presents her belly to the viewer in a posture not unlike that of the upturned small animal displayed to the knife. Darwin flinches away from these connections, seeking to put a space between the body of the woman and of the 'small animal'. Thus he half-consciously protects the innocence of his own touching eye, which in memory glances between male and female, between wild body and encultured body, both of them become teasing objects of desire and consternation.

As Evelyn Fox Keller observes in the passage quoted at the outset of this essay, 'some scientists see their endeavour in predominantly adversarial terms ... others see it as a primarily erotic activity'. Darwin inclined to eroticism yet found himself sometimes engaged in 'exercises in domination'. So it is that the other images – of autochthonous inhabitant, of woman displayed for the pleasure of the gaze – lie behind that of the small animal: just as the word 'guts' is concealed behind the word 'gusto', and the more dignified 'entrails' is substituted: 'I shall not be able tomorrow to pick out the entrails of some small animal, with half my usual gusto.'

The analyst W. R. Bion, in his post-Kleinian essay 'Attacks on Linking' describes the personality that eschews connection.[16] Darwin's bent seems to have been at the opposite end of the spectrum, seeking

[*facing*] 1 Titian, *Venus and Cupid with a Lute-Player*. Fitzwilliam Museum, Cambridge

kinship in the unlike, making links, making *more* than links since that suggests both connection and distance – immersing himself in sensation. And then seeking to taxonomise and describe. In this passage he experiences the terrors of estrangement, of sexual and aesthetic yearning and also of empathy.

Sex and sexual congress is central to Darwinian evolutionary theory. The pairing of *unlike* in the couple produces diversity of offspring – and that diversity increases exponentially. Other forms of reproduction – hermaphroditism, parthenogenesis, division, for example – produce offspring that replicate the previous generation.[17] Sexual reproduction inclines *away* from any such standard identity. So unlikeness and empathy were as important to him theoretically as emotionally.

When Darwin did eventually precipitate his theory of evolutionary descent, however, he paradoxically did away with the sexual pair as an initiating origin. For Darwin, the originary parental dyad is figured as the one, sexually undifferentiated – and irretrievable: 'the single progenitor'. This move allowed Darwin to distinguish his theory from that, for example, of Edward Forbes who proposed aboriginal pairs reproducing and populating specific biogeographical zones.[18] But it had a further emotional advantage for Darwin. It did away with fixed difference. It also avoided debating the prior claims of male or female parent (perhaps a consolation in his own case).

In his imagination, at the start, there was an 'It': 'the ancient progenitor, the archetype as it may be called, of all mammals, had its limbs constructed on the existing general pattern'.[19] Male and female, masculine and feminine, human and animal, are not yet disparted. 'The first creature' (p. 458), 'the single progenitor', 'one primordial form' (p. 455), 'the common parent' (p. 413): the 'one parent' (p. 457) is never sexed male or female in his writing. It is *hors-sexe*, and almost *hors-texte*.

The progenitor is undescried, irretrievable, but not sexually distanced: both self and mother, self and father identically. Epistemophilia, driving back towards an unaskable question which may include the search for the lost mother, fuels the pleasures and anxieties of Darwin's work. The intensity of his nostalgia for a lost England, a foregone self, shades in the letter to Whitley into an imaging of primary nakednesses: man, woman, animal. The fascination with taxonomy as well as the desire to be at one with the physical world is gratified for Darwin in his *Beagle* voyage, not only by the sensory riches of the journey but by writing.

In writing, the physical hand makes contact with a repertoire of scenes, figures and emotions already, even amidst the tumult of current impressions, *not* before his eyes. Among these is his old friend Whitley, less figureable to him now than the Fuegian he has encountered: 'I neither know, where you are living or what you are doing'. Whitley represents a familiar world grown exotic: a picturesque and primitive place of green cottages and white petticoats where young men, anticipating priesthood, ate owls together.[20] Darwin's writing hand conjures Whitley as an absence, a point of identification that will now be for ever fictional: *disembodied*.

Notes

1 *The Poems of John Keats*, ed. Miriam Allott, London, 1970, pp. 657–8.
2 *Reflections on Gender and Science*, New Haven and London, 1985, p. 125.
3 *Realism, Writing, Disfiguration: On Thomas Eakins and Stephen Crane*, Chicago, 1987, p. 65.
4 *The Seminar of Jacques Lacan*, ed. Jacques-Alain Miller, trans. John Forrester, Cambridge, 1988: Book I, 'Freud's Papers on Technique', p. 227.
5 I have written about the racial politics involved in a pamphlet essay *Can the Native Return?*, London, 1989, and about the uses of the first person in such accounts in 'Speaking for the Others: Relativism and Authority in Victorian Anthropological Literature', in R. Fraser, ed., *Sir James Frazer and the Literary Imagination*, London, 1990, pp. 38–60.
6 See Sir Charles Bell, *The Hand, its Mechanisms and Vital Endowments as Evincing Desgn*, London, 1833 (Bridgewater Treatises, no. 4). This work went through six editions by 1860. It is quite likely that it was among the books sent to Darwin while he was on the *Beagle* – but this is not necessary to my argument.
7 See Charles Bell, *A System of Dissections, Explaining the Anatomy of the Human Body*, Edinburgh, 1798–9, and *Essays on the Anatomy and Philosophy of Expression*, London, 1806 – from the third edition onwards, this book was called *The Anatomy and Philosophy of Expression as Connected with the Fine Arts*.
8 I cite page-references to the fourth edition (London, 1837).
9 *Journal of Researches into the Geological and Natural History of the Various Countries visited by H.M.S. Beagle, under the command of Captain Fitzroy, R.N. from 1832 to 1836* by Charles Darwin, Esq., M.A., F.R.S., Secretary to the Geological Society, London, 1839, p. 586. The work had first appeared as volume three of the *Narrative of the Surveying Voyages of His Majesty's Ships Adventure and Beagle*, under the editorship of Fitzroy. I quote from the first edition published independently. Soon afterwards it was re-issued and became known by the title *The Voyage of the Beagle*.
10 *The Life and Letters of Charles Darwin, Including an Autobiographical Chapter*, edited by his son, Francis Darwin, in three volumes, London, 1887 (vol. I, pp. 169–70). See also *The Correspondence of Charles Darwin*, ed. Frederick Burkhardt and Sydney Smith, Cambridge, 1985. In a letter of reminiscences written to Francis Darwin, Watkins (then Archdeacon of York) described the Club as making 'a devouring raid on birds & beasts which were before unknown to human palate . . . I think the Club came to an untimely end by endeavouring to eat an old brown owl', vol. I, p. 160, note 1.

11 *Journal of Researches*, pp. 308–9. Chapter 14 ends thus: 'One sight of such a coast is enough to make a landsman dream for a week about shipwreck, peril, and death; and with this in sight, we bade farewell for ever to Tierra del Fuego' (p. 307). Chapter 15 opens: 'July 23. – The Beagle anchored late at night in the bay of Valparaiso, the chief seaport of Chile. When morning came everything seemed delightful' (p. 308).

12 *Correspondence*, I, pp. 396–7. The oddities of spelling are Darwin's own.

13 See Charles Darwin, *The Expression of the Emotions in Man and Animals*, London, 1872.

14 In *Journal of Researches*, this becomes: 'A group of Fuegians partly concealed by the entangled forest, were perched on a wild point overlooking the sea; and as we passed by, they sprang up, and waving their tattered cloaks, sent forth a loud and sonorous shout' (p. 227). The following page gives a detailed description of their first close encounter with the group.

15 Francis Darwin, op. cit., records a friend's memory of the young Darwin's physical response to music: ' "What gave him the greatest delight was some grand symphony or overture of Mozart's of Beethoven's, with their full harmonies." On one occasion Herbert remembers "accompanying him to the afternoon service at King's, when we heard a very beautiful anthem. At the end of one of the parts, which was exceedingly impressive, he turned to me and said, with a deep sigh: "How's your backbone?". He often spoke of a feeling of coldness or shivering in his back on hearing beautiful music', p. 170.

16 See W. R. Bion, *Second Thoughts: Selected Papers on Psychoanalysis*, London, 1967, pp. 93–109. See also my *Forging the Missing Link: Interdisciplinary Stories*, Cambridge, 1992.

17 On the voyage, Darwin observed in detail other such forms of reproduction, writing with particular fascination about 'compound animals'; see pp. 15–16, p. 31, and, especially, pp. 258–62.

18 See Janet Browne, *The Secular Ark: Studies in the History of Biogeography*, New Haven and London, 1983 for discussion of Edward Forbes's theories.

19 Charles Darwin, *On the Origin of the Species by Means of Natural Selection or The Preservation of Favoured Races in the Struggle for Life* (1859), p. 416. Page references are to the Penguin Classics edition, ed. John Burrow, Harmondsworth, 1968.

20 Francis Darwin (op. cit.) records that the other members of the Glutton or Gourmet Club, besides Darwin and his friend Herbert, were 'Whitley of St. John's, now Honorary Canon of Durham; Heaviside of Sidney now Canon of Norwich; Lovett Cameron of Trinity, now vicar of Shoreham; Blane of Trinity, who held a high post during the Crimean war; H. Lowe (now Sherbrooke) of Trinity Hall; and Watkins of Emmanuel, now Archdeacon of York' (I, p. 169). Darwin had a lucky escape.

George and Georgina Sand: realist gender in *Indiana*

Sandy Petrey

George Sand, Honoré de Balzac, Stendhal: when Sand's novel *Indiana* appeared in 1832, readers hailed it as a superb contribution to the new fictional form developed by *The Wild Ass's Skin* and *Scarlet and Black*. The assimilation of Sand to Stendhal is especially striking, for it came during a period when *Scarlet and Black* was far from a stock literary reference. Bernard Weinberg's classic study of critical reactions to French realism defines the period 1831–8 as 'seven years of an almost absolute silence' concerning Stendhal.[1] It's therefore all the more noteworthy that a large percentage of those who reviewed *Indiana* were impelled to break the silence to tell their readers what Sand's work was like.

For one reviewer, *Indiana*'s characters are 'drawn with that vigour of observation you admire in *Scarlet and Black*'.[2] For another, Sand represents the world in the 'raw and bold tones of Beyle'.[3] Even when the reviewer got the spelling wrong, he had enough confidence in generic identity to set Sand's work among those novels in the process of establishing 'the school of Sthendal [sic]'.[4] *Scarlet and Black* stands commandingly at the origin of French social realism by virtue of its comprehensive integration of contemporary society into the novel form. Two years after *Scarlet and Black*, *Indiana* assumed a prominent place beside it as the prototype of fiction in which literary creation and historical insight are reciprocally invigorating.

In the years since 1832, two currents of literary scholarship with little else in common have collaborated in distancing Sand's work from the foundational realist texts with which it was first equated. The masculinist operations of traditional criticism put Balzac and Stendhal far above their female colleague, and the revisionist impulse of feminist criticism has tended to maintain the opposition while refusing the hierarchy. Different though their attitudes toward Sand's achievement have been, critics have generally agreed that it's not Balzac and Stendhal's. The most striking aspect of Sand's first reception, however, is that invocation of realist authors proceeded from an unexceptionable understanding of realist achievement. The reasons *Indiana* and *Scarlet and Black* were originally put together are the same as those subsequently invoked to set them apart.

Realism's most consequential innovation – its foundational vision of the world – was awareness that the socio-historical conditions in which human existence unfolds have determinant impact on its course. Characters and age constitute a single whole to effect precisely the integration of individual and collective that furnished the leitmotif of Sand's reviewers. *Indiana*'s representation of the human heart, mind and soul was seen as credible because this novel historicises inner states as thoroughly as conventional fictions historicise outer appearance. '*Indiana* is the story of modern passion'.[5] 'The particular merit of *Indiana* [...] resides above all in a profoundly true sentiment of the sufferings and moral turpitudes of our epoch'.[6] '*Indiana* is our story, the story of the human heart as it is now' (Boussuge). 'On opening this book, we saw ourselves introduced into a world that was true, living, *ours* [...] we found customs and characters as they exist around us'.[7] To the eternal and universal paradigms of psychological delineation consecrated by classical humanism, realist fiction opposes the time-bound model of a selfhood formed by the forces that also define an era. That lesson was schematised again and again in the discussion provoked by *Indiana*.

Besides their impressive proclivity for the language that would identify realism as a whole, reviews of *Indiana* were also characterised by speculation on the author's sex. Much of this sexual commentary simply recycles inherited ideas on male and female writing: 'this is a novel written with all the strength of a man's grip and all the grace of a woman's pen'.[8] But the experience of reading *Indiana* stimulated some critics to open a consequential inquiry into the cultural practices that produce (rather than express) masculine and feminine sensibilities. Like hearts, thought, passion and suffering, for some of *Indiana*'s first readers gender too figured among the components of human existence that vary with time, place and customs. To the list of prophetic tropes organising early reactions to *Indiana* must be added a complex of issues with intense contemporary resonance, those addressing the interrelationship of gender and genre.

That George Sand and Aurore Dudevant were the same person was anything but a closely guarded secret in the small world of Paris literary circles in 1832, and reviewers with interesting things to say about the sexual identity of the authorial voice knew or suspected that the actual author was a woman who had taken a man's name. As Sainte-Beuve put it, this transsexual gesture was by itself enough to destabilise the narrating voice and integrate the author and his/her gender into the fictional universe: 'The author of *Indiana*, we are assured, is a woman [...] as far as we're concerned, everything in this harrowing production justifies the suspicion that has been circulating and creates a reading that is doubly novelistic, through the interest of the story in itself and through some mysterious and living identity, invincibly imagined behind the story by the reader' (pp. 473–4). For Sainte-Beuve, the author is as much caught up as characters in the socialised representation configuring the fictional world of *Indiana*. Cross-naming brought the person named into the novel, where his and/or her 'mysterious and living identity' underpins the contemporary reality enclosing Indiana and her supporting cast. Because a woman had written herself as a man by taking a masculine name and mastering a masculine style, the fictions of gender were brought into dynamic interaction with those of love.

While Sainte-Beuve located the novel of the author in the novel proper, Gustave Planche went farther. He took the combination of a name and a writing that both reverse gender expectations as demanding their own narrative, and he amenably provided it. Planche's protagonist is Georgina Sand, a name he derived from 'translating' the 'mysterious anonymity' on *Indiana*'s title page (p. 701). Georgina's biography can be effortlessly inferred from her compositional techniques:

> This must be a woman with an acute sensibility, but one who early on acquired personal direction of her actions. Such premature freedom gave her mind a somewhat virile character. Beside an idea that could come only from eiderdown, from under the laces of a bonnet, next to an emotion that springs from a heart imprisoned by a corset, there are others indicating a daring horseman, riding crop in hand, tearing across fields in the early morning, pulling in great gulps of air, leaping ditches at the risk of his horse's neck. (p. 701)[9]

Why does Georgina sound like George? She led the life George would have had if he existed. If sex is given and gender constructed, Planche's George and Georgina Sand exemplify gender alone. They/she/he write the way they do not because their bodies so dictate but because society has marked their bodies with corsets and bonnets or the chance not to sit sidesaddle.

While Planche sees George and Georgina as the product of androgynous socialisation, he believes Georgina ultimately had to betray herself.

By definition, androgynous socialisation can't be completely masculine, and the author of *Indiana* doesn't display some of the traits male
instruction necessarily conveys. 'A man, on the contrary, introduces
his mind and the artifice of his thought into expression of his every
feeling. He schemes, he organises each outpouring of emotion. Often
he even prefers effects to truth in a tête-à-tête; all the more reason to
do so in a book' (pp. 701–2). When they confront a choice between
truth and effect, men are trained to choose effect, and the author of
Indiana takes truth instead.

Planche gives two instances of unseemly and unmasculine candour:
delineation of Raymon de Ramière, the man with whom Indiana falls
in love, and the narrator's misogynistic remarks on women's lack
of intelligence. 'A man would never have agreed to paint Raymon's
selfishness so pitilessly, or to pronounce this brutal aphorism: Woman
is imbecilic by nature' (p. 700). However imbecilic he considers
women, however selfish he considers other men, a man doesn't say
so in books.

Sainte-Beuve, who also found Raymon too real a man to have been
invented by one, crowns his reasons why a woman must have written
Indiana like this: 'above all the character of Raymon, this disappointing
character brought to light and exposed in detail with all his miserable
selfishness in a way no man, not even a Raymon, would ever have
been able to see or dared to say' (p. 473). The author of *Indiana* got
Raymon exactly right, and that's something no man could have
possibly done.

Which features of Raymon's textual presence are incompatible
with character delineation as men practise it? The question is crucial,
for it asks what 'truth' about themselves men are so unwilling to
reveal that only a woman would put it into words. I believe the
answer is that Sand represents Raymon's manhood as a social performance rather than a natural fact and thus challenges every claim that
men's social position merely recognises their natural capabilities.
In the terms of the essentialist/constructionist debate on identity,
Indiana sets itself squarely on the constructionist side. It depicts –
and enacts – male and female *being* as the consequence of culturally
circumscribed patterns of masculine and feminine *behaviour*, a compelling repudiation of received ideas that goes far towards explaining
early reader response. Reviewers' consistent attention to both the
author's sexual identity and the setting's historical specificity was
the appropriate response to a text that takes social production of men

and women as its dominant concern. The narrator and characters of *Indiana* collaborate in a sustained demonstration that gender is no less a social phenomenon than the class distinctions so prominent in the works of Sand's realist colleagues.

The opposite of realist gender is naturally – physiologically, corporeally – determined sex, and *Indiana* takes pains to show that what looks like natural sexuality is in fact a social role. Raymon de Ramière, the character Planche and Sainte-Beuve saw as revealing the limits on a woman's ability to write like a man, is a perfect example. Raymon is a hugely successful lover, the sort of man whose standard depiction exalts manhood. In Sand's representation, however, Raymon's amatory prowess derives not from his manhood but from his discourse. He talks his desire into existence and in so doing separates desire from its supposed origin in male hormones. The sequence isn't lust followed by seductive language but seductive language followed by lust. 'He expressed passion with art, and he felt it with warmth. Only it was not passion that made him eloquent, it was eloquence that made him passionate' (p. 62).[10] Like that of sex, the essentialist vision of sexuality posits the control of behaviour by anatomy. In the realist vision of *Indiana*, Raymon's behaviour is cause rather than effect. He comes to feel with intensity what he articulates with skill, fabricating successive selfhoods that are simultaneously solid and factitious. What he is derives from how he acts.

As readers have long recognised, Raymon acts like an exemplary avatar of Don Juan. To my knowledge, however, no one has ever thought that Don Juan must be the creation of a woman because no man could ever depict a fellow male in so unflattering a light. On the contrary: Don Juanism is more like a secret ambition than a secret shame in masculinist ruminations on the subject. By no stretch of the imagination is a male character who seduces and abandons women a figure that 'a man would never have agreed to paint'. Too many men have painted such characters with too much success for any reviewer, much less one with the credentials of Planche and Sainte-Beuve, to argue that a man actually wouldn't do any such thing.

What sets Raymon apart from other Don Juans is that his treatment of women doesn't derive from his character but institutes it, which is why the rules of manly writing decreed that he be left undepicted. The eternal masculine mythologised in figures like Don Juan becomes a silly bit of nonsense as *Indiana* severs what counts as masculine from everything that could conceivably be considered eternal. 'Since his first literary creation, the definitive expression and determination of Don Juan has been precise: *a man without a name*, which is to say a sex and not an individual'.[11] By giving her Don Juan a local habitation and a name that are responsible for everything he does, Sand was equally precise: Raymon embodies a gender and not a sex. He becomes a Don Juan not through surging testosterone but through interactive dynamics.

Yet the desire produced by those dynamics is powerful and substanial, for Sand's vision of realist gender pays close attention to the fact that what society imposes on its members becomes their lived reality. When men and women come together in *Indiana*, the sparks still fly. The novel's specificity is ascribing the heat to ideology rather than physiology. Characters' mutual attraction is a social fabrication, their indulgence of it a social rite; the novel consequently makes its only representation of the sexual act its most powerful figuration of gendered desire.

When Noun senses that she's losing Raymon, she makes a final effort to keep him by dressing herself in Indiana's clothes before bringing her lover into Indiana's bedroom. Raymon's response is satisfactorily erotic. What turns him on, however, isn't the body he takes but the setting in which it's presented, a setting filled with the signs of a socio-economic status far superior to Noun's. Physically with the maid, emotionally taking the mistress, Raymon sees Indiana in her mirrors, feels her in her clothes, senses her in her curtains, caresses her on her bed: 'Noun took all these transports for herself, when Raymon saw of her nothing except Indiana's dress' (p. 86).

Like Indiana, Noun is a paragon of female beauty, but her anatomical perfection is erotically non-functional. Her beauty is in fact inimical to her lover's desire: every time Indiana's possessions convince Raymon he's with the woman he wants, one of Noun's body parts pushes itself forward and reminds him he's not.

> It was but a momentary error: Indiana would have been more hidden ... her modest breast would not have been revealed through the triple gauze of her bodice; she might perhaps have adorned her hair with natural camellias, but it would not have lain on her head in such exciting disorder; she could have enclosed her feet in satin slippers, but her chaste dress would not have thus revealed the mysteries of her darling leg. (p. 83)

However Don Juan might react to them, women's breasts, legs and hair turn Raymon off. He's excited not by female flesh but by feminine clothes, pictures, crystal and lace. Anatomy is not destiny. Ideology is, and the ideology of gender activating Raymon's desire leaves anatomical attributes out.

For Don Juan, any female body reflects every other. For Raymon, the desired reflection comes not from female bodies but from feminine signifiers. When he wants 'a purer reflection of Indiana' (p. 83), he looks away from the body before him and to the musical instruments and embroidery behind it, ignoring the physical identity that sets Noun and Indiana together for the social identity that sets them apart. The substitution culminates, famously, when sex with the maid produces a hallucinatory vision of sex with the mistress. 'The two panels of mirrors sending Noun's image back and forth between them an infinite number of times seemed to be filled with a thousand shadows. In the depths of this double reverberation, he made out a slimmer form, and it seemed to him that, in the last misty, vague shadow of Noun reflected there, he saw the slender and elegant body of Madame Delmare' (p. 86). Clothes ordinarily manifest social position in ways a naked body does not. In *Indiana*, however, nakedness too is socially defined. Even when engaged in the most undeniably physiological component of gendered relations, Raymon demonstrates that physiology can never inform a serious understanding of either their causes or their effects.

Although Noun has 'a beauty of the first order,' (p. 52), she isn't desirable to Raymon because her beauty doesn't matter unless it's combined with first-order status. 'The wife of a peer of the realm who would so immolate herself would be a precious conquest; but a chambermaid!' (p. 52) Social standing and gendered desirability are both collective fabrications that interact to generate libido as well as protocol. Physically, Noun and Indiana are alike. Socially, they are a world apart, and Raymon's hallucinatory vision of the socially validated mistress while he engages in physical love with her maid is a striking feature of *Indiana*'s realist view of men and women together. *Every* component of gendered interaction is socially marked.

Indiana replaces Noun in Raymon's mirror because France's social organisation defines her as more desirable. Since social organisation is fluid rather than fixed, sexual desirability vacillates as well, which means that the woman adored can always become a woman scorned if she loses the status responsible for her appeal. Indiana can herself be replaced, as she is when the novel repeats substitution of one woman for another in its title character's bedroom. Raymon is again the figure for whom the substitution occurs, but Indiana becomes the woman expelled instead of the woman invoked when she returns from the Ile Bourbon to find Raymon married to Laure de Nangy. The political revolution that occurred between Indiana's miraculous appearance and ignominious expulsion from the same space figures a different sort of social change: like forms of government, gendered relations vary with historical conditions.

Noun vanishes despite a physical beauty and a loving heart the narrator exalts unreservedly, Indiana despite qualities with analogous certification. As if to show that what actually gets to men has little to do with women's physical or emotional attributes, the prologue to Indiana's rejection by Raymon is her total surrender to him of her body, mind and heart.

> 'Won't you recognise me,' she exclaimed; 'it's me, it's your Indiana, it's your slave [...] Dispose of me, of my blood, of my life; I'm yours, body and soul; I came three thousand leagues to belong to you, to tell you so; take me, I'm your property, you're my master.' [...] She attached herself to him with the terror of a child who does not want to be left alone one instant and dragged herself on her knees to follow him. (pp. 300–2)

The abjection is spectacular, the offer of sexual slavery verbally explicit and gesturally confirmed. Raymon can't respond because – unlike Don Juan – he's not a sexual but a social being.

The same site, Indiana's bedroom, encloses two of the novel's most dramatic sexual encounters, and the outcome of both is a lesson on how much more than sex is involved in each. On a first level, the display could be understood as a simple instance of the dominance of property over human relations in realist fiction. Who gets the man? The woman who owns the bedroom. Nothing else counts – not beauty, not sacrifice, not intensity of desire, not magnitude of devotion. The absent Indiana is present in the space she possesses, the present Indiana might as well be absent from the space Laure has bought. Sand's novel incorporates classic tropes of standard bedroom plots, but it refuses to let them determine what happens in bed.

Although Sand appropriates the economic vision that a certain Marxist tradition has ascribed to Balzac's works, economics alone is far from exhausting the realist configuration of Laure de Nangy's mastery over the man other women beg to master them. Laure rules not just because she's rich but because she's noble as well, a combination with special importance in making *Indiana* what its readers

saw as the 'infallible history' (Pyat, p. 194) of their age. Laure, the
only descendant of an imposing aristocratic family, is also the only
heir to an imposing bourgeois fortune. She thus enjoys superior status
in both the elite groups recognized under the early July Monarchy,
when aristocratic and financial notables were coming to rule side by
side. In the high realist tradition, Laure's person manifests the global
configuration of her age.

The importance in *Indiana* of the July Revolution's social and
political transformation of France is largely responsible for contemporary readers' penchant for describing the novel in the language used
for masterpieces of realism. Laure's special status in relation to July
Monarchy elites foregrounds the reciprocal impact of genre and gender
establishing the specificity of *Indiana* within the realist corpus, for
the power granted Laure by historical changes effects nothing less
than the obliteration of male hegemony. In describing Raymon's
relations with Noun and Indiana, Sand socialises (and thus demystifies)
masculine authority but leaves the man in the controlling role. In
Raymon's relation with Laure, demystification completes itself by
making the male the submissive rather than the dominant partner.
Society may well restrict gendered contact to exercises of dominance
and submission, Sand seems to be saying, but nothing requires either
sex always to occupy the same position. Because the world validates
hierarchies other than those of gender, a woman like Laure need
not be a 'woman' when she's with her man. Her contact with Raymon
is the studied, systematic reversal of Noun and Indiana's because her
position in the France of the early 1830s precludes her assumption
of anything vaguely like their gender roles.

Which of course means that Raymon's gender role must be cast
aside as well. In the fable of Don Juan's sexual drive, every woman is a
point on a line that never ends. In the realist narrative of gendered
identity that is *Indiana*, the woman who stands above Raymon in
collective perception orders that the line be cut, and she is obeyed.
When Don Juan is between two women, he takes the new and leaves
the old behind. When Raymon, 'his eyes sparkling' and 'a terrible
smile playing on his lips' (pp. 301–2), has Indiana at his feet, Laure
pronounces his desire null and void. The pronouncement's impact is
the ultimate demonstration that gender roles and sexual physiology
are independent variables. Laure 'was the woman who was to subjugate
Raymon, for she was as far above him in skill as he was above Indiana'
(p. 293). Much more than his sexual exploitation *of* women, it's

Raymon's exploitation *by* one that makes him the kind of man no other man would have 'agreed to paint'.

On finding Indiana in despair, Laure's reaction – anything but sisterly – is a 'bitter, cold and contemptuous smile' (p. 302). Female solidarity would affirm the fundamentalist, anatomical vision of female identity repudiated by Laure, who can no more sympathise with the woman at Raymon's feet than she could put herself there. She therefore withdraws, 'triumphing in secret over the position of inferiority and dependence in which this incident had placed her husband in relation to herself' (p. 303). The tableau created when Indiana is at Raymon's feet and Raymon under Laure's thumb encapsulates substitution of gender for sex in Sand's first novel. The roles to be assumed in sexual contact are set by society, but no extra-social feature like bodily attributes can determine who will play them. Two characters – Indiana and Raymon, a woman and a man – take the feminine 'position of inferiority and dependence'. Two characters – a man and a woman, Raymon and Laure – take the masculine role of 'subjugating' their partners. The message all characters convey is that formulated when Noun's perfect beauty disappears during her socially imperfect love affair: the body counts only in so far as society decrees that it shall.

Accordingly, it's after Raymon's standing in society has been compromised by his political miscalculations that his body stops making him a man. His phallic superiority turns out to be not genital but political. Among the principal defenders of 'a royal house that was degrading itself and bearing him with it as it fell' (p. 260), Raymon experienced France's expulsion of that house during the July Revolution as a catastrophic end. His marriage to Laure was an effort to align himself with those for whom the events of July were an exhilarating beginning. Revolutionary transformations of governmental and gendered hierarchies coincide because both depend absolutely on a societal acquiescence that can always be withdrawn. Neither kings nor men actually rule by divine right.

There's another way *Indiana* employs the standard tropes of realist history to represent gendered existence: its depiction of the human consequences of France's marriage laws, which placed women in a permanently inferior position to their men. In one of the novel's most quoted passages, Indiana makes an eloquent protest against the French marital system, defending all women's right to disobey their husbands by forcing hers to consider the contrast between legal

bondage and spiritual freedom. 'I know that I am the slave and you
are the lord; the law of this country has made you my master [...]
You have the right of the strongest, and society confirms it for you;
but over my will, sir, you have no rights' (p. 225). Marital relations
are in *Indiana* as pointed and precise a historical reference as dynastic
successions, and the title character repeatedly defines revolution in
the home as no less important than revolution in the palace.

Yet France's legal codification of unjust marital relations is far from
the most significant component of realist gender in Sand's first novel,
which understands perfectly that women's emancipation as traditionally understood would be only a part of the solution to their gendered
submission. The end of juridical subservience to Delmare would do
nothing about moral subjection to Raymon, as the text emphasises by
repeating the key terms of Indiana's protest against being one man's
wife in her abject plea to become another man's lover. The same
woman who indignantly announces to Delmare that the law makes
him the master and her the slave piteously cries out to Raymon that she
has come three thousand leagues to say that she is his slave, he her
master. Gender is an internal mystification as well as an external constraint, and the parallel between Indiana's pleas for freedom and for
slavery pointedly define her womanhood as something she enacts as
well as endures. Sand's men and women are a pulsating agglomeration
of internalised ideologemes. Indiana makes herself Raymon's *woman* as
surely – as ignominiously – as the laws make her Delmare's wife.

Indiana's enthusiastic performance of feminine submission has been
hard for some of Sand's feminist readers to take. Conventional concepts
of femininity seem to structure character delineation throughout this
novel, in which women sometimes conform to time-dishonoured roles
with at least as much commitment as men. My argument is that anything less would betray the fundamental principle of realist gender, an
internalised reality as well as an ideological mystification. Indiana can't
just say no to feminine emotions because her experience of them has
been a constant feature of the processes establishing her selfhood. The
revolution marking the contrast between Laure and Indiana also
expresses the magnitude of the social cataclysm necessary for a meaningful change in gender roles. Laure can assume masculinity because
great upheavals have defined her as a person in whom feminine traits
are ludicrously incongruous. The upheavals in Indiana's life have the
opposite effect, that of exaggerating her 'position of inferiority and
dependence'.

Although Indiana's femininity meshes smoothly with Sand's representation of realist gender, the characters whom reviewers saw as betraying the author's actual identity were both male: Raymon and the narrator. In Planche's comments on the latter, the telltale clue was open contempt for the sex defined as 'imbecilic by nature' in the opening clause of a classically misogynistic authorial comment on the action being described. 'Woman is imbecilic by nature; it seems that, in order to counterbalance the eminent superiority over us given her by her delicate perception, heaven expressly set in her heart a blind vanity, an idiotic credulousness' (p. 245). What distinguishes this from innumerable similar distinctions between men's intellect and women's sensitivity? Why does this particular definition of women's delicate perception and dull brain stand so far apart from those written by hosts of men that its writer couldn't possibly be a man?

The answer is a variant on the reason why Raymon is radically unlike all the other Don Juans in Western literature: the narrator's masculinity too is performative instead of natural, and the more male it sounds the more it problematises maleness. Identical to the intensity of Raymon's sexual drives, George's patriarchal judgements of women are a discursive fabrication deconstructed by the very fact of their expression. What Sainte-Beuve called the narrator's 'mysterious and living identity, invincibly imagined behind the story', is an androgynous being whose self-classification as naturally intelligent rather than perceptive refutes the idea that either men or women are by nature anything whatever. It's because the author identified on the original title page as G. Sand writes so much like George that Georgina's message comes through. The more sexualised the narrative voice, the more forcefully it reveals that all human voices are in fact gendered. Like Indiana's feminine subservience, like Raymon's masculine impetuousness, the phallic resonance of the narrator's voice configures gender by its very success in validating sex. Sand's narrator wrote his manhood as a blend of substance and artifice. Whereas the ideology men absorb from the cradle up has no difficulty with either sexual substance or gendered artifice in isolation, it provides no way to think the blend.

And that blend is central to *Indiana*, in which Raymon is both a raging bull and a henpecked wimp, in which George writes like a woman-hating pig and Georgina's mysterious, living identity undoes all he says. The *effects* of gendered existence are here overpoweringly conventional, their *cause* radically problematised. Raymon isn't just a man, he's a Don Juan; Indiana isn't just a woman, she's a groveling masochist; the narrator doesn't just recount, he does so in the Voice of the Father to cry out 'Shame on this imbecilic woman!' (p. 213) whenever female masochism warrants it. But because Don Juan and George are also the opposite of the male horrors they present themselves as being, the text dissociates all gendered features from sexual physiology. What they are comes not from anatomical attributes but from received ideas.

One of the novel's most forceful dissociations of gender from genitals occurs when Sir Ralph tells Indiana that he was placed with the 'eunuchs' (p. 332) because her behaviour towards him had nothing in common with standard male–female interaction. Eunuchs here come from communal rather than surgical operations. Prevented from performing masculinity by his determination to conceal what he feels for Indiana, Ralph can't be a man despite possessing manhood's consecrated attributes. His assimilation of himself to a eunuch immediately precedes his complaint that Indiana acted as if he lacked 'a soul and senses' (p. 332). He doesn't come right out and say what else eunuchs don't have, but his recognition that *everything* constituting maleness disappears unless masculinity is continuously performed remains striking.

Ralph's confession of his castrated feeling, however, comes at a point in the novel where the feeling has left him because masculine and feminine gender roles are reattaching themselves to male and female bodies. Ralph and Indiana are about to leave France for a tropical island where they will live happily ever after, about to enter a world where soul and senses reacquire their conventional association with anatomical distinctions. Sand's conclusion refuses the realist setting of its first four parts for an exotic elsewhere, so insulated from collective dynamics that Ralph and Indiana prosper in a slave economy while having no contact with slaves except to buy and set free 'poor enfeebled blacks' (p. 352). The novel's last words, spoken by Ralph and Indiana in unison, contrast their home to *le monde*, the term France and its realists consecrated to signal that society *was* the world for those within it. Where there is no *monde* there is no realism, and the happy couple's valedictory address perfectly caps the idyllic story they at last come to live.

The characters' removal from the realist universe coincides with the end of their performance of realist gender. Whereas Indiana continues to play the submissive woman, it now seems *natural* for her to do so because her man is so worthy of her respect. Raymon was only a gendered creature, 'true in his acting' (p. 213); Ralph is a sexual creature 'true in his passion' (p. 337). As a consequence, Indiana's assumption of conventional feminine submissiveness comes to appear as intelligent as it was formerly 'imbecilic'. At the conclusion of *Indiana*, the Couple reappears, purged of historically contingent behaviour, resplendent with forever unchanging devotion. Like Raymon, Indiana enacts the Couple Plot with three different partners. But whereas Raymon ends up with the ultimate figure for existence as socially defined − Laure de Nangy − Indiana's final partner categorically repudiates social definition of whatever kind. Ralph and Indiana are 'returned to truth, to nature' (p. 337) and thus removed from society and history. Conventional masculinity and femininity retain their textual force, but the text organises itself so that they seem to be not conventional but innate. In one of her last novelistic appearances, Indiana − smiling sweetly and silently − removes herself while one man, Ralph, tells her story to another, the narrator. The phallic order is preserved.

Except that, once more, the phallic order is eerily unnatural because one of the men performing it is also a woman. Ralph's progress from the state of a eunuch to triumphant testicularity is chronicled by a figure who undoes all his story's essentialist messages, George/Georgina Sand. Ralph and the narrator's exchange of Indiana's story, a classic instance of male bonding, also disassembles maleness by severing it from foundationalist thought. George Sand joins Sir Ralph in an offensively paternalistic exchange of stories culminating in the frequently misogynistic novel coming to a close; Georgina Sand remains a living identity that detaches paternalism and misogyny from any conceivable ground. Identical to the intensity of Indiana's desire for Raymon, the narrator's complacent masculinity is, despite appearances, a dramatically feminist proclamation. Although it finally abandons realist history, *Indiana* never stops exploring realist gender.

The significance of George Sand's performative masculinity increases in the works that followed *Indiana*, almost all of which perpetuate the refusal of realist techniques that marks *Indiana*'s conclusion. The demarcation of realism from idyll in Sand's first novel holds good well beyond it, for her subsequent works establish an ever-greater distance from the realist project. Naomi Schor's validation of what she calls Sand's idealism attends to the refusal of French society effected when Indiana and *Indiana* leave France behind for an 'epilogue which so spectacularly exceeds the bounds of bourgeois realism'.[12] Schor's emphasis is appropriate, for *Indiana's* abandonment of history was the beginning of Sand's lifelong commitment to developing an alternative to the realist style with which she began her career.

Yet throughout that career Sand's narrative voice clearly and insistently declared its masculinity. Proper and common nouns, adjectives, pronouns – every gendered mark of the French language represented George Sand as a man until he and his creator died. The principal product of realist gender in *Indiana*, the narrative presence of George Sand, remains a central constituent of the works that subsequently called realism to task. The radical destabilisation of the ideology of sex accomplished by *Indiana* continues throughout the writing career of that novel's most celebrated character, whose realist gender never ceases to repeat that sexual identity is constructed rather than inherited.

Notes

1 Bernard Weinberg, *French Realism: The Critical Reaction*, New York, 1937, p. 12.
2 Félix Pyat, review of *Indiana*, *L'Artiste*, 27 may 1832, p. 195. All further references to this review are given in the text. All translations are my own.
3 Gustave Planche, 'Georges Sand', *Revue des Deux Mondes*, 30 November 1832, pp. 687–702 (p. 701). All further references to this review are given in the text.
4 H. Boussuge, review of *Indiana*, *Cabinet de lecture*, 24 June 1832, p. 13. All further references to this review are given in the text.
5 H. de Latouche, Review of *Indiana*, *Le Figaro*, 31 May 1832, no page numbers.
6 Anonymous, review of *Indiana*, *Le Temps*, 14 June 1832, no page numbers.
7 Charles-Augustin de Sainte-Beuve, review of *Indiana* reprinted in his *Portraits contemporains*, Paris, 1870, I, pp. 470–81 (p. 471). All further references to this review are given in the text.
8 Edouard d'Anglemont, review of *Indiana*, *La France littéraire*, IV, 1832, pp. 454–7 (p. 457).
9 Since Planche knew Sand quite well and may even have helped her write the preface to *Indiana*, his claim to have intuited her life from her writing is spurious. The important point, however, isn't whether he was actually deriving gender from style but the steps he saw as enabling someone to do so.
10 George Sand, *Indiana*, Paris, 1962. All page references are given in the text.
11 Gregorio Marañon, *Don Juan et le donjuanisme*, trans. Marie-Berthe Lacombe, Paris, 1958, p. 24.
12 Naomi Schor, 'Idealism in the Novel: Recanonising Sand', *Yale French Studies*, LV, 1988, pp. 56–73 (p. 71).

Reading states of climax: masculine expression and the language of orgasm in the writing of the Surrealist philosopher and poet André Breton

Jennifer Patterson

As a movement, Surrealism seeks to break through the barriers imposed by conscious logic and to liberate the imagination by freeing language from standardised denotational values. From the first page of the *Manifestos*, Breton uses the generic 'man' for 'humankind' but as his discourse proceeds this would-be grammatically neutral term with its exclusionary semantic residue becomes increasingly identified with a masculine experience from which 'woman' is eventually displaced and described as a separate entity. For the Surrealists, words make love, and as a theoretician Breton sexualises language, according value to images which conjoin. Although such images are stated to be all-powerful and man a passive receiver and recorder, he is also a dis-contented dreamer searching to find liberation through the expression of spontaneous abandon. Indeed Breton describes language as a tool controlled by man which has been 'given' to him 'so that he may make a surrealist use of it'.[1]

Breton presents surrealist language as a revolutionary means of attacking, conquering and dominating literary values, and of substi-tuting new and exciting textual experience. His theoretical discourse presents Surrealist activity as an experience of desire and satisfaction, expressed in a masculine language of orgasm:

> It should therefore come as no surprise to see Surrealism situate itself primarily and almost uniquely within language and not, returning from some incursion or other, to come back to that place for the pleasure of lording it over a conquered country. In fact, nothing can any longer prevent this country from being, in the main, conquered. Hordes of words, literally unleashed, for which Dada and Surrealism have engaged to open doors [...] will slowly and deliberately penetrate the small stupid little towns of literature with sure thrusts [...] They will calmly effect a fair consummation

of turrets [...] We pretend not to notice that the logical mechanism of phrases reveals itself to be increasingly impotent, in man's case, to set off the emotive spasm which really makes his life worthwhile. (*M*, pp. 51–2)

Language is used here in a climactic way, exhibiting an external position moving inward in an articulation of desire, to satisfy the aim of that desire which is an eventual projection outside of the individual: 'incursion ... pleasure ... open doors ... penetrate ... sure thrusts ... consummation ... set off the spasm'. Yet the organisation of the language is more complex than progressive and full of gaps and returns. Surrealism is situated 'almost uniquely', but not entirely, 'within language'. After 'incursions' or movements into hostile country, Surrealism will not return to language to flaunt its victory.

The sensation of twisting and knotting created by these incursions and negated returns is analogous to the psychoanalytic notion of a defence mechanism. Breton writes a defence of his surrealist territory into the text ('returning', 'not' 'to come back'). In textual fact, Breton has returned in his discourse and to the conquered country, to state firmly that it is indeed conquered: 'Nothing can any longer prevent this country from being ... conquered'. The complexity of this sentence with its negation of negative forces reads as an over-emphatic affirmative return, a paradoxical negation of the intentions expressed in the previous sentence.

Words are 'literally unleashed', released from prison and madhouse. Set free by Dada and Surrealism, they penetrate, consume towers and in their frenzied liberation 'set off the emotive spasm' which gives value to man's life. Breton's textual desires result in pronominal manipulation and confusion since Surrealism (masculine noun) conquers and liberates, and elsewhere aims guns and projectors and provides keys. This textual construction which identifies with traditional perceptions of masculine roles, opens doors for hordes (feminine plural noun). The feminine plural is constructed as powerful in its liberation; penetrating (a male experience) rival towns (traditionally symbolised as feminine) and consuming towers to achieve a singular climax for 'man' (an 'expressed' male fantasy within this phallocratic state). Hence power is connoted by penetration, yet the liberated feminine noun services the greater excitement of a release described in ejaculatory terms. Engaging with logic is presented as a masculine engagement with a rival mechanism which seems 'impotent' in contrast with the 'simultaneous products of the activity I call Surrealist', liberated by the poet (*M*, p. 37).

While Surrealist liberation is presented as desirable, it is accompanied by anxiety about loss, since the value of the product relates to the masculine ego through the textuality of patriarchy, leaving authority with its masculine ego vulnerable to fear of attack and even castration, to fear of not producing and reproducing. Breton, who transfers his potency to the realm of language, equally transfers his need to make language reproductive, a self-perpetuating line: 'the noun must germinate' (M, p. 299).

Woman is both vassal and vessel in the service of massaging a poetic and linguistic ego: 'Everywhere woman is no more than a chalice overflowing with vowels in liaison with the inimitable night magnolia'.[2] Her reproductive capacity is abstracted; she is subordinate to language, its slave and that of the author, a sex object to be sacrificed or 'consumed' by language: 'woman of pleasure, object of consumption'.[3] Yet her externalised state is necessary to the phallic 'I'. She is a 'promise' which endures in those terms; a catalyst or facilitator of expression reduced to mere 'subsistence': 'In Surrealism, woman will have been loved and celebrated as the great promise, that which subsists after it has been kept' (M, p. 307).

In her summary of modern feminist theorists, Dale Spender discusses the phallic 'I' which demands woman's willing co-operation, holds her responsible and hates her for its needs.[4] Anxiety about a projected and externalised dependency is a gendered political construction which imposes ideas about 'her' objectified and subservient value from this negative perception.

Surrealism offers a drug which promises to satisfy all palates and give ultimate pleasure: 'like hashish, it has the ability to satisfy all manner of tastes' (M, p. 36). It also inscribes a state of need, tension and anger and thereby justifies violence: 'Surrealism ... There is every reason to believe that it acts on the mind in the same way as drugs; like them it creates a certain state of need and can push man to terrible revolts' (M, pp. 35–6).

Evacuating and externalising choice or responsibility from the pressing demands of instant satisfaction, it is perhaps hardly surprising that the same man co-authors a definition of rape as 'love of speed'.[5] The poet's reward for Surrealist products? 'He will be truly elected and the most gentle and submissive women will love him violently' (M, p. 31).

Surrealism seeks to give new life to language and deliberately sets out to destroy the stereotypes of image association. In feminist terms, this could be a positive step, particularly for female gender stereotyping. The Surrealist text relies heavily on the female body as an echo-image of the text and destroys many of the familiar clichés associated with such imaging. However, Surrealism perpetuates and celebrates the more sinister image of the female body as an ideal locus for/on which to perpetrate violent acts.

Breton's poem 'L'Union libre' depicts the body of Suzanne Muzard, his wife whose only identity is as the property of the poet, as an unnamed woman, 'my woman/wife'.[6] The woman is a textual possession of her poetic representation, pornographed by the reification of a male self-pleasuring gaze. She is robbed of space and presence and her body is separated into a list of parts. These parts of the body are images to be used for individual poetic and linguistic associations, objects to be played with. The dislocation of her body parts is mirrored by the disruptive and manipulative violence done to the images imposed on it to demonstrate Surrealist principles of language, images which themselves violently present the representational act.

By fragmenting the woman's body, the author gains greater control over its exhibition. The reader views through the eyes of the author in the viewing sequence which functions as an optical control over presentation, selection of image (and word) order and what is perceived as exciting. In this way, the textual fragmentation and objectification of female body parts is a visual reflection of Surrealist fragmentation of the image systems with which they copulate.

The language of 'L'Union libre' is further subject to the imposition of a cabbalistic alchemical programme which is in turn subject to the 'ruling' author, Breton. Linguistic manipulations exhibit alchemical metaphors and form part of the textual realisation of Breton's cultural quests, thereby confirming the dominance of his identity as theoretician with regard to an 'alchemy of the word' (M, pp. 173–4). Surrealist 'liberation' is perceived and constructed as a linguistic concept whose effect is primary: the woman's body is merely a surface on which authors project their own desire. There is no 'freedom' for woman, merely a series of imprisoning structures, each built around the other, with the represented and fragmented female body at the centre.

As a woman and a feminist, I found it difficult to identify with this expression of desire, because of the violent disfiguring and incarceration of (metaphorical) women which leaves me no space. I would like to emphasise that this is an emotional response to the *manner* of presenting these images of male aggression as love-making, many of which I identify with violation and, indeed, rape. Surrealist images of women are often extremely cruel, and they reify the women they represent, using them to embody the creative process. These texts reflect and refract their author's attitudes towards woman as an object to be flattered, celebrated, confined, manipulated, disfigured – and finally effaced.

Women are seen in new ways, they are no longer untouchable, yet for Breton they often read as sex objects to be used for pleasure, subservience being the price of 'liberation': 'Surrealism has never been tempted to veil itself from the gleam of fascination which shines in the love of man and woman. It could have done so, at least according to its first investigations which clearly introduced it into a country where desire was king' (M, p. 300). The veil is historically related to ownership, concealing the property of one man from the gaze of others. It is transparent from within and opaque from without, an object of non-penetration from the outside. It is also an erotic device, a barrier to that which is concealed and secret and therefore all the more desirable. Were Surrealism to veil itself, it would be on the inside of the veil, able to perceive the fascination it provokes. In fact by veiling itself it becomes desirable. However, a veiled Surrealism would be a feminine vassal in a country where desire was king.

Thus the veil is a seductive textual device, a deceptive image of safety. Veiled or unveiled, a feminised Surrealism is prey to a violent desire grounded in scopophilic sight. Another image of veiling appears in the *Second Manifesto*, where a pretty young woman does the dance of the veils before a bored sultan (M, pp. 185 – 6). The veil reads as a seductive prelude to sadistic violence for when she is naked, he orders her to be skinned alive, her flesh to be stripped off, after which the text narrates her continual dancing presence. The sultan's pleasure demands the woman's murder which is used to illustrate and complement the potency of the poet in creating a textual 'exegi monumentum'. For me, this image indicates rivalry of the sort where sexual strength is expressed by power and domination. Hence the gratuitous sacrifice of the woman is echoed by the use of the 'illustration' (the dancing dead skeleton) to substantiate a dominant authoritarian ego.

For Breton desire is 'unconstrainedly erect', constant and ceaseless as a powerful king in a conquered country (M, p. 299). Kingship is presented in patriarchal heroic style.[7] By repeatedly making references to a shared cultural inheritance, Breton authenticates the archetypal nature of his quest and also claims a literary identity (M, pp. 292 and 288–9). The naming of 'ancestors' (M, p. 285) is similar to classical rules for identifying epic narrative, which derived from the social functions of naming ancestors in burial rites of primitive societies. Breton situates his text firmly in this conceptualisation of the 'masculine' heroic, identifying with it and indeed 'invoking' it to contextualise his own cause and status as a writer.

Breton's Surrealist quest is situated within a tradition which focuses on a (male) hero's trajectory towards that which is sought or desired. The narrative of the quest is perceived from this (limited) viewpoint which established and politicised the cult of the male hero in literary, social, cultural and religious tradition. The image of the archetypal hero is associated with the search for gold, an object of value and liberation, be it the Golden Fleece or the gold of alchemy. The social status of the male in Western culture is a function (amongst other things) of financial worth and success, linked to his ability to own and to provide. In very basic terms these uphold the precepts of dominance and authority upon which patriarchy is founded.

A re-reading of Freudian theory could usefully situate Freud's reading and writing of the money/faeces/gift equation within the same heroic quest tradition. The connection between writing, reading and quest is aptly observed by Stanley Edgar Hyman with regard to the relationship between Freud's quest to resolve the enigma of dreaming and the emblematic content of the stylistic organisation of this pursuit discussed in *The Interpretation of Dreams*.[8] Freud offers a topological map of his quest through the uncharted terrain of the unconscious mind which is comparable to textual maps left by Breton.

Theseus, with whom Breton often identifies, is read in patriarchal tradition as he who, with the virgin's gift, treads the path of reason. Breton's Theseus is presented as a hero who has no need for the 'gift' of rationality, since his labyrinth is a creation of Surrealist activity: 'Without thread [...] these kind of markers [...] sometimes create the illusion of attempting the great adventure, of being a sort of gold seeker: I am looking for the gold of time. What then do these words [...] evoke? [...] Crete, where I must be Theseus, but a Theseus locked for ever in his crystal labyrinth'.[9] This masculine tradition contextualises heroic success in terms of the individual: for the man, there is faecal birth and monetary success, for the woman, there is reproductive efficiency. So the social culture of the labyrinthine intestinal city state, the working of the minds reflecting that culture and the image of social function could be described as meeting in 'obscure' excremental confusion in a psychoanalytic reading of social values.

For Breton, light is the product of Surrealist activity, a Surrealist 'gold'. It erupts spontaneously in an outward spurting movement: 'From the somewhat fortuitous bringing together of the two terms, a particular light sprang forth, *the light of the image* [...] the value of the image depends on the beauty of the spark obtained' (*M*, p. 37). Value is here a function of visual appreciation. Breton presents the 'supreme reality' of Surrealist images which enable man to intuit a place of limitless desire as a Surrealist gift for all:

> automatic writing, which I have undertaken to put within reach of everyone [...] lends itself to the production of the most beautiful images [...] the mind is convinced of the supreme reality of these images [...] it soon realises that they flatter its reason [...] It becomes aware of the limitless expanses where its desires are manifest [...] it goes on, carried along by these images which ravish it [...] This is the most beautiful night, *the night of flashing lightning*; day, by comparison, is night. (*M*, pp. 37–8)

This textual experience is the product of gender stereotypes, a self-perpetuating and enclosed system of visual affirmation of text production.

Freud uses the image of light rays passing through the lens of a periscope, together with the physical reality and invisibility of the lens as a 'figurative image of the two systems', as a 'dynamic' replacement of his 'topographical way of representing things', to describe the relationship between the conscious and the imperceptible systems of the unconscious and preconscious.[10] Hence the 'two kinds of processes of excitation or modes of its discharge' displace a cruder conception of 'two localities in the mental apparatus – conceptions which have left their traces in the expressions *to repress* and *to force a way through*'. The statement which follows this image may be read with an ironic circularity: 'so far we have been psychologising on our own account'.[11]

Wilhelm Reich's description of the orgasm is expressed in terms of electric energy, a theory which he regards as an evolution fecunded by his association with Freud: 'The orgasm formula which directs sex-economic research is as follows: MECHANICAL TENSION → BIOELECTRIC CHARGE → BIOELECTRIC DISCHARGE → MECHANICAL RELAXATION'.[12] Reich stresses that '*procreation is a function of sexuality* and not vice versa' and that 'Freud had maintained the same thing with respect to psychosexuality, when he separated the concepts *sexual* and *genital*' (p. 283). Yet the discourse of his theory, like that of Breton and Freud, 'testifies' to his genitalia. In Reich's model, pressure builds in a 'bladder' likened to a 'pumping system' which in a rigid, compressed state requires 'tossing ... kneading ... stabbing ... injury' and, at worst, 'dissolving, perishing, disintegrating (Nirvana, sacrificial death)', or becomes 'armoured' and 'hostile towards nature' (pp. 279–80). Since he sites the orgasm primarily in the genitals, his anxieties about 'misdirected' or 'bound' genital energy are hardly surprising (p. 153). He describes a fear of 'coitus interruptus' which produces 'sexual stasis and nervousness en masse' and relates this problem to social conditions, family and housing. Within the Freudian language of gifts, that which is 'gold' for men may well be 'shit' for women. And unfortunately the counterpart of Reich's testicular bladder is the (already fertilised) egg, whose development reflects the structure of his orgasm theory which sites woman's orgasm back in the womb (and in the Middle Ages!). This represents a return to the economic theory that 'men make money and women produce babies'.

Patriarchal culture literally placed its balls on the line when it promoted definitions of sexuality for both men and women based on the male genitalia and lack thereof. Freud's neurotic obsession with normative sexuality is projected on to woman whose anxieties other than her 'innate disposition', are defined by masculine performance.[13] In other words the Freudian 'she' is a textually constructed location for male anxieties centred on ejaculation and potency fears. Patriarchy locates the masculine orgasm outside of the male body. Success is placed on perceived existence, the visible presence of the product be it sperm, sparks or orgone energy (Reich). The masculine concept of external reality is a projected reality experienced as a negative object, a loss of its 'other'.

Surrealism presents a love affair between the author and language. It evaluates reciprocal attraction in terms of subject/object unity ('absolute complementarity') grounded in fulfilment of that masculine desire for 'integral unity, both organic and psychic' (*M*, pp. 301–3). For Breton, the ultimate quest is a masculine endeavour to find the path of Gnosis defined as 'knowledge of supra-sensitive reality, invisibly visible in an eternal mystery' (*M*, p. 304). Woman is throughout represented only in terms of a masculine need to perceive 'by himself' that the outside and the inside identify with each other.

Freud defines a similar 'sexual aim' as the 'incorporation of the object'.[14]

In his formulation of the mirror stage, Lacan presents subjectivity as a fictive creation structured by 'the social dialectic which structures human knowledge as paranoiac', giving it 'greater autonomy than animal knowledge in relation to the field of force of desire' and conversely determines such knowledge as an organic insufficiency comparable to the Surrealist dissatisfaction with 'that little reality'.[15] He describes the mirror stage as: 'a drama whose internal thrust is precipitated from insufficiency to anticipation – and which manufactures for the subject, caught up in the lure of spatial identification, the succession of phantasies that extends from a fragmented body-image to a form of its totality' (p. 4). This masculine discourse is presented as the formation of the linguistic individual (the singular 'I'). Tension and anxiety about the dialectic of identification with a masculine other is fictively and subjectively restored by language whose hierarchical nature determines the singular authoritative 'I'.

In her account of the mirror stage, Jacqueline Rose discusses the veiling of the phallus in which Lacan locates the fundamental duplicity of the sign.[16] Within the construction of this mimetic image, the subjective phallic 'I' is dependent on the gaze of its subordinated object, being itself a fictive creation. Juliet Mitchell and Jacqueline Rose stress the child's dependency on the 'look of the mother' who thereby guarantees the child's reality (image of a coherent identity).[17]

Margaret Whitford sites the value placed on seeing as contextual to the work of Luce Irigaray: 'Western systems of representation privilege *seeing*: what can be seen (presence) is privileged over what cannot be seen (absence) and guarantees Being, hence the privilege of the penis which is elevated to the status of the Phallus'.[18] Hence 'the ontological status assigned to women in western metaphysics is equivalent to an imaginary which does not recognise sexual difference'. Women's sexuality and the conceptualisation of the feminine are defined within masculine culture as 'lack' or negativity. Within this system, light plays an important part since lack of light implies invisibility, a negative space associated with the feminine and female sexuality which has been defined as 'castrated'. In Western masculine culture, the discourse of light and of seeing confirms the products of the textualised masculine ego. As products of patriarchal culture, they are inherently dangerous and injurious to the nurture and growth of a female construction of 'femininity'.

Irigaray deconstructs Lacan's mirror, questioning its form and shape and the way in which Lacan sites woman as the reflecting glass.[19] However, woman's gaze does not reflect the exteriority of her own internal subjectivity but a masculine appearance constructed by a dominant phallic 'I'. The violence of externalisation imposed on woman's inner space creates the false appearance of an alien and singular construction of herself. As masculine other, this image is a fictive projection constructed by the emotive tensions of ego verification insecurities. Accepting this position, her violated being will reflect dominant power projections, perpetuating the self-destruction of her *différance*.

Woman's internal reality has been subjected to untold violence and this has been imposed by the external textuality forced down her throat, blocking her voice. The acceptance of a textuality constructed by masculine discourse creates an internalised state of feminine anorexic illness with all the related distorted and fragmented self-perceptions.

That which provides good food for the masculine ego is destructive to a feminine denied a subject space. A concept of the feminine which is a masculinised external perception is destructive and dangerous to the internal feminine 'I', leaving it starving, regurgitating alien masculine products which destroy internal digestion leading to annihilation, in what Irigaray describes as 'this infernal and rigorous gangrene of the phallocratic patriarchal order'.[20] Mitchell and Rose define subjectivity as 'the condition of a social being, aware of her separate existence and the laws of her culture' (p. 117). Irigaray describes women as 'deprived of a subjective order with which to unify their corporal vitality' (p. 130). Whitford reads Irigaray's work as restructuring the construction of the rational subject and reclaiming a feminine imaginary, deconstructing the dominant conceptualisation of sexual difference, creating circular discourses which turn masculine images and presentations on themselves.

Irigaray expresses a need to construct feminine identity through a feminine education, involving respect for life and food, which would come about through mother and daughter relations (p. 59). Woman's sexuality would be a healing of the self, neither dependent on the phallus nor necessary for procreation. It is plural and multiple and purely pleasurable. Women need to recuperate and heal their own sexual identities through a retouching of self with other. Recovery is a surfacing of awareness, of choice of nourishment, of nurturing a healthy space for the self.

For me, that means contextualising discourse with its textual
sexual identity, refusing to consume and regurgitate an alien language
of criticism based on 'clarification' or 'perception', the language of
penetration and subordination, of the authoritative and judging eye.
It also means choosing content which feels internally healthy and
constantly questioning and rewriting my own textuality, retouching
myself and acknowledging that what I utter is personally true but by
no means true for all women. A part of that self for me is the separation
of two kinds of 'I', whole unto themselves which 'I' personally echo
in collaborative agreement with a textual feminine voiced by Irigaray:

> Humanity is composed of two differing subjective identities, each with
> their own objects and objectives. It is profoundly pathological and pathogenic
> that subjective and objective rights should be so unequally shared out.
> A subjective initiation would help women to heal themselves. That would
> need at least: understanding of the question, mutual friendship and respect
> in order to resolve it, rigorous cultural information and sometimes recourse
> to therapeutic psychological help. (p. 130)

Notes

1 André Breton, *The Surrealist Manifestos*, trans. Richard Seaver and Helen Lane, Ann
  Arbor, 1969, p. 32. I have found this translation to be inadequate for detailed examination and biased in its transposition of gendered writing. I have modified it in order
  to expose the full metaphoric functioning of Breton's language and to offer a more
  neutral translation, closer to the original text. Quotations in the text include these
  modifications and are followed by the abbreviation *M*, and page references to the
  published translation. All other translations are my own unless otherwise stated.
2 Breton, 'Femme et Oiseau', *Signe Ascendant*, Paris, 1968, p. 143.
3 *Le Surréalisme au Service de la Révolution*, IV, 1932, p. 14.
4 Dale Spender, 'Modern Feminist Theorists: Reinventing Rebellion', in *Feminist
  Theorists*, London, 1983, pp. 372–3.
5 *La Révolution Surréaliste*, XI, 1928, p. 8.
6 Breton, 'L'Union Libre', in *Clair de Terre*, Paris, 1966, pp. 93–5.
7 See Susan Brownmiller, *Against Our Will*, Harmondsworth, 1986, pp. 31–113 and
  Gerda Lerner, *The Creation of Patriarchy*, New York, 1987.
8 Stanley Edgar Hyman, 'The Interpretation of Dreams' in Perry Meisel, ed., *Freud and
  Literature*, New Jersey, 1981.
9 Breton, *Point du Jour*, Paris, 1970, p. 7.
10 *The Interpretation of Dreams*, Pelican Freud Library, IV, Harmondsworth, 1983,
  pp. 770–1.
11 Idem.
12 Wilhelm Reich, *The Function of the Orgasm*, London, 1983, p. 9. Subsequent
  references in the text refer to this edition.
13 Sigmund Freud, *On Psychopathology*, Pelican Freud Library, IX, Harmondsworth,
  1983, p. 46.

14 Sigmund Freud, *On Sexuality*, Pelican Freud Library, VII, Harmondsworth, 1977, p. 117.
15 Jacques Lacan, *Ecrits*, trans. Alan Sheridan, London, 1977, p. 3. Subsequent references are given in the text.
16 Jacqueline Rose, *Sexuality in the Field of Vision*, London, 1989, p. 66.
17 Juliet Mitchell and Jacqueline Rose, *Feminine Sexuality*, London, 1990, p. 30.
18 Margaret Whitford, *Luce Irigaray: Philosophy in the Feminine*, London, 1991, p. 88.
19 See *This Sex Which is Not One*, New York, 1985, for example p. 151.
20 Luce Irigaray, *Je, Tu, Nous*, Paris, 1990, p. 57. Subsequent references are given in the text.

The injured sex: Hemingway's voice of masculine anxiety

Gregory Woods

This is a sentence which Ernest Hemingway could not have written:

> And every year, when we arrived at Combray, on Easter morning, after the sermon, if the weather was fine, I would run there to see (amid all the disorder that prevails on the morning of a great festival, the gorgeous preparations for which make the everyday household utensils that they have not contrived to banish seem more sordid than ever) the river flowing past, sky-blue already between banks still black and bare, its only companions a clump of daffodils, come out before their time, a few primroses, the first in flower, while here and there burned the blue flame of a violet, its stem bent beneath the weight of the drop of perfume stored in its tiny horn.[1]

And this is a sentence which Marcel Proust could not have written:

> The river looked nice.[2]

What I may be rehearsing, here, is an act as banal as the differentiation between two styles. Ernest Hemingway did not write as Marcel Proust used to write. I could have made the point even more clearly if I had quoted Proust in the original language.

Each is, in its way, a 'good' sentence. Each performs its own allotted task efficiently and even elegantly. In isolation, however, there is no question but that the former is more expressive than the latter, if only because, literally, it has more to say. If readers are to derive any depth of feeling from the latter, commensurate with that which the former delivers of its own accord, they must infer a good deal more from it than it makes explicit. To do so, they must delve beyond the ungenerous text itself, into its context. The words are – according to the fictional conventions to which readers adhere, if they are not to contrive a bizarre misunderstanding of the whole book in which the sentence appears – 'spoken' by an identifiable 'voice' which, although ultimately traceable to the agency of the name below the title (Ernest Hemingway), belongs to a hypothetical human character, a white American heterosexual male, called Jake Barnes. The 'meaning' of the sentence, beyond its obvious denotation, will emerge from consideration, first, of the nature of Jake's 'character', second, of how his character is manifested in the way he 'speaks' (that is, both how he speaks to other characters and how he narrates) and, third, of how he is deemed to be feeling in the moment which he is narrating (not necessarily the same as the moment *in* which he is doing so). Fourth, fifth and sixth, of course, readers may seek similar information from what they know of the author himself, thereby routinely moving from the textual reading, through the contextual, to the intertextual.

To measure each author's antipathy to the other's method, we can allow ourselves the luxury of imagining – which may be to say, of *inventing* – their personalities in conflict. Even through the cork lining of his walls, we can hear Proust's shriek of horrified hilarity at the phrase 'looked nice'. On the other hand, it is not difficult to imagine Hemingway measuring his own style against Proust's and, in partial anticipation of Hélène Cixous's later espousal of Proust and Genet, characterising Proust's prose as *écriture efféminée*.

The Sun Also Rises, whose narrator says 'The river looked nice', offers a classic case of a supposedly hetero-erotic fiction in which the relationship between man and woman is, for the most part, subordinated to relationships between the men who desire the woman. In other words, to use Eve Kosofsky Sedgwick's terminology, the book's main emotional dynamic is located, not in heterosexuality, but in 'male homosocial desire'.[3] A diagrammatic representation of its relationships would not appear as one of those erotic triangles which Sedgwick has delineated in texts from Shakespeare's sonnets to Dickens's *Edwin Drood*, triangles involving one woman and the two men who are rivals for her love, but as an erotic polygon, with Lady Brett Ashley at its apex and with Jake Barnes, Mike Campbell, Robert Cohn and Pedro Romero at its other points. These male points would be linked by straight lines, not only directly to the Brett apex, but, just as significantly, to each other.

When Brett makes her first appearance in the novel, she is surrounded, not by all her straight admirers, but by gay men:

A crowd of young men, some in jerseys and some in their shirt-sleeves, got out [of two taxis]. I could see their hands and newly washed, wavy hair in the light from the door. The policeman standing at the door looked at me and smiled. They came in. As they went in, under the light I saw

white hands, wavy hair, white faces, grimacing, gesturing, talking. With
them was Brett. She looked very lovely, and she was very much with
them. (p. 20)

Jake takes as an affront the pallor of their faces and hands, together
with the fact that their hair is well looked after. Everything about
them is too mobile: their faces ('grimacing'), their hands ('gesturing'),
their tongues ('talking'). Real men, it seems, do not gesture or grimace;
real men do not 'talk'. Instead, like Jake and the policeman, they
exchange silent, meaningful glances, expressing their superiority.

Jake is not unaware of his own homophobia, and he knows that,
as a worldly member of the expatriate American 'lost generation'
adrift in the Bohemian milieu of post-war Paris, he is expected to
control it. The fact is, however, that his first instinct is that of a
queerbasher: 'I was very angry. Somehow they always made me angry.
I know they are supposed to be amusing, and you should be tolerant,
but I wanted to swing on one, any one, anything to shatter that
superior, simpering composure' (p. 20). Jake may be satisfactorily
masculine in so far as he is heterosexual, but his credentials have
been irrevocably compromised by a wound he sustained in the war:
he has been castrated, or, at the very least, rendered impotent.[4]
We cannot help but associate his reactions to Brett's social infidelity
in this scene with what he knows to be the impossibility of his
desire for her. That she prefers gay men's company (for the moment)
to his seems to make him identify himself as a real eunuch among
perversely symbolic eunuchs – and he is not amused.[5] The glance
he exchanges with the cop is not, in fact, as reassuring as it might
have seemed at first: for Jake seems desperate for such moments of
confirmation that he is not a queen, yet the policeman's grin, if Jake
(or the reader) had read it as being *informed*, could have been a threaten-
ing accusation instead. In that case, it would mean: I know your
secret, and you belong with *them*.

There follows the most extraordinary display of stunted interiority
to have emerged from the golden age of the 'stream of consciousness'.
Jake goes home and looks at his body in the mirror. Even if the reader
is not vouchsafed a view, Jake's wound is visible, not a mere case of
shell-shocked impotence.[6] When he goes to bed, alcohol and sleepless-
ness conspire to do their worst:

I lay awake thinking and my mind jumping around. Then I couldn't keep
away from it, and I started to think about Brett and all the rest of it went

away. I was thinking about Brett and my mind stopped jumping around and started to go in sort of smooth waves. *Then all of a sudden I started to cry. Then after a while it was better* and I lay in bed and listened to the heavy trams go by and way down the street, and then I went to sleep. (p. 31, my emphasis)

There is, here, a remarkably forthright, if implicit, repudiation of the experiment to which the likes of James Joyce, Marcel Proust, Dorothy Richardson and Virginia Woolf had devoted so much effort. The exteriority of the passage is, considering its place in literary history, obtrusive and insistent. As far as I know, one does not meet such skin-deep accounts of feeling anywhere else but in pornography. What I find particularly striking is that gnomic account of the *emissio lacrymarum* which precedes Jake's drifting off to sleep. His tears replace the semen he might have shed, had he been capable of masturbating in appreciation of his fantasy of Brett.

Like any pornographic account of ejaculation (where we are shown the semen, but are expected, on the assumption that all readers are men, to know the feeling), this vignette of emotional outpouring relies on an active, explanatory identification with Jake on the reader's part. It also suggests how the castrated Jake means to behave in all future emotional crises. Since the refined etiquette of masculinity requires him to grieve over his double loss (of potency and of Brett) but forbids him to enlist the comfort of a sympathetic hearer, he knows he must internalise everything. He must seem, from outside, to display equanimity and balance at all times. This rugged but passive acceptance of fate is akin, in some respects, to the plight of the tragic hero; the major difference being, however, that Jake is not granted the power to soliloquise.

Hemingway's narrators often seem embarrassed by their own aesthetic sensitivities. One of the most frequent signs of this unease, as Richard Peterson has shown, is the stylistic tic whereby any potentially pompous or precious term is deflated by being yoked to a 'tough' word, as in a phrase like 'damned beautiful'.[7] Above all, a real man must not *gush*. One of the things that sets Brett apart from other women, in addition to her trend-setting, boyish crop and sleek sweaters ('She started all that'), is the way she talks. Her willingness to swear – albeit in the genteel, bourgeois fashion of which Hemingway seems to approve – makes her one of the boys. She, too, says things like 'damned romantic' (p. 23). She, too, clips her sentences: 'Told him I was in love with you. True, too. Don't look like that. He was damn

nice about it. Wants to drive us out to dinner tomorrow night. Like
to go?' (p. 33). Above all, she says the most virile thing in the book:
'Let's not talk. Talking's all bilge' (p. 55).[8]

It is worth turning, at this point, from Hemingway's first novel to his
last: from *The Sun Also Rises* to *The Garden of Eden*, posthumously
published in 1987. As framing works to a career which iconised The
Masculine with such enormous popular success, these are peculiar
novels indeed, the latter especially so. As in the earlier book, Hemingway retains, in the later, his hermetic sexual discretion to a degree
which hardly matches the surface values of his narrative method in
all other respects. Two of the book's three main characters, Catherine
and David Bourne, are honeymooning in the Camargue. They make a
lot of love, day and night. But the sex 'scenes' are brutally cut, in a
filmic manner, as if by a censor's scissors, drawing attention to their
presence by abrupt absence. For instance:

> Her hair was spread out over the pillow and her eyes were laughing and
> he lifted the sheet and she said, 'Hello, darling. Did you have a nice
> lunch?'
>   Afterwards they lay together with his arm under her head and were
> happy and lazy and he felt her turn her head from side to side and stroke it
> against his cheek.[9]

Everything happens in that caesura between paragraphs. Even to
notice that the characters have made love at all, the reader is obliged,
literally, to read between the lines, just as a movie viewer is accustomed
to 'seeing' the orgasm within the interstices of a quick cut. What we
see here, in a book which is really *about* sex and not much else, is a
moment of voluble silence which might seem to contradict what
Michel Foucault used to say (so often) about the modern propensity –
or compulsion, rather – to chatter about sex.

There are times, however, when it is important to the fabric of the
book that we should know exactly what is going on when David and
Catherine make love. Yet, even in these circumstances, Hemingway
is maddeningly reticent. We are still in the first chapter on the same
afternoon: without giving David any warning, Catherine has her hair
'cropped as short as a boy's. It was cut with no compromises'. Showing
her new look to him, she says: 'I'm a girl. But now I'm a boy too and
I can do anything and anything and anything.' And she adds: 'You see
why it's dangerous, don't you?' He says he does (pp. 14–15). When
they go to bed after dinner, they make love in a new manner:

He had shut his eyes and he could feel the long light weight of her on him and her breasts pressing against him and her lips on his. He lay there and felt something and then her hand holding him and searching lower and he helped with his hands and then lay back in the dark and did not think at all and only felt the weight and the strangeness inside and she said, 'Now you can't tell who is who can you?'

'No.'

'You are changing,' she said. 'Oh you are. You are. Yes you are and you're my girl Catherine. Will you change and be my girl and let me take you?' (p. 17)

This is, perhaps, the most interesting sexual event in Hemingway's work, and it is over so soon. Despite the exteriority of the narrative consciousness, which I have already compared to that of pornographic fiction, it is still difficult to 'see' exactly what has happened. The fact is that Catherine is on top ('the long light weight of her on him') and she fucks David with something, whether vegetable or mineral we are not told. He is aware of it before it enters him ('and felt something'); she feels his erection ('her hand holding him') and then moves between his legs to his anus ('and searching lower'). He helps her as she manoeuvres the object into him. Having thus successfully fucked him, she pronounces him not only unmanned, but female, 'my girl Catherine'.

Not that the reversal of roles – which they go on to develop, despite David's continuing unease – liberates both partners from inhibition and social constraint. There is a later moment when Catherine, as a 'boy', asks to kiss David; but here he draws the line. His reply is securely conventional: 'Not if you're a boy and I'm a boy' (p. 67). Even when a man has toyed with his own femininity – which here means his heterosexual passivity – he still dare not subject his manhood to the threat of an imaginary homosexuality. As the novel progresses, and the couple befriend a young woman, Marita, the book turns into a straight man's fantasy of making love, alternately, with two women. Far from effecting a radical inversion of the customary homosocial triangle – whereby two women might relate to each other by way of a male intermediary – Hemingway presents David with a somewhat banal adulterer's charter: a mistress by kind permission of a loving wife.

The problem (if that is what it is) with the book's voluble silences at crucial moments in its sexual narrative is not simply one of self-censorship by the author, but of the kinds of thing he can allow to be heard in his own tone of voice. He does not want to sound, or he does not want his virtuous narrators – for 'true' virility is always virtuous in his books – to sound like gossips, least of all when they are impotent or sexually passive. Gossip is the discourse of the inadequate: women, gay men, and straight men who do not pass muster. Moreover, since gossip is notorious for overstating its cases, he who does not wish to be mistaken for a gossip must make a virtue of understatement. Hence such obscure moments of unstated tension and release as I have cited.

It is at these moments of emotional and sexual litotes that Hemingway most obviously requires an active reader. Adopting Roland Barthes's terminology, Arnold and Cathy Davidson have called *The Sun Also Rises* a 'writerly' text (*scriptible*), in relation to which 'the reader must [actively] cope with missing connections, contradictory value judgements, and textual inconsistencies'.[10] This formulation is not unhelpful in disclosing the paradox at the heart of the Hemingway project. Suppose we accept that the book is indeed 'writerly'. It may have to follow that Jake Barnes's manhood, silently ambiguous as it is, is likewise in need of scripting. Impassive and passive, he requires a range of hermeneutic interventions by the active reader. He can only bring himself to imply what the reader needs to infer. In doing so, the reader adopts an inquisitive and loquacious role, thereby mastering Jake's scarred masculinity with the active effeminacy of gossip.

The same brand of taciturn, wounded heroism effects the closure – the famous endings – of a number of Hemingway's books. Virility under stress turns not to words of complaint (God forbid) but to silence. In *A Farewell to Arms* (1929), Frederic Henry narrates his grief at the death of Catherine Barkley with the notoriously terse-but-expressive sentence, 'After a while I went out and left the hospital and walked back to the hotel in the rain'. The novel ends here. As we are told in all the orthodox critical accounts, and all the A-level essays, the flatness of the syntax represents Frederic's emotional numbness, and the rain represents the tears he cannot shed. Whether he cried when he returned to the privacy of his hotel room – to enjoin, for a moment, the fallacy of a plot which continues after the book has ended – Frederic is not saying. This is a classic instance of what Hemingway's style is all about: he attempts to make readers feel more than they fully understand.

Having been nursed, and courted, back to health by Catherine, after being wounded in the legs and head by a mortar shell, Frederic is left to perform his manly rituals of loss in solitary silence. Jake Barnes's situation at the end of *The Sun Also Rises* is, of course, quite different: for Brett can do nothing to heal him. Having been deprived of his genitals, and *because* this is the case, he now loses Brett as well, not to death, but to a half-hearted marriage with Mike Campbell and presumably (judging by her record and his sensitivity to it) to a sequence of other men. Their final exchange ('Oh, Jake ... we could have had such a damned good time together.' 'Yes ... Isn't it pretty to think so?'), which ends the book, gives an impression of sentiment stoically borne. The child/aesthete's word 'pretty' is all the more emphatic for its not being preceded by the adult/macho 'damned'. Its prettiness is annihilated by the concentric irony of Jake and Hemingway himself. Sharpened thus, it is every bit a real man's word.

The degree to which sentiment is stifled in these books is a good measure of the extent of the fears they express for aestheticism and its sexual and textual concomitants, paradox and sodomy. It is as if Hemingway had never heard of Oscar Wilde, whose work, although mapping out the relatively new arterials of inversion, was no less consistently resistant to sentimentality. A massive shift in cultural attitudes separates the moment when Wilde laughed at the death of Little Nell in *The Old Curiosity Shop* from Ezra Pound's masculinist/ modernist trimming of the language under the aegis of Imagism. Suddenly, it was no longer legitimate for a heterosexual man to gush. This shift partly predates, but largely coincides with, the First World War, the known cause of Jake Barnes's troubles. And yet, who can truly affirm that, for all the book's tight-lipped hardness, sentiment has actually been extirpated from *The Sun Also Rises*?

While discussing the issue of gay men's rehabilitation of sentimentality as a cornerstone in their cultural effectiveness, Eve Kosofsky Sedgwick identifies 'an extraordinarily high level of self-pity in nongay men' in contemporary American society. It is in this context that I would like to locate Jake Barnes's tears. Sedgwick might have had them in mind when she shaped the following account: 'The sacred tears of the heterosexual man: rare and precious liquor whose properties, we are led to believe, are rivaled only by the *lacrimae Christi* whose secretion is such a specialty of religious kitsch. What charm, compared to this chrism of the gratuitous, can reside in the all too predictable tears of women, of gay men, of people with something to cry about?' [11] As pure sign, the tears of the heterosexual man, like the ejaculation of his semen, require no elucidation. Like any token of universal value – here endorsed by the 'universal' cachet of maleness and heterosexuality – they inspire awe merely by being seen or mentioned. As Sedgwick implies, the full shock of this effect is felt in the Bible's briefest utterance, 'Jesus wept', which becomes an oath as obscene in its evocation of divine but human bodily fluids as 'Jesus urinated' would be, but as intense an expression of divine involvement in earthly feeling as 'Jesus came'. Two things are proved by this dramatic emotional event and its recording: Christ's manhood, in both senses. His tears prove him human; and the fact that they are worth mentioning, but too moving to dwell on at length, proves him *all man* – which is to say, hetero.[12]

This immense overvaluation of the pomp and posturings of virility has paradoxical effects. It encourages a vanity in men which corresponds closely with so many of the vices which men have so often attributed to women: shallowness, narcissism, flirtatiousness, immodesty, lack of critical distance, sentimentality and so on. Such signals as the flexing of a muscle or a John Wayne strut eventually become laughable because they are expected to carry so heavy a burden of significance. Intended as signs of strength (to mask the fear of lacking strength), they betray the insecurity within. And it is this discrepancy between intention and effect that leaves machismo so precariously liable to teeter over into the style it most abhors: camp.

In every sense, then, our culture has allowed masculinity to become *precious*. Jacques Lacan once spoke of the 'curious' circumstance in which 'virile display in the human being itself seem[s] feminine'.[13] In fiction, the great promoter of this view is Jean Genet. However, at the risk of questioning new and fashionable canons, one inevitably circles back to the fact that two of the *grandes maîtresses* of what Hélène Cixous calls *écriture féminine* are Proust and Genet, both homosexual. The latter's surname, indeed, is respectfully inscribed in a feminised form within the very title of Cixous's and Catherine Clément's book *La Jeune Née* (1975). But which came first in the process of this decision: the ornateness of their written style, or the unmanly phallolatry with which it lays bare their 'personal' lives? Is what is *féminine* about their *écriture* related to the fact that they liked being fucked by men?[14]

Cixous's crucial sentence on this topic has mysteriously become, in its English manifestation, slippery and elusive. One version reads as follows: 'what is inscribed under Jean Genet's name, in the movement of a text that divides itself, pulls itself to pieces, dismembers itself, regroups, remembers itself, is a proliferating, maternal femininity'.[15] A second translation reads: 'under the name of Jean Genet, what is inscribed in the movement of a text which divides itself, breaks itself into bits, regroups itself, is an abundant, maternal, pederastic femininity'.[16] It does not take the latter, more explicit rendering to disclose the sentence's blithe heterosexism, dependent on the condescending idea that a gay man's cultural productions are mercifully less flawed by his being male – which is to say, they are *less manly*, in senses both positive and negative – than a straight man's. Indeed, coming from anyone other than Cixous, one could be forgiven for assuming the sentiment was not only heterosexist but anti-feminist to boot. Other ideas in the same essay might be taken to support such a reading: 'woman is body more than man is', for instance; which feeds into the *aperçu*: 'More body hence more writing' (p. 95). Such essentialism is virtually indistinguishable from the proudly and explicitly anti-feminist (though much less fashionable) work of Camille Paglia, which also associates gay men's writing with the amorphous fluency of the feminine.[17]

I am irresistibly reminded of the moment in *A Room of One's Own* when Virginia Woolf complains that Marcel Proust is 'a little too much of a woman'.[18] Despite Sandra M. Gilbert's patronising remark that 'even the witty and rational Virginia Woolf may be seen as a crucial feminist precursor of Cixous',[19] it is clear that Woolf is not 'even' but *especially* relevant to the descent of these lines of thought. When she raises the idea of the female sentence, she does so in a manner predetermined by the prejudices she is trying to undermine. The daring rhetorical thrust of Woolf's book excuses the fact that this link in her argument comes apart if one thinks about it at any length. It may be that to take her at her word, and take her seriously, on the question of the 'woman's sentence', one is best advised to follow Gilbert and Gubar in reading the phrase as a metaphor, 'a *fantasy* about a utopian linguistic structure', revealing Woolf's aim 'to revise not woman's language but woman's relation to language'.[20] Otherwise, the idea belongs within a tradition of sexist differentiation with which men have felt comfortable, since it was easily used to prove male superiority. Again, we are led on a firmly established track through intellectual history, backwards.

From the idea of 'masculine' language in a written text – or, for that matter, recorded in quotidian speech by the linguistic anthropologist – it is a precarious task to track backwards to a viable theoretical position without slipping clumsily into the promotion of sexist stereotypes. One can observe the basic problem in any critical work which incautiously attempts to prescribe what women writers are and are not capable of writing.

One of the most sustained of these attempts, and probably the most unguarded in its certainties, is Samuel Butler's thesis, not only that the *Iliad* and the *Odyssey* had different authors, but that the latter was written by a woman. *The Authoress of the Odyssey* (1897) proceeds along a determined path of internal 'evidence', from the proposition that the epic poem 'could not have been' written by a man towards what satisfies Butler, if few others, as its proof.[21] There are several lines of argument, the main ones being (a) that, in contrast with the *Iliad*, which is 'strong', the *Odyssey* is 'sweet'; (b) that the main subjects foregrounded in the *Odyssey* – women, money and religion – are not those which a male author would have chosen; and (c) that certain details, often errors, could not have been written by a man – as, for instance, when a ship is described as having a rudder at each end. Expecting a male 'Homer' to share his own Victorian sexist values, Butler cannot bring himself to imagine a culture in which a man might think otherwise. ('When Ulysses and Penelope are in bed ... and are telling their stories to one another, Penelope tells hers first. I believe a male writer would have made Ulysses' story come first and Penelope's second', p. 157.) Butler's views are forthright and often very funny ('Argus [...] is not a very good name for a dog', p. 151) and they cut an eccentric swathe through the scholarship of his day – not so eccentric, however, that they failed to confirm the dominant masculinist ethos of the time.

It was within this system of essentialist stereotyping that Ernest Hemingway's abrupt telegraphese was developed. Governed by the congruent extremities of its torso (genitalia and larynx), the male body engendered a repressed voice, characterised by pride and sadness. Much as the physique had to be constantly honed, tested and proven, in sports if not in warfare, the voice, too, had to be both exercised and held in check. Its equivocal tendency to veer into poetry, like the risk that male friendship might swerve across the line distinguishing it from love, had to be monitored and suppressed at all times.

What this broken voice expresses best, in its struggle against effeminate eloquence, is the nagging anxiety which is the true condition (in both senses) of masculinity. Unlike the voices of out gay men, which tend to express fears of being forced back into the silence from which they have already made such an effort to emerge, the voice of heterosexual masculinity is, on the contrary, to be compared with that of *closeted* gay men, to the extent that it is terrified of indiscretion. To say too much might be to sound queer.

This is a situation with the ironies of which Marcel Proust was very familiar. There is a moment in the *Recherche* when Proust's narrator says, of the homosexual Baron de Charlus, 'it is almost impossible for men of his sort to hold their tongues'.[22] The joke is, of course, that Marcel, who likes to speak of himself as being impregnably heterosexual, has already been narrating continuously for more than 2,950 pages. It is not the only time that Proust has a homophile joke at the expense of his narrator's homophobia. Marcel seems to have developed a mistaken image of himself – if only for the duration of a passing phase – as the kind of man to whom, after all, a river might look, merely, 'nice'.

Notes

1 *Swann's Way*, London, 1922, p. 229.

2 *The Sun Also Rises*, New York, 1926, p. 41.

3 *Between Men: English Literature and Male Homosocial Desire*, New York, 1985.

4 When a literary critic writes, as late as 1991, that 'Guilt and impotence are, of course, strange traits to be associated with an American hero', one wonders which American literature he has been reading – Guy Cardwell, *The Man Who Was Mark Twain: Images and Ideologies*, New Haven and London, 1991, p. 144.

5 For a quick survey of homosexual male characters in Hemingway's fiction, see Scott Donaldson, *By Force of Will: The Life and Art of Ernest Hemingway*, New York, 1977, pp. 182–8. Donaldson calls this section of his book 'The Mincing Gentry', a characteristic phrase of Hemingway's.

6 In a letter to Maxwell Perkins of Scribner's, Scott Fitzgerald wrote: 'In the mutilated man I thought Ernest bit off more than can yet be chewn between the covers of a book, then lost his nerve a little and edited the more vitalizing details out. He has since told me that something like this happened' – quoted in Matthew J. Bruccoli, *Scott and Ernest: The Authority of Failure and the Authority of Success*, London, 1978, p. 50. Those of us who teach this book have learned not to be surprised when students overlook Jake's wound completely.

7 *Hemingway: Direct and Oblique*, The Hague and Paris, 1974, p. 12.

8 When Jake asks her about the end of her affair with Pedro Romero, she reduces that, too, to a stoical refusal to gush: 'Oh, hell! ... let's not talk about it. Let's never talk about it' (p. 242).

9 *The Garden of Eden*, London, 1987, p. 11.

10 'Decoding the Hemingway Hero in *The Sun Also Rises*', in Linda Wagner-Martin, ed., *New Essays on The Sun Also Rises*, Cambridge, 1987, p. 84. Other than for present purposes, I am not endorsing this use of Barthes. If a 'writerly' text is, merely, ambiguous enough to be open to its readers' interpretations, one can hardly envisage *any* text's failing to qualify, barring certain functional messages such as road signs

and fire escape instructions. Indeed, going by this definition, how could one help concluding that Barthes himself had gravely underestimated the texts he called 'readerly'?

11 *Epistemology of the Closet*, New York and London, 1991, pp. 145–6.

12 Compare this effect with that of the frequent ostentation of the Christ Child's genitals in Renaissance painting. See Leo Steinberg, 'The Sexuality of Christ in Renaissance Art and in Modern Oblivion', *October XXV*, 1983.

13 'The Signification of the Phallus', *Ecrits: A Selection*, London, 1977, p. 291.

14 At this stage in my argument, I am insisting on a reassertion of social usages. Notwithstanding the *sang froid* with which Hélène Cixous performs her redefinitions of the feminine, the fact remains that no one – not even a theorist – can abandon the social meanings of words. As a gay man, I have some difficulty applying the epithet *féminin*, indiscriminately, to Proust on the one hand and Joyce on the other; let alone retaining much respect for the term as still, subsequently, being applicable to women writers like Marina Tsvetayeva and Clarice Lispector. Moreover, when Cixous describes as *féminin* both the texts of homosexual writers (Proust, Genet) and other texts which are clearly amenable to 'gay readings' (Shakespeare, Rilke) she is not released from the fact that homophobic discourse takes as its starting point an equation of male homosexuality with femininity. In short, the terms Cixous has adopted have problematic resonances in which she appears not to be particularly interested.

15 Hélène Cixous and Catherine Clément, *The Newly Born Woman*, Manchester, 1987, p. 84, trans. Betsy Wing.

16 Elaine Marks and Isabelle de Courtivron, *New French Feminisms: An Anthology*, New York, 1981, p. 98. For good measure, Ann Liddle, the translator, footnotes the name of Jean Genet as follows: 'French novelist and playwright, to whose writing Hélène Cixous refers when she gives examples of the inscription of pederastic femininity'. It is this version that is quoted, slightly misprinted, in Nelly Furman's essay 'The Politics of Language: Beyond the Gender Principle?' in Gayle Greene and Coppélia Kahn, ed., *Making a Difference: Feminist Literary Criticism*, London, 1985, p. 74. The original sentence reads as follows: 'Ainsi sous le nom de Jean Genet, ce qui s'inscrit dans le mouvement d'un texte qui se divise, se met en pièces, se remembre, c'est une feminité foisonnante, maternelle', *La Jeune Née*, Paris, 1975, p. 154. The notion of 'pederasty' – which has quite different cultural resonances in French and English – is shifted into the sentence from elsewhere by its translators.

17 Camille Paglia, *Sexual Personae: Art and Decadence from Nefertiti to Emily Dickinson*, New Haven and London, 1990.

18 *A Room of One's Own*, London, 1977, p. 99.

19 'Introduction: A Tarantella of Theory', in Hélène Cixous and Catherine Clément, *The Newly Born Woman*, Manchester, 1987, p. xv. The remark is particularly unwise in so far as it overlooks the dynamically productive relation between the depressive and irrational Woolf and her best fiction.

20 Sandra M. Gilbert and Susan Gubar, *No Man's Land: The Place of the Woman Writer in the Twentieth Century. Volume I: The War of the Words*, New Haven and London, 1988, p. 230.

21 *The Authoress of the Odyssey*, Chicago, 1967.

22 *The Captive I*, London, 1968, p. 57.

The fourth form girls go camping: sexual identity and ambivalence in girls' school stories

Jan Montefiore

> The history of children's fiction should be written, not in terms of its themes or the content of its stories, but in terms of the relation to language which different children's writers establish for the child.
>
> Jacqueline Rose, *The Case of Peter Pan*[1]

> Suddenly Jean flung her arms around her, hugging her tight, till Dimsie shook herself free and wiped away a tear.
>
> '*Jean*!' she said sternly. 'Do let's at least *try* to remember we're Anti-Soppists!'
>
> Dorita Fairlie Bruce, *Dimsie: Head Girl*[2]

Fantasy, parody and gender

School stories are marketed as reading for young girls who have not yet graduated to consuming boy-meets-girl romances. Mainly dating from the inter-war years, girls' school stories remain highly saleable, for surprisingly large numbers of them are still in print. More than half of the sixty titles of Elinor Brent-Dyer's Chalet School series are currently published by Armada, the largest children's paperback publishers, who also sell Enid Blyton's school series about Malory Towers and St Clare's, and Anne Digby's Trebizond book.[3] School stories also feature in magazines for girls, notably the Four Marys strip in *Bunty* – a descendant of the inter-war Harmsworth girls' magazines *School Friend* and *Schoolgirls' Own*.[4]

These commercially successful stories for girls have since the 1950s been the object of a camp cult of parody which has also become part of popular culture. Because camp is, as Susan Sontag has argued, a sensibility and a style, rather than an object or an institution,[5] this cult of boarding-school stories cannot be assessed in terms of reprints and publication figures. Although the number of adult connoisseurs of Angela Brazil and Dorita Fairlie Bruce must be small, the parody of the girls' school story has entered popular culture, inspiring films, the highly successful 'St Trinians' series, the cartoons of Ronald Searle, and more recently the 'Recycled Images' series and the work of Glen Baxter, and even drama – the parody play *Daisy Pulls It Off* ran in London from 1982 for five years and has been widely produced since. Literary camping-up of school stories rarely results in full-length narratives:[6] it is usually found in glancing moments of parody and allusion, most notably in the reviews and skits of the humorous writer Arthur Marshall;[7] in John Betjeman's erotic celebrations of Myfanwy, 'ringleader, tomboy and chum to the weak'; in the 'gurls skools' mentioned in the musings of Geoffrey Willans's hero Nigel Molesworth ('Ho for bat Ho for ball / Ho for hockey and lax and all'); in squibs like Stevie Smith's 'Girls!';[8] and in delighted conversations between lovers of the genre. It even occurs in the more sophisticated school stories, where the characters parody more conventional narratives:

> 'Will you treat what I'm going to say as absolutely secret?'
> 'Now look,' said Lois, mildly alarmed. 'You haven't come across an Epidemic of Cribbing in your form and shall you go to Miss Keith and Sneak, have you? Because that's not my cup of tea at all. Try a prefect.'[9]

Boys' school stories, the older genre on which the girls' story is based, have not been subjected to a comparable parodic cult. Arthur Marshall, one of the first people to read girls' school stories for their unintentional comedy, writes that 'I had always thought that school-girls and schoolmistresses were funny' (*Girls*, p. ix). Schoolboys and schoolmasters didn't, apparently, seem so comic. This suggests to me that the pleasure of these texts, both for the girls who read them 'straight' and for the adults who laugh at them, is tied up with their representations of feminine identity. But for neither audience is this identity a straightforwardly 'given' fact: the characters in the all-female world of the stories can actually be construed – and in a camp reading are so construed – as shifting the terms of gender in ways that bring into question the notion of gender identity as fixed and stable. (Alastair Sim's drag performance as the Headmistress in *The Belles of St Trinians* (1953) is an obvious instance of camp humour unfixing gender categories.) Angela McRobbie has pointed out in a recent article on stories for girls that the 'continual working and re-working within the texts of the question of what it is to be a girl, points to the kind of ambivalence and uncertainty which psycho-analysts [...] have seen as part of the intractable difficulties in the fixing of female identities'.[10] Conversely, camp humour brings out the uncertainty and ambivalence of sexual identity by emphasising the taboo subjects of sexuality and violence which the girls' school story at once denies and indulges. This may be done overtly, as in the Glen Baxter cartoon reproduced here (Fig. 2), or it may be done by innuendo. Arthur Marshall was a master of this genre when he reviewed school stories:

> In *The Lower School Leader*, Miss Veronica Marlow has not hesitated to make full use of realism and the scene where a stubborn junior called Margaret refuses to eat up her gristle is strangely powerful.
>
> 'But that's all gristle!' protested the junior, 'really it is.'
> 'Nonsense. Eat it up at once. There's nothing put before you in this school that is not entirely digestible,' snapped Miss Beckett.
> But Margaret did not move, nor did she try to eat it.
> 'If you want me to be sick, I will,' she said defiantly, 'but it's just cruelty to animals.'
> This seemed to enrage Miss Beckett. 'Take her out, please,' she ordered; and immediately two prefects left their places and more or less dragged the junior by brute force off her chair and out of the dining room. (*Girls*, p. 27)

Arthur Marshall is of course sending up the language of blurbs or puff reviews; he also, by emphasising the violent dragging away of the disobedient girl, discreetly suggests a possible sexual interpretation. His praise of the scene as 'strangely powerful' amounts to a humorous, distanced gesture in the direction of Freud's essay 'A Child Is Being Beaten'.[11] The scene from *The Belles of St Trinians* (1953), reproduced here (Fig. 3), works by similar innuendo.

The way that such camp mockery can bring into focus the contra-dictory representations of gender in a school story is disturbingly brought out in a passage from a classic feminist novel of the 1970s: Doris Lessing's *The Golden Notebook*.[12] Mid-way through the 'Free Women' narrative, Anna Wulf enters her daughter Janet's room while the lodger, Ivor, is reading aloud a story about a girls' school:

> Ivor winked and raised his voice as he read: 'And so Betty put her name down for the hockey team. Would she be chosen? Would she be lucky?' He said to Anna in his normal voice, 'We'll call you when we're finished,' and went on: 'Everything depended on Miss Jackson. Betty wondered if she had been sincere when she wished her luck after the match? Had she

really meant it?' Anna paused outside the door listening: there was a new
note in Ivor's voice: mockery. The mockery was aimed at the world of the
girls' school, at the feminine world, not at the absurdity of the story; and
had started from the moment Ivor had become aware of Anna's presence.
(*Golden Notebook*, p. 335)

This is, clearly, a complex, nasty moment of sexual politics (and a
reminder that the uses of camp are not necessarily benign). Although
the scene of the reading is represented as sexually 'innocent' before
the adult Anna enters, it also stages, for her benefit, Janet's assertion
and Ivor's bargain. Janet's pleasure in this very stereotyped, English
story – just the kind of book her mother dislikes – represents a mild
defiance of Anna's post-Communist avant-gardism. Ivor meanwhile
has an ulterior motive for pandering to Janet's pleasure: he has moved
his male lover Ronnie into his room, and his friendship with Janet
in general, and the reading in particular, constitute his pay-off to
Anna for her tolerance of Ronnie's presence as a non-paying fixture
in her flat (*Golden Notebook*, p. 334). His dependence on Anna's
goodwill is mimicked by the words describing the heroine's anxiety,
'Everything depended on Miss Jackson'; the malicious edge to his
voice is presumably overdetermined by his awareness of being dependent on Anna's goodwill – a reversal of the traditional power-relations
obtaining between man and woman. This camp misogyny is not, Anna
perceives, caused by Ivor's homosexuality, or anyway not primarily;
the hostility and the self-distancing attitude which he is manifesting
are precisely equivalent to those characteristics of a ' "real" [i.e. hetero-
sexual] man who intends to set bounds to his relationship with a
woman [. . .] It was the same cold evasive emotion, taken a step further'
(*Golden Notebook*, p. 335).

Yet when Ivor reads without mockery, before Anna enters and after
she goes, there is no hint of sexual tension between the male reader
and the young girl listener, not so much because Ivor is sexually
uninterested in women as because of the story's language, themes
and structure which all imply a world in which people (i.e. girls) are
preoccupied exclusively with success at sports and with popularity
among their peers. Or, to put it in more overtly theoretical terms,
the language of the story interpellates a readerly subjectivity that is
simultaneously feminised and sexless.[13] This is the contradiction on
which Ivor's *double entendre*, like so much camp, turns; his mockery
evokes precisely that problematic femininity which is erased from
the language of the story he reads. The scene corresponds, then, to

GLADYS HAD NOT REALIZED THAT VIRGINIA
WAS UNABLE TO ACCEPT DEFEAT GRACEFULLY

2 Glen Baxter, 'Gladys had not realized', © Glen Baxter 1990

Jacqueline Rose's diagnosis of the Victorian cult of childish innocence: 'the child [is] always innocent and yet sexualised by that very focusing of attention' (*Peter Pan*, p. 98). If a 'feminine' story and its female listeners are mocked for their gender, then they cannot be sexless – something Janet becomes uneasily aware of as she senses 'the mockery being directed at herself, a female' (*Golden Notebook*, p. 335). Yet the target of the mockery does not seem to be sexuality so much as femininity – emotionalism and 'a female world'. It seems that whereas the pleasure of the story, for its female listener, is bound up with its representation of feminine identity, its comic potential is related to feminine powerlessness and inequality. This essay aims to explore the tension between these differing readerly pleasures in the school story, beginning with the question of sexuality.

Feminine identity and the reader's pleasure

Like my namesake in *The Golden Notebook*, I was in my early teens an addict of school stories. Elinor Brent-Dyer's Chalet School sagas, Enid Blyton's Malory Towers and St Clare's series, and especially Dorita Fairlie Bruce's Dimsie stories: I read them all again and again, with deep satisfaction and a pleasure like that of sinking into a warm bath. (In fact, I often did read them in the bathroom, since, although they weren't exactly illicit reading at home, they certainly weren't approved of.) The appeal of these stories was not that they corresponded with my own experience or even expectations of school; the whole point was that they didn't. I had no desire at all actually to attend a boarding school; the social miseries of the Perse School for Girls were bad enough from 9 to 4 on weekdays. But the knowledge of my own unpopularity and incompetence at sports only increased the pleasure of reading again how Darrell scored the winning goal for Malory Towers, or how the girls of the Jane Willard School cheered Dimsie after yet another spectacular rescue.

In my repetitive reading of what I knew to be fantasies, I seem to have been completely typical of girls who are addicted to the genre; a category which is not confined to the middle class. Gill Frith has shown how girls reading school stories 'knew it was a fantasy structure they were reading over and over again, but they enjoyed both the

[facing] 3 *The Belles of St Trinians* (film still). BFI Stills, Posters and Designs

exciting plots and the predictable endings. The highly ordered, rou-
tinised world of the boarding school was at once reassuring and
thrilling'.[14] Discussing Frith's essay, Angela McRobbie has suggested
that school stories are pleasurable because they both provide readers
with a world outside the family and enable them to 'experiment with
non-gender-specific activities. In the ballet school or boarding school,
there are echoes and replays of the child's original bisexual disposition
played out here as a kind of *grand finale* before the real world once
again intrudes' (*Feminism and Youth Culture*, pp. 205–6).

The appeal of the school story is also tied up with the way its
fantasies are articulated in the mode of realist fiction, a form which
subtly effaces its ideology by its claim to describe only 'reality'. In
classic realism, subjectivity is all-important: character causes action,
the characters themselves being implicitly defined as unchanging
essences, at once stereotyped and individualised.[15] So school stories
present a range of characters who persist from story to story (sporty
girl, studious girl, Irish rebel, weepy girl, etc.), from whose interactions
the plot invariably comes. The predominance of character is emphasised by what Catherine Belsey calls the 'illusionism' of classic
realism (*Critical Practice*, p. 70) – that is, its effacement of its own
fictionality in favour of what purports to be a 'real' world; this enables
fans of the genre to imagine that 'the characters are their friends'.[16]
And because the reader of the realist text shares the author–narrator's
omniscience, reading the texts enables one to enjoy a fantasy position
of knowledge and power, which must be particularly attractive to
relatively inexperienced and powerless readers.

These observations could apply to almost any work of popular
fiction for children; the difference of the school story lies in its representation of a female world with a wide variety of possible identities,
not all of them conventionally feminine. There are male-identified
girls like Enid Blyton's horse-loving 'Bill' or Elsie J. Oxenham's
'Rena';[17] furthermore, the girls' proficiency in sports and their frequent acts of heroism in dangerous places identify them as active,
powerful and courageous: qualities traditionally reserved for men.
But all this activity and independence is also combined with more
traditionally feminine physical and emotional vulnerability. The
fantasy of damaged heroism is apparent in the recurring theme of
the heroine's rescue of another girl from death by drowning, fire,
avalanche or precipice, almost but not quite at the cost of the heroine's
own life.[18] The other girl is usually an outsider at odds with the

school, often a rebellious junior, whose reckless folly or selfishness causes the danger. The transgressor's subjectivity in these narratives is quite as important as the heroine's: the latter tends, after the rescue, to become unconscious and disappear from the narrative, which then dwells on the culprit's gratitude and remorse, these emotions being a prelude to her complete integration into the school community. This scenario is played out so often in Elinor Brent-Dyer's Chalet School stories that the cliffhanger rescue finally appears to be an initiation ritual whereby all except the most innately virtuous newcomers learn to accept the wise values of the Chalet School. Its potential for melodrama is handled more forcefully in Dorita Fairlie Bruce's Dimsie stories: for example the chapter called 'The Price That Dimsie Paid' in *Dimsie Among the Prefects* where Dimsie holds Hilary Garth over a cliff – 'Dimsie felt as if her body was on the rack' (p. 185) – followed by two harrowing chapters in which it appears that Dimsie may be crippled for life (she isn't, of course), and above all, the final scene of *Dimsie: Head Girl*. Here, Dimsie turns out to have badly burnt her hand by rescuing her friend Jean Gordon's box of manuscript poems from a blazing shed accidentally set on fire by some younger girls smoking out a wasps' nest. This is a particularly selfless act, since these poems have already caused Dimsie's estrangement from Jean, who has neglected her duties to the school in order to write them. Jean has been demoted mid-way through the book, and the reluctant Dimsie made Head Girl in her stead, and though Jean admits her fault, she meanly resents Dimsie's promotion. Not until she notices Dimsie's pallor and her hand 'swathed in a large silk scarf' (*Dimsie: Head Girl*, p. 229) does she repent, undoing the bandage and applying some healing ointment with 'deft tender fingers' (p. 231).

This scene, even more than other rescue melodramas, clearly plays out a masochistic revenge fantasy in which the pain of estrangement is represented, as in conversion hysteria, by literal physical damage. This latent content ('If only she could see how she's hurt me') explains the cause and location of the fire: the wasps' nest in the potting shed where Jean keeps her poems metonymically signifies the hurtful nuisance they are felt to be, while the thoughtless juniors scolded by Dimsie for starting the fire (p. 226) represent a displacement of irresponsibility and of unconscious malice – qualities unthinkable in a heroine. The scene thus also half-entertains a more straightforward dream of revenge, since the guilty party *almost* loses her most precious possession (in other versions, her life), yet by restoring the loss, the already wronged one is damaged again. The narrative focuses not on Dimsie's feelings but on Jean's gradual perceptions of Dimsie's injuries and of their cause, so that the pleasurable fantasy of the victim pitied by the one who has caused her pain is sharpened by the reader's access to the guilty party's embarrassment and remorse.

Furthermore, from a psychoanalytical point of view, this fantasy of emotional revenge itself both masks and stages another fantasy of lesbian pleasure and punishment. The motif of the heroine's danger and the other girl's precious box on fire is remarkably similar to Dora's dream of the house on fire (famously recounted by Freud). In particular, her father's dream words *I refuse to let myself and my two children be burnt for the sake of your jewel-case*[19] relate interestingly to the damage incurred by Dimsie for the sake of Jean's manuscript box. The desires, paternal treacheries and sexual exchanges represented and interpreted in Dora's dream are of course absent from Fairlie Bruce's text (families hardly signify in school stories); however, the text mobilises a cruder version of this dream symbolism whereby the box representing female genitals, together with the fire and its implied opposite, moisture (Jean's ointment), signifying danger and sexual inflammation, represent the perilous desires of girls who touch one another. In this fantasy, the vulva appears as the site of damage and wounding, symbolically replicated in the burnt fingers; to touch the other girl's fiery box is to incur an injury (which itself represents an inscription on the girl's body of the mark of her castration). But punishment yields to forgiveness: the wound, emphasised as much as veiled by the white silk scarf swathing it, is then viewed, touched and relieved by the other girl's 'deft, tender fingers'. The cycle could continue indefinitely.

I don't wish to offer this post-Freudian exegesis of seduction/castration symbolism as the hidden truth which explains the essential emotional dynamics of the school story. Fairlie Bruce's narrative, like all school stories, represents her schoolgirls as essentially sexless, and to ignore this is to lose the text's meaning. Yet the fantasy of pleasure and punishment is not so much censored as actually made possible through the text's total erasure of feminine sexuality as an issue. (For example, it is never admitted in these stories, even discreetly, that girl's menstruate.[20])

Nevertheless, my reading obviously raises the question whether school stories ought to be read as lesbian fiction. Rosemary Auchmuty has argued forcefully that they should. She rightly emphasises the significance of the school story's focus on 'a female world. All authority figures as well as colleagues and comrades were women. The action was carried on by women, and all decisions were made by women [...] All emotional and social energies were directed at women, and women's frienships were presented as positive, not destructive or competitive, and sufficient in themselves' (*Not a Passing Phase*, p. 126). Arguing that these friendships are essentially lesbian, Auchmuty quotes a suggestive passage:

> Jen's eager eyes widened in delight when Rhoda appeared, followed up the drive by a tall, sunny-faced girl in khaki tunic and breeches and big boots, a shady hat covering her yellow hair, which was tied in a bunch of curls behind. Rena was tanned and healthy and straight, strong with a year's work in the moorland garden at Rocklands, and very pleasant to look at [...] She touched her hat in a boyish salute, as she came up to the couch. Jen stretched out her hands with an eager cry ... (*Not a Passing Phase*, p. 119)

This passage is strong evidence for Auchmuty's claims. She also points out that the school story's representation of the female world of school as the happiest time of one's life flatly contradicts the orthodoxy that marriage should be a woman's joyful destiny. As she rightly argues, this orthodoxy is piously but uncomfortably endorsed in the stories; the girls are admonished that marriage is 'one of the ends for which God made woman',[21] and the main characters marry young and are prolifically fertile (except in the stories of Enid Blyton, who doesn't follow her characters after they leave school), but the emotional interest of the stories is all directed at girls' relationships. It is, however, not clear how far these relationships are to be interpreted as sexual, and Auchmuty's essay is contradictory on this point. Her essay oscillates between interpreting girls' school stories as coded fictions of lesbian desire and reading them as sexually innocent celebrations of female friendship, in which girls sharing beds do so only out of 'a very conscious love for women' (p. 140) and an over-intense crush is judged 'unhealthy, of course, and silly; but it isn't vicious' (p. 136). These ambiguities are, as I have argued above, themselves inscribed in the school stories; if their representations of sexless femininity do constitute a 'working and re-working [...] of the question of what it is to be a girl' (*Feminism and Youth Culture*, p. 208), they certainly don't offer a settled answer. Furthermore, school stories are read largely by girls on their way to heterosexual romance, to most of whom (as, probably, to the writers of the stories themselves) the term 'lesbian' means an accusation, if it's recognised at all. Yet to interpret the pleasure of these texts as intrinsically lesbian must mean interpreting the reader's response in the same terms, which in turn would mean that school stories belong to what Adrienne Rich has independently defined as the 'lesbian continuum'. This notion insists on female identity as essentially lesbian, defining the 'lesbian continuum' not as a matter of sexual practice but as intensity of feeling between women, denied but never totally suppressed by the institutions of compulsory heterosexuality.[22] Rich's argument is radical and valuable in its refusal of the categories of patriarchal 'normality' and its insistence on lesbian identity as basic to female sexual identity, and there clearly is something in it; not enough, though, to be accepted without question. What, for instance, about female heterosexual desire?

This last question is raised forcibly by a much more prestigious genre of fiction related to and mostly contemporaneous with the school story: namely, the novel set in a girls' school. Unlike the school story, which is not a literary genre, these novels, all written by women, are definitely and consciously part of a tradition of high culture: they include Charlotte Bronte's *Villette*, Antonia White's *Frost in May*, Kate O'Brien's *The Land of Spices*, Muriel Spark's *The Prime of Miss Jean Brodie*, H.H. Richardson's *The Getting of Wisdom* and more recently A.S. Byatt's short story 'Racine and the Tablecloth'. (Antonia Forest's 'Kingscote' stories, which participate both in pleasurably escapist fantasy and high culture, exist somewhere between these two genres.) The thematic difference between these and the conventional school stories (the difference in literary quality is not my concern here), is not only their emphasis on the emotional pain of the educational process but their insistent connection of the closed world of the girls' school with other institutions and practices, notably the family, the world of art and literature, and – sometimes – heterosexual romance. In contrast to the exclusive concentration on girls' relationships in the school story, the effect of the all-female setting in the novel of the girls' school is often, paradoxically, to highlight the feminine experience of heterosexual desire and loss. These stories turn either on traumatic family loves (the heroine's negotiation of her loss, by death or estrangement, of a loved father or brother)[23] or on a heroine living out a fantasy of romantic heterosexual desire which never finds its object.[24] The possibility of lesbian desire is imagined in some of these texts, but it is never the main concern; where such narratives dramatise one girl's surprised perception of another as beautiful, her beauty is articulated through images or allusions to the realm of visual or literary art, which turns the girl into an aesthetic object.[25] Such comparisons both dramatise and sublimate desire, transmuting sexual feeling into aesthetic perception. The tradition of visual and literary art on which these texts draw is of course exclusively masculine (Mantegna, Giotto, Goya, Milton, Shakespeare) but it is represented as a transcendent world of genderless imagination. When Kate O'Brien's heroine sees the girl Pilar 'ironically, delightedly, as a motive in art' (*The Land of Spices*, p. 272), the purity of her vision is guaranteed by the authority of Western art; she thus occupies the position of the male gaze, objectifying female beauty, making the girl's identity disappear into what she signifies.[26] In other words, these texts participate in the masculine privilege of defining feminine identity without changing or even questioning the terms of the definition: a paradox of powerless privilege which appears in all stories about girls' schools, even the most naively celebratory.

Privilege, inequality and the 'queens of the schoolroom'

'I had always thought that schoolgirls and schoolmistresses were funny' (*Girls*, p. ix)

It is a truism of feminist thought that in the Western patriarchal tradition women represent sexuality and feeling as against the male's reasoned superiority. Parodies of girls' school stories confirm this point, sometimes by an overtly sexual *double entendre*, but more often by guying the convention of feminine emotionalism. Thus Nigel Molesworth on gender equivalence:

Imagine wot would hapen at st custard's if we were like gurls and got a CRUSH on somebody, e.g.
FOTHERINGTON-TOMAS: oh, nigel, may i take yore books to the fr. class this morning?
NIGEL: foolish little thing. peason hav already offered.
FOTHERINGTON-TOMAS: (*blubbing*): oh.[27]

Girls' school stories do not actually correspond to this parody of feminine intensity, for 'crushes' are disapproved of (Dimsie's 'Anti-Soppist League') or ignored altogether (the Chalet School stories). It is true, though, that these stories do concentrate on feelings and relationships. Friendships, rivalries, jealousies, rebukes are all intense affairs, especially the last. The following passage in which Deira O'Hagan is told off by the Headmistress, is typical: ' "You may go, Deira," she said at length. "I am disappointed in you." Deira went – and [...] just managed to get up to her cubicle before her self-control vanished and, lying on her bed, she cried heart-brokenly. That last sentence of the Head's had cut home' (*The Head Girl*, p. 68). Deira, however, is a headstrong Irish girl. It is rare or unknown for the heroine of a school story to cry so passionately; she may understandably wince when rebuked 'in a tone of cold contempt that cut like a knife' (*Dimsie Among the Prefects*, p. 113), but she is likely to manifest hurt feelings by nothing more than 'catching her breath with a short sob' (p. 229). But the sob betrays her vulnerability, and in fact, this deadly serious emphasis on reserve paradoxically emphasises the feminine emotionalism which it denies. Dimsie's 'Anti-Soppist League' aims to suppress feminine 'soppiness'; it nevertheless defines the girls who belong to it in relation to emotional intensity.

This contradictory relationship between ideals of self-control and vulnerability in the girls' school story is produced by the asymmetrical relation between gender and class privilege. To attend a girls' public school is to participate in a form of educational privilege. To read girls' school stories is therefore to participate in a fantasy of enjoying such privilege; and whatever the mixture of classes the stories may reach, these narratives endorse the ideological beliefs of the British upper classes whose juvenile social world they represent. Although girls' schools did not, unlike the boys' public schools of which they were copies, enable their ex-pupils to take up positions of economic or political power, they nevertheless enforced a strongly masculine ethos on their pupils. Between 1920 and 1940, the heyday of the girls' school story, girls' boarding schools did notoriously model their educational practices and beliefs (compulsory team games, prefects, the honour of the school, the stiff upper lip, etc.) on those of the boys' public schools whose role was to educate the officer elite who administered the British Empire. The links between imperialist patriotism, militarism and a public school ethos of judicious emotional reserve have since 1970 been much explored by historians, who have theorised and debated the historical connections between the myth of the cricket-playing honourable schoolboy, the actual practices of schools and the needs of an imperialist state.[28] But however good at cricket, however admirable a prefect a girl might be, she would never be told 'Go out and govern New South Wales!';[29] she would at best be a memsahib, enjoying her husband's class privilege but not his power to rule. Excluded from the heroic imperialist destiny, the world of the girls' school was, in terms of the power it enabled women to exercise, a closed circuit: the only way in which women could continue to exercise unquestioned authority after leaving school was to re-enter it as teachers, whose function was to reproduce the ethos of the public school.[30]

It is not, then, that Dorita Fairlie Bruce, Elinor Brent-Dyer and the other writers of school stories were 'reflecting reality' by writing of girls who play hockey ardently and blush if they bring shame on their school; the point is rather that the school stories share and reproduce the class values of the institutions which they idealised. That these values were emphatically masculine is confirmed by many ludicrous anecdotes: the girl who asked permission to play cricket with a tennis ball and was 'sent to the Headmistress, and made to apologise, miss supper and write out "I must try not to be so feeble" fifty times' (Marshall, *Giggling*, pp. 95–6); the girl at Sherborne who said 'I'm glad I'm not pretty'; or the girls at Wycombe Abbey who were reproved by their house captain for lacking 'determination and guts'.[31] As with the 'Anti-Soppist League' which ineluctably defines girls in relation to 'soppiness', these exhortations look silly because a feminine emotionalism is implied in the very intensity of these denials of vulnerability. Stevie Smith makes this point in the anti-school poem 'Girls!', which sends up 'Miss So-and-So' and her exhortations not to sell the pass or let down the side – 'That is what this woman said and a lot of balsy stuff beside / (Oh the awful balsy nonsense that this woman cried)' (p. 167). The discreetly misspelled, repeated obscenity 'balsy', punning on 'balls' (testicles/nonsense) and ball games like hockey, indicates that 'playing the game' is simply an empty charade of masculinity.

These contradictions are exploited in Louis MacNeice's delightful camp letter-diary 'Hetty to Nancy' (*Letters from Iceland*, 1937). This relates the events of a real camping expedition across Iceland, undertaken by MacNeice himself, Wystan Auden, a schoolmaster called Bill Hoyland and four schoolboys including Michael Yates (who later wrote his own memoir of the trip). MacNeice's text, itself a pastiche of disorganised feminine chat, turns the author into 'Hetty', Auden into 'Maisie', and the school party into 'Miss Greenhalge' and her girls. The names Hetty and Nancy are 1930s code for 'straight' and 'gay': 'Nancy' means 'homosexual' and 'Hetty'

is short for 'heterosexual' or 'heter' in the slang of the Auden group.[32]
'Hetty', the supposed writer, is emphatically feminine; she wears
lipstick, silk stockings and crêpe-de-chine knickers (much disapproved
of by the androgynous 'Maisie' as 'a relic of barbarism like men
wearing beards':[33] MacNeice himself was bearded). She is of course
engaged to be married, while the addressee 'Nancy' appears to be a
rock-climbing lesbian: 'I hope you are liking the Dolomites [...] what
about your new girl-friend? I thought she sounded sweet but that may
be just by contrast. With the last I mean; I warned you about her all
along' ('Hetty', p. 156). Inverting the sexes thus enables MacNeice to
write about homosexuality in a coded but fairly overt way, and to
tease his public-school companions by emphasising their failure to
live up to the heroic school ideal. He exploits the conventions that
girls are emotional creatures and that women like to gossip about
feelings and relationships by representing the schoolboys as girls
pretending to be boys – a pretence which frequently comes unstuck:

> We caught up the advance guard in a state of frightful emotion. Anne
> [Michael] had cut her finger and two of the girls were in tears. Greenhalge,
> redder than ever, rushed round the pack-horses tearing open all the panniers
> for iodine; anyone would have thought the girl was going to die. Maisie
> [Auden] was explaining that you usually cut your finger because you
> wanted to – like making Spoonerisms she said. Anne did her best to be a
> lovely martyr but she did not have the whole house with her as both the
> guides and little Hetty were definitely bored. These queens of the schoolroom
> begin to think that anything will go. (p. 174)

The satire is not only aimed at the failure of MacNeice's unfortunate
companions to behave 'as public schoolboys behave in Ian Hay or in
the Mind of God' ('Hetty' p. 161): it also by implication sends up the
public-school ideal as a fake for boys as well. The point of MacNeice's
camp farce is the recognition that the notion of schoolgirl normality –
'I must try not to be so feeble' – is, precisely, a fantasy and an unstable
one at that.

This frivolity, then, sends up the values of the public schools and
the discourse of imperialism. Andrew Ross has argued in 'The Uses
of Camp' that:

> the camp effect is created [...] when the products [...] of a much earlier mode
> of production, which has lost its power to dominate cultural meanings,
> become available, in the present, for definition according to contemporary
> codes of taste [...] That is why the British flag, for Mods and other sub-
> cultures, and Victoriana, for the Sergeant Pepper phase of the later sixties,

became camp objects – precisely because of their historical association with a power that was now in decline.[34]

The asymmetry of power between the sexes (even more marked in 1936 than now) produces the same kind of 'distancing' effect from the institutions and values of imperialism as the actual decline of the British Empire did subsequently.[35]

On the other hand, the misogyny, or at least the contempt for women, implicit in MacNeice's humour cannot be ignored either; his joke works only because boys are demeaned by being represented as girls. It is obviously not enough, then, to praise camp readings of school stories for the mocking deconstruction of sexual stereotypes, or even to note their potential for satire on imperialist identities, without asking whether and how women actually benefit from such mockery. There clearly can't be a single, prescriptive answer to this question; it must depend in particular instances on whether the feminine identities are being problematised to make repressive language and reactionary institutions look silly, or whether, as in *Private Eye*'s notoriously misogynist humour,[36] the joke is on the female victim. Unless this question is addressed, the pleasure of reading school stories may involve collusion, either in the class values of an imperialist patriarchy or in the mockery of its more powerless subjects: the young girls for whom these stories are written.

Notes

1 Jacqueline Rose, *The Case of Peter Pan*, London, 1984, p. 78. Hereafter cited in the text as *Peter Pan*.

2 Dorita Fairlie Bruce, *Dimsie: Head Girl*, London, 1922; the quote is from the revised edition (London, 1984), p. 232. Hereafter cited in the text.

3 Armada Books, Britain's largest publisher of children's paperbacks, have in print thirty-five of Elinor Brent-Dyer's Chalet School stories, plus two of the cheaper 'Three-in-One' volumes in the same series. Armada also print the Enid Blyton 'Malory Towers' and 'St Clare's' series in 'Three in One' books (two volumes for each series); Blyton's three 'Naughtiest Girl' books are also printed individually by Beaver Books. Eleven of Anne Digby's recent 'Trebizond' series are in print as paperbacks, ten in Puffins, one in Swift Books. All nine of Dorita Fairlie Bruce's 'Dimsie' books (1922–45) were reprinted in 1984 in revised editions, with the slang updated and most of the cricket matches taken out, by Goodchild Books, and are still in print. Angela Brazil and Elsie J. Oxenham have not, however, been reprinted. (Source: Whitaker's *Books in Print* microfiche, October 1991.)

4 See Patricia Craig and Mary Cadogan, *You're a Brick, Angela!*, London, 1976, chapters IX–XI, for a full discussion oythese magazine stories.

5 See Susan Sontag's 'Notes on Camp', in *Against Interpretation*, New York, 1967, pp. 275–6.

6 The only exception is *The Girls of Radclyffe Hall* by 'Adela Quebec' (Gerald Berners), privately printed in 1932.

7 See Arthur Marshall, *Girls Will Be Girls*, London, 1974 and *Giggling in the Shrubbery*, London, 1985. Hereafter cited in the text as, respectively, *Girls* and *Giggling*.

8 John Betjeman, 'Myfanwy', *Collected Poems*, London, 1970, p. 86; Geoffrey Willans and Ronald Searle, *How to be Topp*, London, 1959, p. 48; Stevie Smith, *Collected Poems*, London, 1975, p. 167.

9 Antonia Forest, *Autumn Term*, 1948, reprinted London, 1977, p. 221. This kind of parody also features in P. G. Wodehouse's 'Mike'; cf. Psmith's greeting to Mike – 'Are you the Bully, the Pride of the School, or the Boy Who Is Led Astray and takes to drink in Chapter Sixteen?' (*Mike at School*, London, 1922. I am indebted for this example to an unpublished essay on school stories by Louise McConnell). See also Kipling's *Stalky & Co* where the boys are chuckling over the hero's resentment of a beating in *Eric or little by Little* – ' "He burned not with remorse or regret but with shame and violent indignation. He glared" – oh, naughty Eric! Let's go on to the part where he goes in for drink' ('An Unsavoury Interlude', *Stalky & Co*, 1899, also noticed by Joseph Bristow in *Empire Boys*, London, 1991). The effect of such parodies of stereotyped melodramas is to establish the superior realism of the 'containing' text; the passage from Kipling shows clearly how 'realism' can enforce some highly ideological assumptions (e.g. that *real* boys think that violent resentment is an absurd response to being beaten).

10 Angela McRobbie, 'Dance Narratives and Fantasies of Achievement', *Feminism and Youth Culture*, London, 1991, p. 208. Hereafter cited in the text.

11 Penguin Freud Library, X, *On Psychopathology*, London, 1983.

12 Doris Lessing *The Golden Notebook*, London, 1972, p. 335. Hereafter cited in the text as *Golden Notebook*.

13 It is noticeable that when the 'Free Women' text insists on the girl's sexual innocence, it reproduces the language of the school story, describing Janet as 'a black-haired urchin' – exactly the kind of phrase that school stories apply to tousled juniors.

14 Gill Frith, 'The Time of your Life', in G. Weiner and M. Arnot, ed., *Gender Under Scrutiny*, London, 1987, pp. 118–33. The quotation is from Angela McRobbie's summary and citation of Gill Frith in *Feminism and Youth Culture*, p. 206.

15 This account of realism is obviously based on the theories of Roland Barthes (see *S/Z*, London, 1977 and *Image–Music–Text* London, 1978). I have also drawn on 'Addressing the Subject', chapter 3 of Catherine Belsey's *Critical Practice*, London, 1980, which is a clear and detailed exposition of the Barthesian critique of classic realism. I've criticised Belsey elsewhere for the oversimplifications implied by 'classic realism' ('Listening to Minna: Realism, Feminism and the Politics of Reading', *Paragraph*, XIV, 1991, pp. 197–216), but I think her critique describes the reader-relationships set up by the 'realism' of popular fiction remarkably well.

16 Rosemary Auchmuty, 'You're a Dyke, Angela! Elsie J. Oxenham and the Rise and Fall of the Schoolgirl Story', in *Not a Passing Phase: Reclaiming Lesbians in History*, Lesbian History Group, London, 1989, p. 124. Hereafter cited in the text.

17 'Bill' and her horse feature in all the Malory Towers stories. Enid Blyton seems to have had a soft spot for cross-dressing girls; cf. also the girl George in the Famous Five series. The appearance of 'Rena' in her khaki tunic, 'breeches and big boots' (*Not a Passing Phase*, p. 119) is discussed at greater length below.

18 There is also a sporting variant of the theme of damaged heroism, sent up by Antonia Forest in her *End of Term*, London, 1959. Here Lawrie, her most immature character, has bruised her leg just before a netball match. She dreams of being 'the one who saved the game, who was everywhere at once, doing ten people's work ... [like] the people in books who played with broken fingers and sprained ankles, and no one ever knew till they fainted at the end', but sadly realises that this isn't going to

work for her: 'she didn't honestly see how she was going to play as well as usual, let alone better. People in books must have different kinds of bones or something' (p. 153).

19 Sigmund Freud, 'Fragment of an Analysis of a Case of Hysteria (Dora)', Penguin Freud Library, VIII, 'Case Histories', London, 1977, p. 99.

20 Antonia Forest (who has a strong commitment to realism) is, once again, an exception here; when one of her characters is chosen to swim in a school match, she 'calculated – June 30th: no, that was safe – she wouldn't be cursed', *The Cricket Term*, London, 1979, p. 123.

21 Brent-Dyer, *The Head Girl of the Chalet School*, London, 1922, reprinted 1988, p. 112.

22 See 'Compulsory Heterosexuality and Lesbian Existence', in *Blood, Bread and Poetry*, London, 1986, pp. 22–75. This connection is made by myself, not by Rosemary Auchmuty; her essay does not cite Rich, suggesting rather that Oxenham's fictions lost their popularity by being sexualised (i.e. read as lesbian) after the *Well of Loneliness* trial in 1926 – though as its title suggests, her essay also emphasises the lesbian subtext of Oxenham's writing. The point of mapping Auchuty's arguments on to Rich's theories is simply to clarify the issues raised by a reading of school stories as (however subtextually) lesbian.

23 This is true of White's *Frost in May*, London, 1932, reprinted 1978, Kate O'Brien's *The Land of Spices*, London, 1941, reprinted 1988, and Byatt's 'Racine and the Tablecloth', in *Sugar and Other Stories*, London, 1988. *The Land of Spices* links the losses of loved males endured by two very different heroines: the Reverend Mother, emotionally crippled by her estrangement from her beloved father, and the child Anna Murphy who loses her dearest brother. *Frost in May* turns on the heroine's relationships with her father. Though there are moments of romanticism between the girls at the 'Convent of the Five Wounds', the most strongly (and horribly) sexual moment occurs when Nanda's father rejects her in front of the Mother Superior as she feels 'as if he had stripped her naked and beaten her' (*Frost in May*, p. 217). Family relationships are more tenuously present in Byatt's 'Racine and the Tablecloth', a story which engages powerfully though obliquely with the question of women writers' relation to masculine tradition. In this story, Emily's fantasy of a male 'Reader', who will give her not personal love but impartial judgement of her writing, enables her to endure, though not to escape, the bullying of Miss Crichton-Smith, the sanctimonious headmistress. This situation replays, in fantasy, a post-Freudian paradigm of the girl child's position in the family whereby the father's masculinity offers an escape from an overpoweringly dominant mother (see Dorothy Dinnerstein's *The Mermaid and the Minotaur*, New York, 1976, for a powerful theorisation of this paradigm). Miss Crichton-Smith and her school are, figuratively, a bad mother and an oppressive family, from which the benignly impartial (fatherly?) masculinity of the Reader offers escape.

24 Bronte's *Villette* obviously corresponds to this model: Lucy's desire is frustrated because one-sided (Dr John) or doomed (Paul Emanuel's death). *The Prime of Miss Jean Brodie*, London, 1961, sets up a comic version of the same process: Miss Brodie becomes the dull music master's lover as a substitute for the affair she really wants with Teddy Lloyd; Sandy, who does seduce him, gives up sex to become a nun; the adult Jenny never again experiences 'the lost and guileless delight of her eleventh year' except as loss: 'There was nothing whatever to be done about it, for Jenny had been contentedly married for sixteen years past' (Spark, p. 108).

25 See Antonia Forest, *End of Term*, p. 81. Forest's stories deal more sympathetically than most with the 'crush': Janice is also admired by Nicola's friend Miranda West, who in *The Cricket Term* (1978) is able both to dramatise and to sublimate the attachment when she plays a brilliant Ariel to Janice's Prospero in a school production of *The Tempest* – 'Thy thoughts I cleave to; what's thy pleasure?' (*The Cricket Term*, p. 166).

26 For two very different critiques of the objectification of the female body, see Adrienne
    Rich, 'Snapshots of a Daughter-in-Law', *The Fact of a Doorframe and other Poems*,
    1986, and Laura Mulvey, 'Visual Pleasure and Narrative Cinema', 1977, collected
    in Mulvey, *Visual and Other Pleasures*, London, 1990.

27 Geoffrey Willans and Ronald Searle, *Back in the Jug Agane*, London, 1959, p. 89.

28 See Corelli Barnett, *The Collapse of British Power*, London, 1977; Isobel Quigly,
    The Heirs of Tom Brown: The English School Story, London, 1982, and Joseph
    Bristow, *Empire Boys*, London, 1991.

29 Hilaire Belloc, 'Lord Lundy', *Cautionary Tales*, London, 1908.

30 Judith Butler makes a similar point when she argues that the pursuit of equal rights
    is a chimera if the implicit politics of the rights themselves are not thought through:
    'if [the] system can be shown to produce gendered subjects along a differential axis
    of domination or to produce subjects who are presumed to be masculine ... an
    uncritical appeal for the emancipation of "women" will be clearly self-defeating',
    Gender Trouble, London, 1990, p. 2.

31 E. Arnot Robertson, 'Run, Girls, Run!', essay printed in *The Old School*, ed. Graham
    Greene, London, 1934; cited by Quigley, p. 219. The anecdote about Wycombe Abbey
    was told me by my mother.

32 For 'Nancy', cf. Orwell's contemporary jibe at 'the Nancy poets' in *The Road to
    Wigan Pier* (London, 1936, reprinted 1963 by Penguin, p. 31); for 'heter', see *W. H.
    Auden: A Tribute*, ed. S. Spender, London, 1975, p. 79. This volume also contains
    Michael Yate's account of the camping trip.

33 W. H. Auden and Louis MacNeice, *Letters from Iceland*, London, 1937, p. 162.
    'Hetty to Nancy' is cited hereafter as 'Hetty'.

34 Andrew Ross, 'Uses of Camp', in *No Respect: Intellectuals & popular culture*, New
    York, 1989, pp. 139–40.

35 A similar point is made in much more politicised terms in another 1930s camp text:
    Virginia Woolf's *Three Guineas*, London, 1938. Woolf's feminist polemic plays a similar
    game of inverting the sexes to satirise uniforms and the reverence they command:
    'A woman who advertised her motherhood by a tuft of horsehair on the left shoulder
    would scarcely, you will agree, be a venerable object.' *Three Guineas*, republished
    by Penguin, Hammondsworth, 1977, p. 25.

36 I have in mind the 'Sylvie Krin' romances that send up a central feminine conscious-
    ness, particularly 'Love in the Saddle', whose humour at its heroine's expense
    strongly resembles Ivor's mockery in *The Golden Notebook*.

Who's read *Macho Sluts?*

Clare Whatling

The practice and representation of consensual lesbian sadomasochism have been controversial within feminist and lesbian feminist communities since the early 1980s. Arguments both for the attack and the defence have been intense and violent and, though attempts have been made to defuse the terms of the debate,[1] these have largely been unsuccessful and positions have remained polarised. Some feminists wish to claim that S/M, whatever its claims to consensuality and the sex or sexual proclivity of its practitioners, has always been and remains a construction and effect of patriarchy (which is understood as resting upon a sadomasochistic power relation grounded in a presumed but spurious consensuality). Lesbians who engage in consensual S/M are thus merely imitating and even colluding in patriarchal structures. Such a view is propounded most famously (or notoriously) in the radical feminist anthology *Against Sadomasochism* and by Sheila Jeffreys who argues that 'Sm practice comes from nowhere more mysterious than the history of our very real oppression'.[2] This is a view supported by the contributors to *Against Sadomasochism*, one of whom maintains: 'We believe that sadomasochistic impulses are created and sustained by events and images within our society, and that sadomasochistic behaviour reproduces and therefore condones many of the power imbalances and destructive features of our lives.'[3] 'Hence', continues another contributor, 'these are encounters where the patriarchal view of sexuality is played out' (p. 80).

To most practising lesbian sadomasochists, however, consensual S/M does not so much imitate patriarchal relations as parody and indeed occasionally deconstruct them. Over the past decade there have been as many claims made for consensual lesbian S/M as there have been condemnations of it – some of them as dubious. Of particular issue is the reification of S/M as a practice. Where courage is needed to make a maligned identification there is always the danger that this identification is invested in as a totality. In the proliferation of sexual groupings over the last two decades there has been an opening-up of the possibilities for identification, but also a point of closure whereby the sexual act is overburdened with the fiction of total identity. This is a temptation which must be resisted since it postulates identity as an essence and its freedom of expression as the sole requisite of 'the self'. The final ruse, is indeed, as Foucault says, to 'believe that our "liberation" is in the balance'.[4] As a result, any claims made for S/M's revolutionary character must be interrogated. S/M is never *intrinsically* revolutionary. Like all sexual practice, it is a product of its time and context. As with other sexual practices, it may be oppositional under certain conditions, but is never always so. Indeed, like most marginal sexual practices, it is likely to play into, as well as out of, the dominant structures of the society in which it is practised.[5] In this sense, it is true to say that S/M is constructed in relation to the society in which it is played out and cannot be understood without reference to the inequalities that exist there. Nor can it change them without recourse to equivalent change on the infrastructural level. In other words, S/M is in some respects no different to any other practice.

Where S/M does perhaps differ from more conventional sexual practices is in the self-consciousness it brings to encounters. For S/M as a practice does much to foreground the constructedness of all sexuality. It attempts this primarily in the way it denaturalises sex, disputing the romantic myth of sex as natural, mutual and spontaneous. S/M makes it very clear, it is indeed central to its praxis, that sex is also about compromise, negotiation and shared imagination.[6]

On the one hand, then, we have the radical feminist argument that S/M practice is a product of patriarchy and thereby vitiated. On the other, we have the S/M insistence that all sex is shaped by social forms but that power-play need not be oppressive in the forms it takes within sex. The very terms of the debate are, however, a construction – 'both sides' have an investment in the vanilla–S/M distinction, the one side to protect their sexual purity, the other side to fuel their exoticism. Nevertheless, the division is a false one and the differences between the practices involved are much less distinct than many would like to pretend.[7] The distinction is a politically and rhetorically useful one, however, since it allows one side to maintain its political purity at the expense of the other, in constructing an extreme image of S/M practice and practitioners which sometimes seems to make of S/M a repository of all evils.[8] The notion of the moral purity of one group of women (vanilla) is problematic where, as Gayle Rubin has theorised it,[9] a hierarchy of values is set up in our society which makes of one practice 'the norm', and of the rest scales of 'deviance from'. Within dominant society it is married monogamous reproductive heterosexuality which represents the norm. Recently, however, as Jana Sawicki argues, 'as some gays and lesbians achieve a modicum of acceptance [. . .] new norms have been established within these groups through the identification of practices that are deviant relative to theirs'.[10] Lesbian feminism's continued exclusion of 'deviants' from its ranks, its construction of extreme images by which to fuel fear and hatred of certain minorities, demonstrates its complicity with dominant structures of evaluation. The anti-porn activist Andrea Dworkin's support (to the point of testifying at the hearings) for the Attorney General Edwin Meese's 1986 report on pornography is a notorious instance of feminism's collaboration with the moral and political establishment. This report cleverly manipulates feminist rhetoric in order to further the cause of right-wing moral consensus. Although Meese promised that 'there will be no censorship while I am Attorney General'[11] the report has provided the justification for a number of repressive actions against individuals, and is responsible for a general increase in what feminists opposing state censorship believe is a determined erosion of individual and collective minority rights. S/M practitioners have been chief among the victims. In this moral climate, the feminist reception of consensual lesbian S/M becomes an issue of real political importance.

Since its publication in 1988, Pat Califia's book of short stories *Macho Sluts* has been one of the texts at the centre of the sex controversy. Criticised as misogynistic and therefore pornographic,[12] vilified as a product of the lesbian S/M movement, condemned out of hand by some, it is a book more talked about than read. Yet it is a book which *is* read, and enjoyed, by many more women than would admit to it within a public feminist space. The book addresses a much wider community of readers than might have been expected a few years ago, and though many would balk at the label 'lesbian sadomasochist', women are none the less participating in lesbian S/M, at least as a literary-voyeuristic phenomenon. This seems justification enough for extending the current debate outside of the practice of consensual S/M and into a more general framework of reader response.

   Macho Sluts is a text which raises a multitude of questions around the issues of women, sexuality and power. I propose to concentrate on those issues which have received less of an airing within the feminist movement. One which is constantly under erasure within feminist discourse is that of feminists' own use of violence. There has always been a crypto-relation between lesbian feminists and violence in the form of feminist vigilantism. This has a fictional tradition embracing feminist classics from Wittig's *Les Guérillères* to Andrea Dworkin's *Mercy* whose 'reconstructed' heroine gains deep pleasure from her shockingly sadistic anti-male fantasies.[13] Often, however, as has been the case until recently with Dworkin, the more question-able implications of such table-turning have gone unexamined by feminists.

In exploring rather than merely acceding to the deployment of power and controlled violence on a fantasy level, *Macho Sluts* induces women to consider more seriously their own relation to violence. There is a scene in 'The Vampire' where Kerry (the androgynous dominatrix, and the vampire of the tale) wreaks an (almost) deadly revenge on a witless leatherman who has provoked her wrath by his unthinking sexism. Califia sets the scene:

> The fool kept on talking. 'Why Ah don't reckon yew could even make a dent in my hide,' he chuckled. 'Probably be a waste of time. Ah kin take quite a lot, yew know. Wouldn't want ta embarrass a lil gal like yew – yew are a gal, ain'tcha?'
>
> Then the fatuous ass pronounced his own sentence: 'Ah kin take anythin' yew kin dish out, sister.'[14]

What is the reader's response, as witness of the scene that follows? It may be to close the book. However, one may find oneself in a rather more disquieting position, that is as a potentially desiring participant in such a scene. The passage is set up as a revenge fantasy and the reader might experience a certain satisfaction at the victor-ious conclusion of the exchange.[15] Still, how does this fit in with women's relation to violence and, even more controversially, to sadism as it has been theorised within feminism? Hegemonic feminist thought has tended to theorise violence as the prerogative of men and as the abuse of women. This attitude is, of course, fundamental to a certain moment within feminism, but in concentrating on the relation between men and violence to the exclusion of every other power relation, such feminism closes off important avenues of explor-ation. Ellen Willis notes how women are traditionally not supposed to have violent fantasies about men (let alone about other women), most particularly if such fantasies take the form of viciously sadistic impulses.[16] Yet, as Willis asks, in a question which radically opens up the possibilities of female subject identification: 'when a woman is aroused by a rape fantasy is she perhaps identifying with the rapist as well as the victim?'[17] Marion Bower, in a Kleinian reading of Freud, also attempts to show how a 'female sexual sadism exists'.[18] This is in relation to the more traditionally foregrounded female masochism, even perhaps as subservient to this, but none the less able to be accessed 'in its own right' (p. 42) at times. Bower cites evidence from Melanie Klein's research into early childhood fantasies which illustrate instances of female sexual sadism. She argues from these that a female sexual sadism does exist but is rendered invisible by its cultural suppression. Women are not *believed* to be sadistic because they are not *seen* to be, at least if they wish to remain 'womanly'. Bower is aware how unattractive the idea of the existence of a female sadism might be to feminists who prefer to retain an 'illusion of innocence' (p. 52) and confine their understanding of sadism to the ways it operates through masculinity. A partial reading of this sort is, Bower argues, exemplified by Susan Griffin's *Pornography and Silence*.[19] In her book Griffin employs Freud extensively in order to describe sadism as it is manifested in men, but stops short of the applicability of Freud's analysis to women. In this totalising view, women are only ever victims. What *Macho Sluts* suggests (without implying that women are responsible for their victimisation) is that women are always more than only victims, that, in different circumstances, we may be aggressors too. I made the comparison with *Mercy* in order to demonstrate how feminism manifests hypocrisy by designating one sadism as fascistic and the other as righteous feminist indignation. There are few scenes in *Macho Sluts* of the horror of *Mercy* but the book is no easy ride either. *Macho Sluts* shows women being aggressive, standing up for themselves and their desires. It shows how a female sexual sadism both exists and satisfies a variety of impulses in the woman reader. To refuse to acknowledge the insistence of such feelings is to do an injustice to the complicated mix of emotions, desires and fantasies experienced by women in their own lives.

Other desires, equally controversial, but of a rather different order, are also raised by the book, for example, the question of sexual identity and its sometimes complex relation to sexual desire. In 'The Surprise Party', Califia describes a woman who is adamant in her chosen identity as a lesbian butch. As the story unfolds, however, this woman is led to confront what was previously her secret desire for men, and more specifically for the male body: 'Liar, her sex-conscience jeered. You love getting fucked. You fantasize about cock and talk dirty about it all the time. But I'm a lesbian her public persona objected. This doesn't have anything to do with that, the wiser voice replied' (p. 214). Part of this desire is for the strangeness of the male body and much of the language in the story evokes the difference in image, smell and taste of men. However, the woman's desire is further complicated by the fact that she both desires to have a man, that is to have him sexually, and desires to have the body of a man, that is to inhabit the stylistic signifiers of maleness as her own. The fact that all three men available to her are gay only adds a special frisson to her desire:

> Her own experience with straight sex had been as unsatisfying as Mike and Joe's. But this act of penetration was firmly situated within a context of dominance and submission – the core of her eroticism [. . .] And these men were incredibly good at what they did. They liked fucking and they liked being fucked, they knew how to do it and they wanted her to like it. The element of mutual homosexuality made it seem more perverse, yet safe. (p. 233)

The male participants also desire the woman, although they are forbidden to express their desire freely by the scene's co-ordinator, Don. Still, Don is only too willing to play on the men's desire for the boyish lesbian masquerading as male. Thus, he teases: 'Maybe it will help if you don't think of her as a girl. After all, she doesn't want to be a woman. She wants to be a man. She dresses like one, talks like one, walks like one. She's a queer, like you boys. Queers have sex with queers right?' (p. 231). A number of taboos are being addressed when it is suggested that not only can lesbians desire men and gay men desire women, but that gay men and lesbians can also desire each other, those who are twice other, being of the 'wrong' gender and the 'wrong' sexual orientation. What I am arguing here is not an identity free-for-all, not merely another invocation of the old polymorphous perverse. What I am rather seeking to illustrate is the coterminous maintenance and relinquishing of identity within a particular mode of S/M role-play.

'The Surpise Party' is a text which revels in a knowing transgression of traditional lesbian feminist injunctions. From its images of a lesbian desiring the penis and being turned on by the sight of men acting sexually together, to its outrageous play on that most resistant of patriarchal signifiers, the gun as penis as erotic tool, it presents (as the flyleaf to the book promises) 'a WAP [Women Against Pornography] woman's nightmare'. Yet its impulse, I would argue, is not merely to shock but to transform and subvert. Both of these intentions are illustrated by the way Califia twists and shapes conventional pornographic imagery so that the woman's pleasure (which within the S/M dynamic does include fear and uncertainty) is foregrounded. As Lesley Stern (a feminist who wishes to utilise pornography for a feminist end rather than condemn it en masse as Dworkin does) puts it, 'To focus on female pleasure "uncovering" this in what is established as porn',[20] this is what then becomes Califia's strategy. Thus, when the woman performs fellatio, her pleasure is not forced in the sense that she pretends pleasure, nor is her pleasure constructed by a male desire attempting to assuage its own guilt, as would be the conventional pattern. Rather her pleasure is her own, is indeed defiantly her own. Indeed it is this which becomes problematic for her: 'To just suck him off without bargaining sex for freedom – to do it just for the pleasure and the degradation of it – was stupid, perverted, sick, stupid ...' (p. 221). Changing the context, substituting the agency of the female subject for the traditionally acted-upon feminine object, Califia alters what would be the story's conventional focus. She thereby allows her protagonist access to age-old fantasies shaped *her* way. This is made clear at the end of the story when we learn that the entire scene has been staged as a surprise party gift by the woman's lover, Fran, on the basis of her lover's own erotic confessions.[21]

In arguing for this kind of a reading, I am obviously not saying that the sexual gaze (usually associated with voyeurism and fetishism but here opened up to the possibility of other identifications) is rendered innocent and unproblematic. What I am arguing for is a way of reading which allows women access to a multiplicity of subject positions and thus multiple viewing-pleasures, whereas beforehand only one was theorised, namely the masculine. One of the things demonstrated by the story is that sexual identity does not have to correspond with fantasy, since, as Lesley Stern notes, 'the insertion of phantasy as a question provides a challenge to the notion of sexuality as fixed by identity' (p. 55).[22] A much greater freedom of identification is indeed possible within fantasy. For, as Califia observes: 'Many people do not fantasize about the kind of sex they actually have. Fantasy is a realm in which we can embrace pleasures that we may have very good reasons to deny ourselves in real life (like the fact that something might not be nearly as much fun to do as to think about)' (p. 16). It is a mark of feminism's sexual fix,[23] however, that where we can fantasise over Amazons and vampires to our heart's desire, as soon as fantasy enters the realm of the explicitly sexual, a totally other standard pertains and we are required to police our thoughts for signs of political reaction. This is partly a product of sex's over-burdened significance within our culture, our insistence that we make of sex a special case. It is also a hangover from the feminist anti-pornography movement's insistence on a simplistic causality between fantasy and reality. Whatever its origins, this double standard has left us with a misunderstanding of the role of fantasy in sex with little room for manoeuvre.

Yet 'The Surprise Party' is a story which extends and complicates our understanding of fantasy as it operates within the literary text. A number of different levels of fictional reality are activated in this narrative which suggests the difficulty of forging a clear line between fantasy and reality without totally eliding the distinctions between the two. Within the narrative, we first see what we think to be reality brutally invading the reverie of the heroine as she is accosted by three policemen on the street. Reality here appears to intrude upon her private musing. Later, held captive in the police car, the woman finds herself in the morally dubious position of fantasising about the scene she unwillingly finds herself trapped within. Apparent reality provokes fantasy and finds itself in a problematic symbiosis with it. As the narrative progresses, we come to understand that the events depicted are not real 'in themselves', but are the fantasies of the woman, made real, staged for her benefit by police who are not police and acted out within a safe space, namely the consensual S/M encounter. Within the narrative, fantasy and reality thus find themselves in an increasingly complex dynamic with each other, within a relation which neither sets up a direct correlation between the two nor explains fantasy as being simply 'not real'.

The reader has a rather different relation to the text. As readers, we are reminded of our safety (we are reading a book) at the same time as our involvement is confirmed by our responses to the text (we are repulsed, scared, or perhaps aroused). Our distance from the narrative events alongside our participation as reader once again foregrounds the grey area between 'fantasy' and 'reality'.

What needs exploring is the psychological relation between fantasy and desire. This is on one level to ask why some fantasies involve experiences we would absolutely not want to see enacted in 'real life' but are prepared to explore as psychological realities. As Jessica Benjamin poses the question, it is to ask, 'What such fantasies mean and why they hold such power over the imagination'.[24] This is not to condemn but it is to question, to travel towards some understanding of the insistence of fantasy beneath the surface of everyday life. What is really called for is a non-pathologising exploration of the construction of sadomasochistic desire within the individual, an exploration that would be intent to discover as much why some individuals resist the S/M label as why some defiantly take it on.

But are there then no limits? Is everything open to appropriation, fodder for the individual fantasy? Theoretically, there need not be limits. As Stern explains, 'Phantasy, on the level of the Unconscious, does not make neat distinctions between sex and love, between clean and dirty, between pacifism and aggression' (p. 60). This can, however, often induce acute guilt on the conscious level. But one must not then make the leap to the argument that, although fantasy isn't real, it is culpable because it imitates actual events, in other words, that someone's fantasy is someone else's reality. For where content may parallel, context changes fundamentally. Since there is a totally different relation of agency and identity at work within the sexual fantasy, what looks like torture in fantasy bears no active relation to what torture means in reality. To argue it does is indeed to trivialise the fight against torture as it exists today in the world. This is not, however, to argue that our fantasies should be immune from analysis and criticism. When Califia's narrator voices her rhetorical plea, 'What broken-hearted prisoner does not love her torturer after a beating stops?' (p. 239), one is quite justified in demurring. Universalisations, in whatever form, are always susceptible to critique.

> Fiction *differs* from fantasy in that it is constituted by a process of telling, and in the process elicits a response, asks to be read, looked at, listened to, but not necessarily believed. It is also *related* to fantasy – not because it is a direct representation or manifestation, but in terms of function. (Stern, 'The Body as Evidence', p. 57)

Macho Sluts is a work of fantasy, not an instruction booklet.[25] However, *Macho Sluts* (no doubt much to the regret of some feminists – and to the delight of others) is not a private fantasy but a piece of writing making public statements, weaving its fantasies for public consumption. There is always a problem for the reader approaching the literary fantasy, which is that, as an independent cultural product, it may not always 'go' the way you want it to. This is of particular issue with the self-confessed erotic text since it so obviously solicits an effect. There is always the chance that this effect will not be forthcoming since fantasies, even the literary sort, are never universal in their appeal. Feminist readers of *Macho Sluts* may find themselves responding erotically to the text one moment and being repulsed by it the next. We may even wish to disavow our previous erotic response in the light of what we subsequently read. Still, we can surely recognise distaste as a justifiable response while avoiding the placing of a general judgement that a text is merely sick.[26] And of course, one can always alter the text to suit one's own desires. Califia as author is only too willing to open her work to this kind of appropriation. Indeed she positively encourages it.[27] The intersecting of literary fantasy and personal desire is nothing new. Texts always work alongside the individual imagining since 'Fiction is posited on pretence, but not a pretence of plenitude: instead of the image asserting its presence as the only possibility [...] it provokes other possibilities, substitutions' ('The Body as Evidence', p. 58). The reader's response is an active one not only in the sense of how she responds to the text (with desire, laughter, repulsion) but also in terms of what *she does* to the text, how she substitutes her desires for Califia's effects. Such substitutions would be in keeping with Califia's general cavalierism about textual and thematic appropriation. One of the most liberating aspects of *Macho Sluts* is the way it announces that desire does not have to be confined to one's active sexual preference. Lesbians do not have to be 'lesbian separatist masturbators' as Califia puts it (p. 16). Rather, we have endless possibilities for erotic fantasy.

> Hasn't anybody but me wondered why porn produced for lesbian consumption has to be about women only? If the point is simply to turn lesbians on, why limit our sexy literature to lesbian sex? Straights and gay men take it for granted that they can use material about other groups of people to turn themselves on. Why should lesbians get tied up in knots because we have straight fantasies, faggot fantasies, fantasies about animals, and intense fantasy relationships with shoes and other inanimate objects? (p. 16)

One of the fears is that non-lesbian readers will colonise such texts, appropriating them to their own designs. Califia's attitude to this possibility is direct: let them, she says, and we will appropriate back, using representation to undermine representation, turning the dominant back on itself.[28] This is a strategy claimed by Bette Gordon in her conceptualisation of her position after filming *Variety*, the film that succeeds where *Not a Love Story* so decisively fails. Says Gordon:

> I am interested in interrupting the conventions of dominant culture by twisting them around [...] I try to intervene with the way in which the dominant culture presents ideas [...] Other film-makers are interested in creating a separate or alternative feminist erotica. I am not, since that alternative suggests marginality [...] I don't want to maintain that outsided-ness [...] I prefer to work within and through the existing culture by challenging it, especially its constructions of sexuality [...] Pornography provides one more place to investigate how sexuality is constructed.[29]

This is also a strategy I would claim for Califia. What is central to such a strategy is that nothing should remain closed off to lesbians. As Califia insists, 'There ought not to be any subject that we cannot give our attention to', and as lesbians we must look at everything because it all requires transformation 'rearrangement' (p. 17). In this way we beat the dominant at his own game. Not in imitation (the old insult that we are really deluded by our own heterosexual oppression), but in order to take up the old forms (because there is nothing else) and transform them, reconstitute them into something positively, albeit momentarily, lesbian. This is not going to change the world or even for that matter the construction of sex and gender on the political or commercial scene. Different strategies are needed for this. Nor do I believe that this kind of parody has a political import merely *as* parody. It might after all never go anywhere but the bookshelf. But as a representative strategy, it does have some force for it sets up alternatives and allows women a choice. And this, in the face of ubiquitous restrictions on women from feminism as well as from society at large, must be a good thing.

I am not implying that the sadomasochistic relations described in *Macho Sluts* are simply in general better for being honest about their power dynamics (and about the pleasures that can be drawn from the consensual dramatisation of these). I would not wish to extend such a carte blanche to any kind of sexual expression. The claim that S/M merely expresses the old libertarianism of 'anything goes' is a common but facile one. I would rather argue along with Jana Sawicki that 'sex is a pluralism in which nothing goes' (p. 189). My argument thus rests implicitly upon the need to extend a general critique which includes every form of sexual expression, but which will also support and tolerate difference wherever it is found. What I am also arguing is that lesbian S/M as it is reflected in a text like *Macho Sluts* raises issues of importance to the feminist movement and that, as such, the book becomes something which it is surely feminism's task to defend.

Notes

1 See S. Ardill and S. O'Sullivan, 'Upsetting an Applecart: Difference, Desire and Lesbian Sadomasochism', *Feminist Review*, XXIII, 1986, pp. 31–57.

2 'Sado-masochism: The Erotic Cult of Fascism', *Lesbian Ethics*, II, 1986, pp. 65–82 (p. 68).

3 R. Linden et al., ed., *Against Sadomasochism: A Radical Feminist Analysis*, East Palo Alto, 1982, p. 138.

4 *The History of Sexuality: An Introduction*, trans. Robert Hurley, London, 1978, p. 159. There is another risk, as Foucault points out, in locating the 'truth' of one's identity in one's sexual orientation since it is a strategy that can be mobilised by the powerful as well as the weak. Thus, S/M liberationists may be externally constrained so that they are identified only in terms of their 'perversion' (the old category of sexology) while they make a similar claim for singular identification, but this time with the emphasis on their positive transgression of social, and feminist, sexual norms. That is, their practice is their politics is their identity. This is of course so simple an equation that it merely risks co-option by the forces that originally consigned sadomasochists to the realm of the perverse. That such identifications have been made on both sides of the feminist S/M debate is perhaps one of the reasons for the intense volatility of opinion and general contempt for the positions of others that has characterised it for so long. In making this point I do recognise the need to construct a strategic defence against the oppressive incursions of the state and other forces. There are many reasons to believe that in the face of new and more determined anti-S/M feeling it is wise to ensure a strong and vocal community which will defend group rights. But this is not the same as to invest in sexual behaviour as an identity per se. We must question this investment in totalising theories of the self *wherever* they occur.

5 For an expansion of this argument see M. McNair, 'The Contradictory Politics of SM', in S. Shepherd and M. Wallis, ed., *Coming on Strong*, London, 1989, pp. 147–61.

6 Curiously enough, in this sense S/M's understanding of sexuality is very like the revolutionary feminist theorisation of sexuality as a construction. Where the two theorisations do part company of course is in their understanding of how sex can be reconstituted through practice. S/M accepts that there are power dynamics in every sexual relation so the issue becomes one of how best to mobilise them in the most consensual and enjoyable way. Revolutionary feminism sees power differences as a factor of current sexual relations but believes it can reshape sexual practices to erase power. The problem with this conceptualisation is that it presumes either that we all have to stop having sex until society is transformed, or that the majority, still deluded into having patriarchal sex, must for the moment trust to the superior guidance of the elect few to demonstrate the way towards non-patriarchal sex.

7 See McNair, 'The Contradictory Politics of SM'.

8 See Ardill and O'Sullivan, 'Upsetting an Applecart'.

9 In 'Thinking Sex: Notes for a Radical Theory of Sexuality', in C. Vance, (ed.), *Pleasure and Danger*, Boston, 1984, pp. 267–319.

10 'Identity Politics and Sexual Freedom', in I. Diamond and L. Quinby, ed., *Foucault and Feminism*, Boston, 1988, pp. 177–91 (p. 182–3).

11 Quoted in Pat Califia, *Macho Sluts*, Boston, 1988, p. 24.

12 The relation is not necessarily an absolute one. The connection is, however, made in Dworkin's much touted correlation between pornography and male supremacy; see *Pornography: Men Possessing Women*, London, 1981.

13 This example is indicative: 'I've always wanted to see a man beaten to a shit bloody pulp with a high-heeled shoe stuffed up his mouth, sort of pig with the apple' (Dworkin, *Mercy*, London, 1990, p. 327). This is in response, to be sure, to a succession of horrifying episodes where violence is inflicted upon women. Still, one of the questions raised by the book is, how do such description differ from established violent porn? Namely, is Dworkin's conviction of the clarity of her own intentions enough to override the vagaries of reception in this instance?

14 *Macho Sluts*, Boston, 1988, p. 248. All further references are given in the text.

15 This is hardly a startling idea in the light of the recent lesbian reception, and celebration, of the film *Thelma and Louise*.

16 My working definition of sadism attempts to encompass both the variety of interpretations of the sadistic role within consensual S/M and the Freudian understandings of sadism and masochism utilised subsequently by Marion Bower. The two are not necessarily unrelated. Indeed, Freud's argument for the existence of both sadism and masochism in all individuals, regardless of their gender (see for instance, Freud, 'Three Essays on the Theory of Sexuality' in *On Sexuality*, trans. J. Strachey, London, 1977, pp. 72, 142) has interesting reverberations for a lesbian S/M that celebrates the 'switching of keys'.

17 'Feminism, Moralism and Pornography' in A. Snitow (ed.), *Desire*, London, 1984, pp. 82–8 (p. 85). Such fantasies would fit into what Marion Bower calls the contamination theory of fantasy whose best and earliest exponent is Susan Brownmiller. Brownmiller argues that: 'it is a rare woman who can successfully fight the culture and come up with her own non-exploitative, non-sadomasochistic, non-power driven imaginative thrust [. . .] stated another way, when women do fantasize about sex, the fantasies are usually the product of male conditioning and cannot be otherwise' (*Against our Will*, London, 1975, p. 360). While I would not wish to deny that fantasies are a product of social conditioning, to suggest that individual fantasies are wholly determined by patriarchy is not only profoundly disenabling to the subject fantasising but also risks the danger of falling into a pathologising psychology with its bandying of terms like 'healthy' and its implicit correlate 'sick' (see Brownmiller, p. 359).

18 'Daring to Speak its Name: The Relation of Women to Pornography' *Feminist Review*, XXIV, 1986, pp. 40–55 (p. 42).

19 *Pornography and Silence*, London, 1981.

20 'The Body as Evidence', *Screen*, XXIII, 1982, pp. 38–60 (p. 53). All further references are given in the text.

21 The betrayal of trust implied at the end of the story (Fran was not supposed to be so candid in her descriptions to Don) becomes an extension of the game as the story's heroine will be able not only to 'punish' Fran, but to return the challenge through Don's 'houseboy'.

22 Note that the *phantasy* invoked here is an unconscious one. Califia's subsequent use of the term on the other hand is in terms of a conscious working of *fantasy*. The distinction is formal and is not universally observed. Laplanche and Pontalis (who do not maintain the orthographic distinction) argue that in practice the distinction is of limited use when describing the workings of fantasy. They observe: 'the Freudian problematic of phantasy, far from justifying a distinction in kind between unconscious and conscious phantasies, is much more concerned with bringing forward the analogies between them, the close relationship which they share and the transitions which take place between one and the other' (J. Laplanche and J.-B. Pontalis, *The Language of Psycho-Analysis*, London, 1983, p. 317). One of the

difficulties encountered by feminists concerned to 'clean up' fantasy in order to ally its preoccupations with a conscious feminism is the intrusion of the unconscious with its not always obviously feminist desires. As Elizabeth Cowie wryly points out, unreconstructed desires cannot be removed by 'fiat' ('Fantasia', *m/f*, 1984, p. 71–104 (p. 72). Indeed their very ability to unsettle and destabilise our most trusted notions of ego identity testify to their power of insistence. On the other hand, as Freud points out, the debris of conscious life, 'the indifferent refuse left over from the previous day' (Freud, *The Interpretation of Dreams*, trans. J. Strachey, London, 1977) also has its part to play in the secretive workings of the unconscious.

23 I take the term *sexual fix* from Stephen Heath's book of that name, *The Sexual Fix*, London, 1982.

24 J. Benjamin, 'Master and Slave: The Fantasy of Erotic Domination', in A. Snitow, ed., *Desire*, London, 1984, pp. 292–311 (p. 308).

25 For this, see Pat Califia, *The Lesbian S/m Safety Manual*, Boston, 1988.

26 At this point it is pertinent to recall Gayle Rubin's words in 'Thinking Sex': 'Most people find it difficult to grasp that whatever they like to do sexually will be thoroughly repulsive to someone else, and that whatever repels them sexually will be the most treasured delight of someone, somewhere' (p. 283).

27 As when she encourages lesbian readers who are not turned on by descriptions of men to change the male characters to women in strap-ons.

28 This is considerably more effective a strategy than Alison Assiter's suggestion that we appeal to the good will of potentially hostile groups of readers in order to persuade them of 'the impropriety of "stealing" images from a feminist context' (Assiter, *Pornography, Feminism and the Individual*, London, 1989, p. 108). At the same time resistances can be set up within texts which render appropriation by other groups more difficult. It is after all the old criticism levelled at male heterosexual pornography that its images allow so little access to women. Such resistances can also be found in *Macho Sluts*. 'The Surprise Party' with its self-foregrounding lesbian and its three gay male protagonists does not allow easy access to the average heterosexual male!

29 'Variety: The Pleasure in Looking', in C. Vance, ed., *Pleasure and Danger*, pp. 189–203 (p. 194).

Messing around: gayness and loiterature in Alan Hollinghurst's *The Swimming-Pool Library*

Ross Chambers

In Alan Hollinghurst's *The Swimming-Pool Library*,[1] an ironic and witty novel of gay life, set in London during the summer of 1983, there is a fleeting Baudelairean moment – a kind of 'crépuscule du soir' – when the narrator–protagonist (I do not want to say hero), Will Beckwith, finds himself walking 'against the current' as city workers spill from a Tube station 'in the benign vastness of the evening', and contrasts himself, as a 'loafer', with this industrious crowd. 'And then I was a loafer who had hardly ever actually earned money, and they were the eager initiates, the coiners of power and the compromise in which I had unthinkingly been raised' (p. 314). I see here a generic clue: this passing reference to the *flâneur* tradition situates the novel as one of a very large number of texts which, since Sterne's *Tristram Shandy* and *A Sentimental Journey*, have constituted what I like to call the tradition of 'loiterature'.

Loiterature is a genre which, in opposition to dominant forms of narrative, relies on techniques of digression, interruption, deferral and episodicity (cf. the headless, tailless structure of Baudelaire's collection of prose-poems, *Le Spleen de Paris*) to make observations of modern life that are unsystematic, even disordered, and are usually oriented toward the everyday, the ordinary and the trivial (what is called '*flâneur* realism'). Meanwhile the observer himself – almost always a man – is self-presented as an engaging, entertaining ne'er-do-well, a descendant of the ancient *parasitus* and the early modern picaresque hero – a social misfit who, like the Rousseau of the *Reveries of a Solitary Walker*, has time on his hands and uses it to explore the sensations of the present, moment by moment, to recall the experience of the past (he is a man of memory), and to write. Loiterature has much in common with the punning concept of *désoeuvrement* ('idleness'), which Maurice Blanchot used to refer to the inevitable failure of writing, because of linguistic lack, to constitute an *oeuvre* (work);[2]

but the loiterateur is one who 'performs' such failure, and not for its
pathos, but as an oppositional comment on the ambitious pretensions
of aesthetic sublimity, and on the blindness, rigidity and exclusionary
formalism of disciplined and systematic modes of knowledge.[3]

It is as a performance of failure, but also for its insights into the
significance of such a failure, that *The Swimming-Pool Library* interests
me. The novel constructs a relation between its own diary-like structure, as a novel of day-by-day experience and of memory, its narrator's
easy-going and seductive, parasite-like personality, as one who says
'doing nothing ... kept me busy enough' (p. 6) and finally the oppositional status of gay men's sexuality in the 'man's world' of the
patriarchal social formation. In each of these respects – both textually
and sexually, if one will – it is a novel of compromise, for to be
oppositional, it suggests, is to fail in performing the radical acts that
would profoundly change the world, but to do so without, at the same
time, enjoying full integration into or identification with the structures
of power that make the world the way it is. The loiterer's 'work' –
in this case, the work of historical memory – turns out to reveal him
as a functional part of the social system that simultaneously constitutes
him as a misfit, so that his oppositional identity cannot be thought
heroic nor his writing classified as an *oeuvre*, in the sense that it
might *make a difference*. The irony of his 'crépuscule du soir' is then
that, even as he distinguishes himself from the 'alien breed', he
acknowledges kinship with the 'coiners of power' and recognises a
certain 'compromise' to which he has been educated, foreshadowing
in this way the painful discovery he is to make in the course of the
novel, through his exploration of the historical memory of gay men.
The 'benign vastness' of the social order has room not only for submissive workers but also for the more troublesome parasite, who
forms part of the total system, however much that system may treat
him, less than benignly, as 'the flower beneath the foot'.

This last phrase is the title of a Ronald Firbank novel that furnishes
The Swimming-Pool Library with its epigraph:

> 'She reads at such a pace', she complained, 'and when I asked her *where*
> she had learned to read so quickly, she replied on the screens at Cinemas.'

Were one to ask Hollinghurst's narrator, on the other hand, where he
learned to write so charmingly, he would doubtless respond: at the
Swimming-Pool Library, this being a reference to the tradition at his
prep school of calling prefects 'librarians' and to his own responsibility

for monitoring the pool, which he loved, however, as much for the
sexual goings-on in the changing room as for the swimming itself.
He has always had a 'vocation', in short, but it has been a vocation
for what he calls 'messing around' (p. 101): and so, in anti-Proustian
fashion, his writing is a defence and illustration of time lost – that is,
of time spent in 'doing nothing' and 'messing around' – rather than
of time regained. Literature in this book is *not* a way of redeeming a
life of time-wasting, and the novel, more particularly, is 'a book
about why I couldn't write the book' (p. 328) that would have had
such a redemptive function. Far from recruiting memory as a way of
rescuing some essential self from the dissolution of time, Will's
book is itself a book of days, an episodic quasi-diary that records in
apparently linear order the memories of one particular summer, a
work of loiterature without pretension to the status of *oeuvre*. But
the summer in question, 'the last of its kind there was ever to be'
(pp. 5–6), is worth writing about because this remembered summer
was the summer in which, precisely, the loafer was to discover the
dimension of memory and with it the historical condition of his kind.
Why that discovery should entail the inability to adopt a stance of
oppositional heroism or to write a book of redemption from time is
the question the novel invites us to consider.

The swimming-pool library of Will's childhood has its analogue
in the whole subterranean world of London's gay life, flowering beneath
the feet of the passers-by above and centred on the microcosmic space
of the Corinthian Club's basement pool, where 'men of all nations'
(the Club's motto) self-consciously or spontaneously display their
bodies and, surreptitiously or openly, cruise one another. Related
venues are the cellar-like disco called the Shaft, and even the Under-
ground itself, imagined by Will as 'sexy and strange, like a gigantic
game of chance, in which one got jammed up against many queer
kinds of person' (p. 55). But the phrase is completely literalised in
the library of Lord Nantwich's house in the City, which is situated
directly above a cellar containing remains that indicate it was once a
Roman bath; and it is here that the dimension of historical memory first
enters Will's experience of gay life, for Nantwich has symptomatically
adorned both library and cellar with a pornographic modern pastiche
of a classical priapic frieze ('Tom of Finland *avant la lettre*', Will
says); and the old man himself, who in 1983 is 83, has memories that
span the century.

It is in response to Nantwich's request to 'write about me' (p. 95)

that Will begins a lazy and random exploration of his voluminous
diaries and conducts some haphazard investigations among living
people who remember Nantwich's past. Like a Firbank character,
the old man is 'flighty and extravagant in the extreme', but, like a
Firbank novel, he is also 'as tough as nails' (p. 64) – he figures the old
queen as survivor, the 'belated' side of loitering whose 'dilatory' side
is represented by Will. It is Nantwich's account in his diary of his
school days, his Oxford years, his service in the Sudan with the
British colonial administration, the gay London of the 1920s, the
1940s and the 1950s that furnishes Will with a historical memory,
the last diary entry linking with the date of the younger man's birth
so as to extend the span of memory through to the 1980s at one end,
while it nostalgically reaches back at the other towards the 1880s,
the period Nantwich regrets having missed. Will Beckwith and Charles
Nantwich are alter egos, linked in particular, as fellow loiterers, by
their common love of 'swimming' and their taste for Black men, so
that between them – for Will too records his own memories of
school, university and the gay London of the 1980s – they document
the permanence of the 'swimming-pool' and its 'library' throughout
the history of modern England.

Like colonial Africa as described by Charles, the whole of London,
however, is a 'big public school' (p. 283); and, as in such schools, the
swimming-pool library is therefore part of a larger, less surreptitious,
above-ground world – one that is no less all-male, however, figured
as it is by Nantwich's segregated Club with its dining-room redolent
of stale cabbage and bad cooking ('some residual public school thing,
quintessential to Clubs, infected the atmosphere', p. 45). Mentioned
as mothers, sisters or wives, women are otherwise banished from this
segregated novel (although two washing-up women are given a line
of dialogue each on p. 226), with the result that there is a strong sense
of continuity between the 'Corry's' always ambiguously gay environment and the supposedly straight, but similarly equivocal, clothed
'world of jackets and ties, cycle-clips and duffel coats' (p. 20) above
ground.

The world of power, in short, is far from being discontinuous with
the world of the parasite. Thus the staff of Charles's respectable Club
furnishes the actors for pornographic movies, and the sleazy personage
who makes them turns out to be known to Will's straight brother-in-
law for his work on a neighbourhood committee 'about the traffic
and the one-way system' (p. 271) – perhaps not an entirely innocent

reference, if 'one-way system' refers playfully to compulsory heterosexuality. 'You know, some of us lot do have contacts with some of
you lot', says Gavin, who is attending a vernissage of soft-porn gay
photography thinly disguised as art and is, on that occasion, perhaps
the only straight person in the room. But at the Covent Garden
performance of *Billy Budd*, attended by Will and his friend James
with Will's grandfather, Lord Beckwith (the novel's figure of the
enforcement of heterosexuality), the relations are reversed: here it is
homosexuality in the audience, like the 'suppressed or ... deflected
sexuality' of the music (p. 140), that goes unacknowledged and ignored,
and a homophobic remark by the wealthy and powerful peer is allowed,
uncomfortably, to pass. 'The three of us in our hot little box were
trapped with this intensely British problem: the opera that was, but
wasn't gay, the two young friends on good behaviour, the mandarin
patriarch giving nothing of his feelings away' (p. 140).

Will has a sense that 'men really don't want women around much.
I think most men are happiest in a male world, with gangs and best
friends and all that' (p. 283); and the novel explores the paradox of an
officially heterosexual world in which men nevertheless prefer one
another's company, with the consequence that, like the Britten opera,
it has male homosexual desire as its profoundest but 'suppressed' and
'deflected' truth. This is the paradox that gives 'flaunted deviancy' –
such as Will and James enjoyed practising on the streets of Oxford
(p. 76) – its point and its power to disturb, a power now forgone by
James, who has become a hard-working doctor and joined the ranks
of repressed respectability, but still frequently practised by the scan-
dalously loiterly and outrageous Will. The same paradox, however,
accounts for the fact that, although the patterns of Will's scandalous
desire infringe the taboos of a class-conscious and racist power structure
(the 'boys' he falls in love with are exclusively working-class and for
preference Black), they also simultaneously reproduce that structure,
signifying his class-determined positioning within a system of power
that only his desire infringes.

The same is true of James, who subscribes to porn magazines put
out by a 'Third World Press' in Chicago, and of Charles Nantwich,
the 'light' of whose life is a Nuba boy whom he brought back to
London, but as his servant. It is Charles, too, who recalls the complicity
with which the Colonial Service recruited homosexual men, prone
as they were to 'immense idealism and devotion' (p. 282) – his long
years of service to the Empire, in short, betray a 'vocation' (p. 281) for

submission to the structures of power that is an exact counterpart of Will's 'vocation' for messing around, while James's selfless devotion to his patients provides another example of this other, 'service'-oriented side of gayness. The scandal of the gay man as cruisy loiterer and provocative queen is, somehow, *of a piece* with the service rendered by gay men in the world of power and the social formation at large; and the occasional jokes in the novel about the profession of being a 'waiter' (one of the stereotypical gay 'vocations') capture this ambivalence. A waiter both loiters and serves. In emblematic fashion but with sinister à-propos, Will's lover Phil works as a waiter at the Queensberry Hotel, named after the regulator of the boxing that is a mainstay of the boys' club Nantwich supports, but also after the persecutor of Oscar Wilde. The waiter is *available*, whether available for service or in the sense that the cruisy gay loiterer is 'available' – or whether available, finally, for repression and persecution.

Eve Sedgwick would describe the world of the novel, then, as 'homosocial'.[4] It is a world in which relations between men are mediated by women who – as a consequence of that mediating role – are excluded not from the total cultural system (which is one of compulsory heterosexuality) but from the workings of power. The appearance of homosexual desire in such a system therefore has the character of a parasitic disturbance in Michel Serres's sense of the term,[5] arising as unwanted 'noise', a by-product of the exclusion of women. But as such it also signals the very nature of the system itself, since the 'noise' produced in the area of desire by male homosexuality announces the repressed feminine mediation and signals its unwanted return, transformed, in the sphere of power. Homophobic repression of male homosexuality, and what Sedgwick calls 'homosexual panic' on the part of officially straight men, are counterparts, then, of the misogynistic exclusion of women from power; but whereas this exclusion is a systemic phenomenon, the repression of homosexual desire functions to contain a kind of 'local' disturbance arising sporadically and unpredictably, and dangerous only – but therefore also crucially – because of its power to reveal the system's nature.

To demonstrate, as *The Swimming-Pool Library* does, that such noise has been arising in the system, and being contained by it, over a period of a hundred years (or indeed much longer, if one takes account of Charles's Roman-era pool and the archaeological evidence of 'sun-worshipping' Pharaohs he shows Will at one point, p. 89) is to enlist the power of historical memory against the forces of repressive

containment. But it is also to recall the deep intrication of the noise
in the system with the system in which it arises, the inextricable
interdependence existing between them. I read the triangularity
of men's loves, as the novel presents it, as the sign of this interdependence of homosexual desire and the all-male world of homosociality. Will falls for Phil because he knows that Bill is drawn
to him (the similarity of the names shows that the men are each
other's alter egos); similarly, it is James's admiration for Colin that
produces Will's sexual interest in this man. At the vernissage, Will
thinks first of going home with a model named Aldo, is then attracted
to another, 'thick-set' man, and when – in one of the novel's funniest
but also most symptomatic moments – Aldo comes up to them and
says: 'Let's get going', '[i]t was only when the three of us were virtually
through the door that I realised his words had been addressed to
the thick-set man rather than to me' (p. 277). Needless to say, Phil
will eventually turn his attention to Bill, leaving Will as the excluded
mediator of *their* relationship.

There are two points here. One is that these mediating men can
be seen as stand-ins for the women who are absent from the novel,
although mentioned in it, just as they are excluded from the homosocial world: they are stand-ins for the absent go-between. This
substitutive role is demonstrated by the 'transsexual talk' that goes
on at the 'Corry', 'any man in the least attractive being dubbed
a "she" and only males too dire for such a conceit being left an
unadorned "he" or, occasionally, sinisterly, "mister" – as in the
poisonous declaration "I trust you won't be seeing Mister Elizabeth
Arden again?"' (p. 77). It is only inasmuch as they function as object
of desire (and so substitute for the homosocially excluded women)
that males qualify for the personal pronoun that reintroduces the
feminine gender into the situation.

But, as a result of such a substitution, in which it is men who
now stand in for disempowered women, male homosexual desire –
this is the second point – is itself mediated by the power from which
women are excluded and which thus determines its conception of
desirability: as a consequence it takes as its object images of power.
All the body-building and the preoccupation with cocks (preferably
large ones) at the Corry make this point readily enough; and so one
gets conversations like the following, quoted as typical, in which
athleticism and the feminisation of the object of desire go hand
in hand:

'You know that new girl behind the bar?' one square jawed athlete enquired
of his bearded companion.
   'What, the blonde, you mean – no, she's been there a while.'
   '*No*, not her, no, the dark one with the big tits.'
   'I'm not sure I've seen *her*. Nice, is she?' (p. 77)

But the implications of the mediation of gay desire by power are
most strikingly spelled out in the figure of Colin, the man desired
by both Will and James, for Will's brief encounter with Colin reveals
him to be, as he says to James, 'as queer as [...] me, you' (p. 260),
while James's adventure discovers him to be a policeman out to
entrap and arrest people like James. Colin thus stands for the homosexuality inherent in homosocial power, for the attractive role of
power as mediator of the desiring relations between men, and finally
for the homophobic repression on which the maintenance of the
homosocial order depends.

For, obviously, the other side of homosexual fascination with
power is homosocial fear and hatred of homosexuality, as the 'noise'
in the system that betrays the mediated character of homosocial
power. Venturing too far east in a search for his Black lover, Arthur,
Will is brutally beaten up by a group of skinheads, who combine
National Front racism with their homophobia (and who exemplify
the 'gangs' Will says men prefer to the company of women). This is
the flower beneath the foot with a vengeance: a beautiful first-edition
copy of that novel, given by Charles to Will who plans to give it to
James, is destroyed by the booted feet that simultaneously kick in
Will's ribs and break his nose, spoiling the beauty of which he is
vainly proud. And James's arrest by the erotically attractive Colin
replays the event of 1954 to which Will's exploration of homosexual
memory through Nantwich's diaries finally leads him, as the culmi-
nation of his investigations: Charles was himself entrapped by a
handsome policeman near a London 'cottage', and sentenced to six
months of sewing mail-bags. Furthermore, and to complete the sym-
metries, it was during his incarceration that Charles's beloved Taha
was beaten to death by a racist gang ...

These revelations of the danger to gay men of the power that is
simultaneously so attractive to them are completed, however, by
a final and traumatic discovery that awaits Will – the discovery of
his dependency, as a parasite, on that self-same homophobic power.
For the Director of Public Prosecutions of the day, the man who
'more or less sent [Nantwich] to prison' (p. 304) and personally,

vindictively attended the sentencing, was none other than Will's grandfather, Lord Beckwith, the 'mandarin patriarch' with whom Will and James attended the opera in their 'hot little box', whose elevation to the peerage closely followed the sentencing of Nantwich, and whose wealth it is that permits Will to enjoy the life of a loiterer.

The closely triangulated relation that is now displayed between Lord Beckwith, Will Beckwith and Charles Nantwich makes dramatically clear what the novel has been demonstrating all along, the interdependence of the parasite and of power. Will's wealth, and in particular the flat he lives in, comes to him from his grandfather; but the powerful man who indulges his idle grandson once persecuted that grandson's alter ego, the gay man who, rather than disturbing the system with 'flaunted deviancy', served the Empire devotedly. Each relation within the triangle is mediated by the third man: Will would not have discovered his parasitic relation to persecutory power without Nantwich's request to write about him, but the latter would presumably not have approached Will except for the Beckwith connection, figuring as it does the interrelatedness of the homosexual and the homosocial; while the relation between the two peers of the realm, figuring the power that joins heterosexual control and homosexual deviance, is mediated, finally and tellingly, by the parasitic Will, who is kin to the one and friend and alter ego of the other, his identity 'split' between them.

In standing for the intrication of the homosexual and the homosocial, Will simultaneously illustrates the curious rule of agency (known to us from the novels of John Le Carré), which states that every agent is, knowingly or unknowingly, a double agent: to oppose is to be part of what one opposes (but conversely – as the relation of the two peers suggests – to be part of a system of control is also to be in a position to disturb it). If culture is a phenomenon of mediation, the mediators who are its agents – we ourselves – are, in ways we may never fully recognise, both indispensable to its working and the site of inevitable disturbances that disrupt its dynamic of control and gradually change it.

But it is because of Will's double relation, as a cultural agent, to Lord Beckwith and to Lord Nantwich that he both *cannot* write the book that would redeem his own parasitic life and his friend's reputation, and yet *must* write the book 'about why I couldn't write the book', that is, the book of loiterature that we, as readers of *The Swimming-Pool Library*, hold in our hands. It is loyalty to Lord

Beckwith and the 'compromise' in which he has been 'unthinkingly' educated that makes it impossible for Will to write the memoir of Charles's life and times that would vindicate the humiliated and scapegoated peer, symbolically replicating his first act in the novel, when he gives mouth-to-mouth resuscitation and breathes life back into Charles (who has suffered cardiac arrest in a 'cottage'). The scandal of the gay grandson's redeeming the homophobic grandfather's victim cannot be contemplated, and thanks to the 'compromise' in which he has been brought up, Will does not have that form of heroism. But it is loyalty to Charles that requires Will nevertheless to write what he can, and to give an account of what he has learned.

His final 'realisation about life' is the one he had had some present-iment of on the very day of the mouth-to-mouth rescue, a 'realisation [...] obscurely disagreeable and perhaps deserved' (p. 7); and it is the realisation of the parasite's complicity with the power that oppresses him. But this in turn is the very complicity that prevents Will from writing the book that would attack the world of power openly and vindicate its victim, so that it is this loyalty to Charles, as it is inhibited, however, by the parasite's loyalty to patriarchal power (to the homosocial system to which he owes his gay identity), that is readable in the form of the book Will actually writes – not a redeeming *oeuvre* but a work of loiterature and *désoeuvrement* or 'worklessness' – whose episodic, counter-narrative structure is determined by the unwillingness of its protagonist to be a hero, to exert a 'will' of his own. Will's book does not only incorporate long extracts from Nantwich's diary but itself has the form of a diary, simultaneously espousing the dailiness of the loiterer's life in its dilatory, time-wasting, episodic form, and registering memories of its own that extend the belatedness of those registered by Charles. Such a book, by its avoidance of narrative closure, can only confirm the parasite's 'vocation' both for 'messing around' and for dependency on the 'host'; it cannot free him, therefore, of the distressing implications of his work of memory.

For diary-like as it is, the novel is written in a nostalgic, Proustian 'imperfect' tense, the past indefinite of memory: 'My life was in a strange way that summer, the last summer of its kind that was to be. I was riding high on sex and self-esteem – it was my time, my *belle époque* – but all the while with a faint flicker of calamity [...]. I'd surrendered to the prospect of doing nothing, though it kept me busy enough' (pp. 5–6). It is certainly not inappropriate to read into this reference to the 'last summer of its kind' – as the blurb-writer for my edition does – an allusion to AIDS, thereby producing the novel as a sort of document and, like Charles's diaries, a memorial to a period in gay life that is now part of the historical memory. But the metaphor of the *belle époque* should alert us to the danger of putting too precise and local a historical interpretation on the passage, suggesting as it does a certain continuity of gay existence since the period of the formation of modern male homosexual identity. And, it is suggested also, what makes for such continuity is precisely the 'faint flicker of calamity' that is in Will's consciousness here, 'like flames around a photograph, something seen out of the corner of the eye' (p. 6). But this flicker in turn is none other than the 'realisation, disagreeable and perhaps deserved' that makes the conscience of the parasite so uncomfortable a place when its memories turn out to include one that tells of its own complicity with controlling power.

If, in short, it is the vocation of the parasite to be a man of memory, what he recalls is inevitably a reminder of that which, at the edge of his consciousness, he can never quite forget: his compliance with the 'compromise in which [he has] unthinkingly been raised', the compromise that makes him the parasite of power. Beyond the suggestive equivalence of (gay male) sexuality and (loiterly, unheroic) textuality in Hollinghurst's novel, one might conclude that loiterature itself, as *désoeuvrement*, recalls the general rule of agency: we cannot be the 'author' of an *oeuvre* because authorial agency is blind to the ways in which it subserves cultural forces that are beyond its ken. Like Will between Lord Beckwith and Lord Nantwich, the loiterly parasite exists to remind us, inconveniently but incontrovertibly, of that fact.

Notes

1 Alan Hollinghurst, *The Swimming-Pool Library*, London and New York, 1989. Page numbers in parentheses refer to this edition.
2 See Maurice Blanchot, *The Space of Literature*, trans. Ann Smock, Lincoln, Neb., 1982. Smock discusses the translation of *désoeuvrement* on p. 13. In *Lost beyond Telling*, Ithaca, 1990, Richard Stamelman translates it as 'worklessness' (p. 46).
3 This essay is part of a work in progress on loiterature, and the definition proposed here is a partial one only.
4 See Eve Kosofsky Sedgwick, *Between Men: English Literature and Male Homosocial Desire*, New York, 1985 and *Epistemology of the Closet*, Berkeley, 1990.
5 See Michel Serres, *The Parasite*, trans. Lawrence Schehr, Baltimore, 1982.

So what's all this about the mother's body? The aesthetic, gender and the polis

Isobel Armstrong

Prologue. Blake: the aesthetic belongs to Hell

Blake calls the Proverbs of Hell 'sayings' which mark the 'character' of Infernal culture, and which provide the anthropologist of the infernal regions with an understanding of Hell's national identity. Two sayings in particular offer a laconic comment on a product of the late Enlightenment, a new European/infernal category, the aesthetic:

> The head Sublime, the heart Pathos, the genitals Beauty, the hands and feet Proportion.
> Exuberance is Beauty.

Hell is creative and destructive – in Blake's terms, Prolific and Devouring. On the one hand, a new, 'Prolific' language of the beautiful is being created. On the other hand, the body is mapped and charted, repressively ordered into zones and hierarchies. The zone of the sublime is the head, reason, from which both Kant and Burke explicitly excluded women. The head is separated from the heart, the region of pathos, that new affective area of imaginative empathy which, from Shaftesbury on, was to act as the unifying social bond – I understand your suffering through imagining myself in your place. Intuition, not thought, directs social feeling, both assuaging absolutist law and creating a bourgeois subject capable of checking the unbridled desires of the individual self. Beauty belongs to the zone of the genitals because, from the eighteenth century on, the Beautiful was emphatically gendered. For Burke, the Beautiful is associated with the social, and the social is founded on sexual feeling and the desire for procreation. Women, weak, passive, melting, belong to the genital zone because they arouse sexual feeling, not because they experience it. As well as delimiting the erotic, the genital is the source of sensation and somatic life, the world of sensory experience which was beginning, through philosophers such as Hume, to be appropriated for a new sceptical epistemology. Classical proportion is displaced to the hands and feet, reduced to the status of the artefact, the material object at the base of a hierarchical, idealist world. And proportion is also mechanised, product of the 'hands' which are utilised in the division of labour, a division founded on the fragmentation of functions which are inscribed on Blake's partitioned body. Finally, 'Exuberance' is invoked to redress the alienation created by these newly configured parts – energy, creativity, self-delight. Beauty becomes an emancipatory concept, as Blake's proverbs challenge or redress one another. But this is emphatically a Proverb of Hell because the aesthetic escapes from the ethical: it need not belong to the moral order, it can be neutral, it can belong to evil. In its pure self-justifying freedom it is severed from the ethical and may even do violence to it.

But while Blake's beautiful *can* be emancipatory (another reason, of course, why it belongs to Hell), current thinking on the left generally views the category of the aesthetic as, if not fraudulent, deeply suspect. Terry Eagleton's *The Ideology of the Aesthetic*, a study of the category of the aesthetic in post-Enlightenment Europe, for which Blake's two proverbs might have stood as epigraph, is an example of such thinking, despite some gestures to the contrary. It offers a powerful reading of the aesthetic – the book enabled me, for instance, to read Blake's proverbs afresh – but it is pessimistic on the whole. Can the aesthetic be reclaimed for radical thought? Need it be handed over to the right? Can it be reclaimed for feminist thought and praxis? I begin by taking issue with Eagleton's argument (worth challenging because this is a brilliant book), particularly his chapter on Kant, as a preliminary to setting out an alternative account of the aesthetic and the polis.

The ideology of the aesthetic and the seductions of the imaginary

Eagleton's Kant chapter leads up to a moment he seems to have been waiting for, pliant, to be toyed with in the moment of primary narcissism:

> What else, psychoanalytically speaking, is this beautiful object which is unique yet universal [...]? The beautiful representation, like the body of the mother, is an idealised material form [...] with which, in a free play of its faculties, the subject can happily sport. The bliss of the aesthetic subject is the felicity of the small child playing in the bosom of its mother,

enthralled by an utterly indivisible object which is at once intimate and
indeterminate, brimming with purposive life yet plastic enough to put
up no resistance to the subject's own ends. (p. 91)

So that was it after all: the work of Kant's aesthetic comes to this –
the omnipotent infant using for its own purposes the mother's body
and its illusory plenitude and false unity. Kant's imaginary, it is
assumed, will stand as a paradigm for the aesthetic in general. What
is interesting is not that Kant is shackled to the mother's body
(the founding moment of relationship with the mother's body can
perfectly well belong to an account of the aesthetic, as I show later),
but that Eagleton seems to think this is the worst thing he can say
about the aesthetic. Not only does he retain without questioning
(if the irony of the passage is intended to question, it does not work) the
insistently denigrating Enlightenment connection of the aesthetic and
the feminine, but in invoking Lacanian and Althusserian parallels he
manages to ontologise these psychoanalytical structures as universals.

What got into him? Such a clever book, using all the resources of
the aesthetic so exuberantly, has rarely been written on a topic so
uncongenial, so repugnant to its author. While saying that he is
liberating the category of the aesthetic from those on the left for
whom it is simply 'bourgeois ideology' (p. 8), he puts it pretty firmly
back there, and admits that his project is 'hardly' one of the most
urgent facing the Left (p. 11). The first part of the book is actually
a skit on the aesthetic as the product of liberal humanist ideology.
But Marx, who believed passionately in the aesthetic, is a problem,
and will not be assimilated into this Marx Brothers' intellectual slap-
stick or its compulsively carking ironies. So the scene of masquerade
gives way, in the last part of the book, to some of Eagleton's best
critique ever, from Heidegger to Adorno, Freud to Foucault.

Sharing with Derrida and de Man (a strange meeting of the ideologi-
cally incompatible) a thoroughgoing dislike of the category of the
aesthetic, Eagleton is far more insistent than they are, or in de Man's
case ever could be, that a black line runs from the earliest explorations
of the aesthetic in Baumgarten to fascism. He sometimes argues as if
the aesthetic *produced* fascism. Implicit in his discussion is Benjamin's
admonition, that the documents of civilisation are the documents of
barbarism, and Adorno's belief that art after Auschwitz is impossible.
True, this is something we need to be constantly reminded of: the
Gulf War, closely following upon Eagleton's book, produced a coolly

technologised aesthetic destruction on television screens, as smart bombs, autotelic, self-maintaining, like the Kantian aesthetic subject in free play, found their targets.

Eagleton's is a worst-case reading, and has to be attended to. But the best answer to this case might well be to retheorise a flagrantly emancipatory, unapologetically radical aesthetic. This would refuse the conservative reading of the aesthetic as that which stands over and against the political as disinterested Beauty, called in nevertheless to assuage the violence of a system it leaves untouched, and retrieve the radical traditions and possibilities with which the idea of the aesthetic has always been associated. I would regard with dismay a politics which subtracts the aesthetic and refuses it cultural meaning and possibility.

Moreover, it is the aesthetics of Enlightenment Europe, as Eagleton discloses, which first made gender apparent, first made the feminine visible, as a topos in philosophical discussion, albeit as a means of severely restricting the definitions of sexual difference, a limitation of which Blake's proverbs are aware. So a consideration of the aesthetic and the polis must include the category of gender. Without it, we have no means of grasping our history, no means of grasping, analysing and understanding those massive energies of cultural production which are apparently non-instrumental (to put it in the most neutral way). Not to have conceptual tools is disabling. Feminists themselves have enumerated the dangers of an analysis of a gendered aesthetic: the pursuit of an illusory essentialist thoery, naturalising and dehistoricising the constructed category of art, and the privileging of a merely formal avant-garde textual subversion as the site of the semiotic, consent to the false hierarchy of fine art and mass culture. But this should not prevent us from considering the part gender has played in the evolution of the aesthetic, or speculating on what part it will play in the future.

What is wrong with the aesthetic

According to Eagleton, two things are wrong with the aesthetic. First, like a kind of deadly virus, the aesthetic will show up in bourgeois culture only when it is combined with something else, confounding what hosts it. It is viscous enough as a concept already: the *process* of creation, the art object, the experience of its reception, the theorising of it as concept and praxis – all these are comprehended in the term *aesthetic*. But for Eagleton the aesthetic is positively *runny*. It is both everywhere and nowhere. It secretly confounds the distinction between fact and value (because it manipulates affect). It collapses sign and thing (because it proposes to fuse representation with what is represented in organic unity). It dissolves cognition and percept (because it slides particulars under the concept and substitutes them for it). It plays havoc with the separate realms of the cognitive, ethical and political, making them permeable by aestheticising them, so that they are commonly grounded in the aesthetic rather than in propositionality. It pretends to be itself while infiltrating the fiercely contested categories of bourgeois thought – freedom, legality, self-determination, necessity. It adopts the appearance of standing over and against power while being the very essence of the mystified power by which hegemony maintains itself. The virtuosic feats of hegemony, that look-no-hands trick by which hegemony makes people do what it wants by persuading them that they are doing it voluntarily, are performed through the aesthetic.

If hegemony wants a new, free, independent bourgeois subject to facilitate economic competition, the aesthetic offers a pure model of free, self-referential, autotelic, autoaffective being in the work of art in order to lull the conscience of the new subject. If hegemony wants a paradigm of exchange which enables a formal equivalent between human beings and commodities to be developed for the needs of the market place, then the aesthetic will do the reverse of endorsing a full individual subject and make the individual into an abstract entity to provide a model for the capitalist economy of exchange. The aesthetic is always on hand to become a kind of phantom proxy for whatever manoeuvre hegemony conducts. Indeed, it *is* ideology. And because ideology requires a scene of seduction in which the fierceness of power and the brutality of capital can be disguised, hegemony brings on the dancing girls. The aesthetic is a woman. That is the second thing wrong with it.

Here aesthetic epistemology becomes not a paradigm of political structures but an *allegory* of them, not the cause or consequence of the bourgeois/capitalist order, not an element belonging to a material or intellectual structure but an active *agent* in complicity with hegemony, also heavily personified. As naturalising allegoriser, Eagleton not only abolishes the saving conceptual distance which makes critique possible but also accepts the feminine as a marked term (bound up in European accounts of the aesthetic almost from the start) without the grounding of historical explanation. Indeed, he appears to believe that an account of the aesthetic in terms of the feminine *is* a historical explanation. True, inverted commas sometimes surround 'feminine' as a deconstructive gesture but investigation goes no further and he stays with the essentialist feminine. Happiest and at his most lovingly sardonic with those grumpy fellow-allegorisers of, respectively, the Will and the Ironist, Schopenhauer and Kierkegaard, he passes lightly over Kierkegaard's phallophile vengeance on the woman's body, his figuring of woman as sickness. One impetus of the aesthetic in the Enlightenment, the redistribution of gender character-istics across the sexes, and the material explanation for this, gets scant enquiry.

What is wrong with Kant?

Kant instigates the true aesthetic subject of bourgeois ascendancy, the first genuinely hegemonic aesthetics, as opposed to the tyranny which directly controls its subordinates, figured as the unruly somatic life of the body, implicitly the male body. So Kant's aesthetic has to account for, or display, bourgeois ideology, bourgeois morality and bourgeois commodity in homologous relationship. The ruling order, Eagleton says, *needs* Kant's epistemology: it needs a persuasive account of freedom which masks the manoeuvres of the ideology of private capital. The self-identical law of the one, producing the autotelic and abstract free play of the aesthetic as an end in itself, is in dialectical relationship with a regressive, atavistically narcissistic individualist subject which must 'coopt reality' (p. 91) to its own purposes. This individualism is surreptitiously slipped under the protection of the disinterested activity of the aesthetic subject.

Kant, read as cultural symptom, is one of the main actants in the bourgeois farce described in the first part of this book. Thus to remind oneself that Kant's was one of the earliest attempts to see the political and cultural problems around the changed relations between the new civic individual and the modern state, for instance, or the problems around rationality and representation, would be to confuse the genre of the discussion. Systematic, almost coercive, misprision (a little heavy for farce) is part of the game. Nevertheless, it is possible to say that Eagleton constantly situates Kant in comic dilemmas which

Kant has already systematically allowed for: furthermore, in his anxiety to align and critique the seductions of commodity and ideology with Kant's aesthetic, he forces Kant's unwilling texts towards the pleasure principle, ignoring a much more fundamental critique, the connection between the aesthetic and *violence*.

The culminating critique of Kant's aesthetic is that it provides a structure for, and consents, to ideology by privileging concrete particulars which are universalised. The Kantian subject (seen overdramatically) is a split and agonistic being, opening up a series of self-perpetuating fissures which the sensuous and affective life of the aesthetic is invoked to assuage. Thus 'sensus communis', which Eagleton interprets as community of *feeling*, is invoked to assuage both the divided subject, unable to comprehend either itself or the object except in terms of property, and the class division which is a corollary of this state. Acting as a point of exchange between subjects as the only 'non-alienated object' available in society, the aesthetic acts as a 'spiritualised commodity' (p. 78) by the very fact of exchange, thus mystifying the relation between fact and value. A series of consequential and homologous splits opens up, parallel to this 'real' and transcendental commodity: between the phenomenal and the noumenal, between the instrumental and the pure, between the activity of purposeful subordination and the non-purposive end in itself, between the practical and the transcendental, between the free play of formal, abstract morality as pure *Law* on the one hand and nature and praxis on the other. Just like the 'spiritualised commodity' of the aesthetic this pure law of the transcendental signifier, depending on the self-identical one, forces individuals under the same formal category to facilitate contractual exchange. The aesthetic replaces this unbearable totality with immediacy and the manifold concrete. It heals these fractures by persuading us that, like a commodity, the world is *made* for us.

Eagleton does not pause to consider that the Enlightenment move towards parity and exchangeability also instigates the idea of the vote, democracy and representation, but hurries on to the marriage of ideology and the aesthetic. The concrete manifold of the aesthetic, having no access to the concept possessed by transcendental law, can only mimic the form of reason, not the content. Like ideology it slips the concrete under the general. It ignores the *propositionality* of reason, raising the individual to the universal, generalising concrete particulars and short-circuiting the conceptual.

That Kant painfully unpicks the relation between the cognitive and the concrete manifold of the aesthetic and its representations, that he attributes to the orator precisely the short-circuiting of the concept at work in ideology (we can use *reason*, he thinks, to get at this) need not concern Eagleton. He is attending to symptomatic structures rather than to particular arguments. But he is enthralled by the structure of seduction, by Kant's pleasure principle, whereas it is precisely the connection of the aesthetic with the death wish, or with mourning, at least, which is striking in Kant. Containment, stasis, the refusal of difference, is the essence of his aesthetic. The republican potential and critique available to the aesthetic must be muted to individual self-fulfilment in a civic society with 'a low degree of civil freedom'; and if that individualism shows its inbuilt tendency for violence in those 'not capable of *managing* freedom' (my emphasis), then state violence is on hand to manage it with a standing army. This is the modern aesthetic state, and it is worth investigating further.

But bourgeois aesthetics, morality, commodity, ideology, are not connected with transcendental phallic law here. No, it is the mother's body and a founding narcissism which is responsible for all this. Only a Kleinian anger, the infant's resentment of the mother's witholding, could find this explanation plausible.

The fear of metaphor

Can this chapter be right about Kant? But this is not the question to ask: it would be better to ask, why does Kant have to mean this in Eagleton's text? The detour of a parenthesis suggests an answer to the first question: the second demands the first of a series of speculative propositions and zig-zags.

(To begin with the 'Sensus communis': surely this is not the assuaging reciprocity of community (a sentimental account), where class is muted, but an appeal to universal standards of taste, which are the decisions of a social elite? The aesthetic inheres in *taste*, not in the object. Therefore agreement about the rules (and who makes them) is essential, reinforcing rather than assuaging division. This is one of the many occasions on which, in order for the chapter's argument to be sustained, it has to soften the rigidity – the often cold and rather coercive rigidity – of Kant's distinctions. Kant keeps apart the aesthetic idea and the rational idea, just as he

keeps apart representation and nature and art and nature. When he argues
that the imagination puts ideas into motion by quickening the cognitive
faculty; or that the imagination borrows a second nature out of nature,
re-modelling it in a constructed representation; or that the work of art
may *look* like nature but is ordered with a self constituting power which
nature does not possess (para. 49), he is writing with an understanding
of the separateness of these categories in order to sustain the connection
between representation and the aesthetic. An account of representation
does not collapse into ideology but becomes a tool for analysing it. The
problem seems to be the reverse of this chapter's complaint and lies in
the stiffness of Kant's exclusions rather than in a permeable narcissistic
relationship of consciousness and the mother's body: the aesthetic object
is oneness and unity in self-maintaining free play all right, but because
it brings together categories in a static way, without changing them, it
belongs to the phallic one of the self-identical subject rather than to the
imaginary. It *does* matter, and is a crucial difference between the two thinkers,
that Lacan's *subject* experiences lack in the mirror stage but that in Kant's
epistemology the *object* is so often drained of coherence. Lacan's subject
has no sense of the other but the Kantian subject has only too much sense
of the alien and *abstract* other lying outside it, which maintains the subject's
oneness only because it is so thoroughly separate, has been so thoroughly
expelled.)

To cut to Derrida, whose 'Economimesis' in some ways pre-
empts the discussion in *The Ideology of the Aesthetic*: both texts,
in inverse but parallel ways, are intrigued to the point of fascination
with an aesthetic of the one. For Derrida, the self-identical one of
the symbolic order defends itself with nausea against that which
might force it to entertain difference, whereas in *Ideology* the narcissistic one is arrested indivisibly in unity with the mother's body
at the level of the imaginary. In transcendental work over and against
the economic (Derrida's Kantian subject hierarchises play over work
and the salaried subject who is marked by class), the aesthetic labours
on the exclusion of heterogeneity. In an expressive model of taste
predicated on distaste, the aesthetic subject spews forth in untrans-
cendental vomit that which might entertain difference, the other.
The work of mourning, Derrida says, in one of those brilliant insights
he forgets to follow up, is too easily foreclosed, too easily elided
with the self. But for *The Ideology* the work of mourning has never
begun because the narcissistic aesthetic subject, in a reverse but
structurally parallel movement, has fused the other with itself.

Connect this with Paul de Man and his resistance to the Romantic
metaphor and symbol which, he thinks, has an essentially narcissistic

structure. Metaphor fuses mind and world, sign and thing, cognition and percept, in an illusion of unity. Connect this also with a recent extrapolation of both Derrida and de Man to the colonial subject, product of the Kantian exclusion of difference as a positive marker. A formidable unanimity emerges. David Lloyd has recently brought Derrida and de Man together to argue that the Kantian aesthetic produces the colonial subject through the self-identical phallic one because racial difference is excluded as an aspect of the exclusion of heterogeneity. He connects this with a valorising of metaphor in terms of its capacity to produce 'likeness' between categories. The project of metaphor is to elide rather than separate the unlike: 'Whiteness is the metaphor for the metaphorical production of the Subject as one devoid of properties rather than the natural sign of difference' (p. 77).

So metaphor both produces and is produced by the self-identical subject. Narcissism, class, racism: are they all to be founded on the totalising unity of metaphorical activity? Is the aesthetic to produce and be produced by metaphor? Can such opprobrium be heaped upon a trope?

There is an overdetermined and deeply contradictory anxiety about the law of the one and its connection with the aesthetic. At the same time as the law of the one is accepted as a kind of tragic necessity, phallic fate, reintroducing itself at all levels – in the imaginary, even, whose narcissism strangely mimics it, in the cultural order, in language – it appears to be *produced* and sustained by its opposite. The aesthetic is feared as the collapse and elision of categories, as a permeable, dissolving meltdown of difference in the law of the same: the threat of metaphor. Phallic self-identity is at one and the same time shored up and undermined by the aesthetic figuring as metaphor.

Does metaphor trope woman for these writers? Is it the threat of the feminine for them? Hence their opprobrium and anxiety. This is why it is not necessary to ask, is this really what metaphor is about? For the fear of metaphor is performing the work of repression.

(A parenthetical question: Is this powerful convergence of so many masculine texts in the anti-aesthetic related to the present historical moment of feminist thought? This massive attack coincides with the last twenty years, when women's creativity has burgeoned, and aesthetic artefacts, writing and cultural production have been a huge part of the feminist agenda and the energies which have created a feminist counter public sphere. This attack has occurred just when aesthetic productions have been politicised for feminist emancipatory writing, just when discursive networks of feminist production have challenged the managed society, establishing a form of communality despite the fragmentation of feminisms. This is a proper question, not a recrimination, for the project of reclaiming the aesthetic for the left is as important as reclaiming it for feminism: the two are bound together.)

But what does metaphor do? And why is it so closely connected with the aesthetic? Abandon the view of metaphor as deliquescence, the fatal weakening of distinction into likeness. The play of *unlikeness* is essential to metaphor. Some people, including Paul Ricoeur, think that metaphor is about the transformation of categories, not their reconciliation. It is interesting that Lloyd rather wilfully misreads Ricoeur here, forcing an account of metaphor as the one. And yet Ricoeur explores metaphor as a transformation, a discovery of new meaning, new *categories* so important that metaphor is a prerequisite for cognitive thought. 'A tear is an intellectual thing' – Blake makes a stark categorical contradiction here. The precipitation of mental anguish runs down the face as a fluid, pain's material form secreted from the body. Blake's statement arrests with the shock of difference. A tear is expelled (we think of Derrida again) as an *expression* of the body but it is not mere salt water because it *is* grief, and without the tear grief could not find expression, nor could grief begin to understand itself (compare vomit). The puzzling junction of bodily and mental experience is being explored here.

Metaphor is a test case of the aesthetic because it has to do with the questioning of categories. But it is not the aesthetic itself. What would another account of the aesthetic for the left and for feminism look like?

Towards a new aesthetic

First, L. S. Vygotsky (1896–1934), whose work circulated in the 1950s and 1960s in Western Europe. Some core texts are translated in *Mind in Society* (1978). Second, D. W. Winnicott (1896–1971), whose *Playing and Reality* (1971) collected essays from the 1950s on. One a Marxist, one a psychoanalyst, both see *play* as a central activity for investigation. The writings of both, significantly, emerge at the beginnings of the post-war managed society, at the moment when capitalism begins to colonise the life world of individuals ever more systematically.

Play, that fundamental activity, is cognate with aesthetic production. It is part of a vital continuum. I understand play not as a simple binary set against work, not as a hierarchy of activity (as in Schiller) subordinating work, not as an epistemological hierarchy subordinated to knowledge (as often in Kant), but as a form of knowledge itself. Interactive, sensuous, epistemologically charged, play has to do with both the cognitive and the cultural.

How does Vygotsky help?

For him, play is not a symbolic system (as in the translations of abstract geometry). Nor is it an alternative world (an escape), for play and reality often coincide. Sisters play at being sisters, mother is made to play at being mother, playing 'what is actually true' (p. 94). Play is rule-bound. Imaginary situations contain rules of behaviour, and 'every game with rules contains an imaginary situation' (p. 95). Play sets up a constant dialectic between rules and freedom. It is thus a constantly questioning activity. But, more than this, it is only in play that it is possible to make an essential cognitive leap which radically changes one's relation to reality.

Children live in a world of immediacy, unable to separate the visual field from the field of meaning. But in play 'things lose their determining force'. It is the experiment of play alone which 'enables the child to act independently of what she sees' (p. 96). Play achieves an extraordinary reversal, a transformation of the very structure of perception. When one thing begins to stand for another (a stick for a horse), that thing becomes a 'pivot' for severing the idea of a horse from the concrete existence of the horse, and the rule-bound game is determined by ideas, not by objects. Play liberates the child into ideas, into an understanding of categories and their *relation* to objects:

A divergence between fields of meaning and vision first occurs at preschool age. In play thought is separated from objects and action arises from ideas rather than things: a piece of wood begins to be a doll and a stick becomes a horse. Action according to rules begins to be determined by ideas and not by objects themselves. This is such a reversal of the child's relation to the real, immediate, concrete situation that it is hard to underestimate its full significance. The child does not do this all at once because it is terribly difficult for a child to sever thought (the meaning of a word) from object. (p. 98)

The pivotal object is fundamental in providing a transitional stage in cognitive discovery. It is not a substitute, not an abstraction (the emphasis is not on Lacanian absence): there is still a horse in the stick. It is not metaphor either, because it is bound up with immediate material objects, though it is functionally akin to metaphor:

> Play provides a transitional stage in this direction whenever an object (for example, a stick) becomes a pivot for severing the meaning of a horse from a real horse. The child cannot as yet detach thought from object. The child's weakness is that in order to imagine a horse, he needs to define his action by means of using 'the-horse-in-the-stick' as pivot. But all the same, *the basic structure determining the child's relation to reality is radically changed at this crucial point, because the structure of his perceptions changes* (p. 98) (my emphasis)

The child is separating itself out from the world but not escaping from it. It is a materialist and a cognitive account of play. The horse–stick is a pivot for remaking categories and for discovering new perceptions. The stick–horse makes a space which redefines one's relationship to the world and the world itself.

'A child's greatest self control occurs in play' (p. 99), Vygotsky says. At the same time, play is liberating through its capacity to be interactive: because the child can create an alienated meaning within the constraints of a specific, concrete situation, play occupies 'the realm of spontaneity and freedom'. This is not simply a semiotic space for subversion/freedom any more than it can be the experience of omnipotence. Nor is it that Kantian form without content, particulars divorced from concepts. It is a cognitive negotiation. Spinoza provides Vygotsky with the notion of 'an idea which has become a desire, a concept which has turned into a passion'. A new perception actually ignites desire and desire creates the possibility of new perceptions, constantly discovering new thresholds of experience. (Elsewhere Vygotsky describes intellectual growth in terms of a zone of proximal development in very much the same way.)

Of course, I am reading Vygotsky partly against the grain. There are repressive implications to his thought. Play is ultimately 'a rule that has become desire' (p. 99), and the experiment that has brought about a 'new relation' can be made to perform the function of cultural conditioning. A child grows out of play – it transfers to the world of work all that it has discovered. Play is a transitional stage between the situational constraints of childhood and the freedom of the adult and leads straight to work, to compulsory activity based on rules – and to competitive games. But Vygotsky does make play intrinsic to cognitive experience: the function of the essentially double-sided pivotal object (the aesthetic object?), acting within the constraints of material experience yet able to envisage new categories, emancipates us from the tyranny of the one and the primal ooze of the imaginary. And it is in itself emancipatory.

The piece of blanket and the stick–horse

How does Winnicott help?

He redresses some of Vygotsky's limitations. For example, it is crucial that play continues into adulthood. *Playing and Reality* seeks to find in play a non-orgiastic, non-omnipotent experience (Winnicott insists that he is not writing about narcissism), an intra-subjective space in which meanings are renegotiated. The piece of blanket, the transitional object the child clings to when it is releasing itself from the mother, leads him to speculate on this and the way we relate to and revise cultural tradition. For play is and creates a shared cultural reality ('The Location of Cultural Experience'). The transitional object, a thing of paradox, neither subject nor object, opens up a third space, the site of play.

The transitional object has an aspect of interiority and indeterminacy lacking in the pivotal stick–horse, but it has an isomorphic relation to it and is functionally similar. It opens up and contains, however, the contradictions only implicit in the pivotal object. 'But the term "transitional object", according to my suggestion, gives room for the process of being able to accept difference and similarity' (p. 7). It is not me *and* part of me; it is neither subject nor object; it is neither inner psychic reality nor external reality; it is the union of the baby and mother and the point at which their separation occurs. The transitional object enables the baby to do without the mother yet recalls her. It is adopted, not created ab initio. It is not a symbol because it is a real, literal object, but it can stand in as the symbol; it can stand in for the mother's breast.

The transitional object is the primal experience of culture, the beginnings of representation and its phantasmic mobility and resourcefulness. 'The place where cultural experience is located is in the *potential space* between the individual and the environment (originally the object). The same can be said of playing' (p. 118).

A mode of release from, not a fetishistic encounter with, the mother's body, not at the mercy of the body's functions but attentive to its experiences, moving from continuity to contiguity, to non-omnipotent relations and to the renegotiation of *boundaries*, the transitional object mediates a life-creating, culture-modifying space which is at once transgressive and communal. 'In order to study the play and then the cultural life of the individual, one must study the fate of the potential space between any one baby and the human (and therefore fallible) mother figure who is essentially adaptive because of love' (p. 118). The transitional object cannot be a fetish except where it fails to be a transitional object, for, as Kristeva has reminded us, the fetish stops with the literal. It is where meaning ends, not where *meanings* are infinitely remade.

Where now?

So between them, the pivotal and transitional objects (do these relate respectively to the symbolic order and the imaginary? and does the aesthetic conflate these two orders?) establish the category of the aesthetic as *play*, with all its cognitive and representational potential, its specific cultural space, its interactive possibilities. Yet, as Winnicott emphasises, the transitional object can be part of a continuum which includes madness. The prolonged absence of the loved object causes the infant's derangement. When the transitional state goes badly the toleration of anxiety and ambiguity passes over into fetishising and persecution. Such an admonition reminds us that if we accept the aesthetic state on these terms it is not a privileged condition producing privileged objects, but is amorphous, part of a continuum in which madness subsists at one end and ideology at the other – and only becomes art, perhaps, when we *choose* to call it so, just as the infant's possession of the transitional object occurs by a priori agreement. Nevertheless, our play is *play*, not simply subversive linguistic play, but the transformation of categories which constitutes a change in the structure of thought itself: it is not only an aspect of knowledge but the prerequisite of political change.

A number of theses concerning the aesthetic and the polis can be generated from what has been said, going in a number of directions. They are all capable of further development. But since this discussion is a prolegomenon, they will be expressed laconically.

1. The aesthetic is emancipatory because access to the change of categories is possible in many ways and in many different areas of our culture and its productions. Categorical experiment – new

kinds of knowledge – breaks down the binary of high and low culture because it is produced incessantly.

(In parenthesis, two examples: (i) Rave: dancing, that almost universal activity because all it needs is the body, and other bodies, reinvents the body and subverts its function in the pure instrumentality of labour. The body plays at being the body, and in Rave's preoccupation with styles of *posing*, the categories of commodified display find themselves not only mocked by exaggeration and hyperbole but also transposed from the beckoning allure of *objects*. They are manipulated by subjects, by people who are in control of their bodies, recognising and changing the rules of commodity. (ii) Veronica Forrest-Thomson's poststructuralist poem 'Ducks & Rabbits', a 'dialogue' with Wittgenstein, whose impossible hybrids, Duck/Rabbits, one representation only for two mutually exclusive figures, take on a bizarre literal being as it/they swim in the river at Cambridge. The poem is a meditation on the transformation of categories in metaphor, on the impossible/ possible coexistence of difference, and the kind of knowledge it creates. Just like the Duck/Rabbit, it flickers between two figures for metaphor. Note: neither dance nor avant-garde poem has a special dispensation from mania or ideology.)

2. If the aesthetic enables and empowers, then this implies profound educational change. That is, men and women need to be able to create and tolerate paradox in order to create change.

3. If revisionary ambiguity is at the heart of cognitive experience, then it looks as if a truly populist manifestation of the aesthetic (yet to come) will discover a cultural production which will be as *different* as possible from what Rita Felski calls 'the pragmatic constraints of everyday discourse'. Like Felski, I do not see the Adorno-endorsed high modernist avant-garde as intrinsically revolutionary simply because it exists. But, in my view, the further away some of our discourses are from everyday discourse through the transformation of categories, the nearer they are to critique. It is harder to make a critique from within a discourse than through the drama of difference in linguistic experiment.

4. This then presupposes that everyone needs to be freed into language.

5. But at this point in our culture men and women enter into language, into the symbolic, in different ways and on different terms: as Cora Kaplan has argued convincingly, girls enter into language circuitously, with more complex negotiations with repression and absence than do boys. I wonder if as a consequence girls are asked to take the strain of language, to tolerate linguistic ambiguity, uncertainty,

paradox. Language's affinity with the pivotal and transitionxl objvct would be foregrounded for them as the site of paradof and diysolve. I wonder if those who do learn to speak are made more aware both of the uncertainty and the *possibilities*, through metaphor and metonymy, of language's connection with those vital cognitive shifts and the transformation of categories which I have called a central component of the aesthetic and the prerequisite of all revisionary thought, all cultural transmission which is capable of redefinition as well as assimilation. I wonder if women of different class and colour are subject to the same conditions – whether there is a greater under-standing of difference and contradiction as a result of our culturally learned roles. Women may well have a greater responsibility to *play* with contradiction as critique.

6. If women at this specific cultural moment are hypersensitive to contradiction, then a feminist aesthetic will not be one which is confined within pre-given feminine experience (always the problem with a feminist counter public sphere) but one which changes the polis because sexual difference itself is what is being redefined. (This also means finding new modes of aesthetic production and dissemination – networks, informal groups – circumventing com-modified processes.)

7. It is surely our present task to *play* with contradictions. If, at this moment of upsurge in neo-conservatism, when hypertext and virtual reality in particular encourage the union of art and ideology, then that is not an argument for an anti-aesthetic but for more of it. A counter-aesthetic, using the aesthetic against itself rather than banishing it from the polis (though not as a Lyotardian guerrilla but as a political subject) is the answer. And women, with, if I am right, that heightened sense of contradiction, may have a great part of the work to do in redefining communality and formulating critique. Women's first object must be to disband the gender-neutral language round the classless society built on privilege, with its free choice predicated on an underclass, and to ask where women function in this structure – poor women, Black and Asian women. We will not do this if we lose one of our strengths, a politicised aesthetic. The aesthetic is not the political, but it may make the political possible.

Coda: to return to Blake ...

'Infant Joy': a *reciprocal* dyadic relation. If the aesthetic belongs to Hell, then *Songs of Innocence* at least afford a glimpse of an emancipatory aesthetic, a revisionary creativity so radical but so immediate that – an essential for that rare thing, a populist reading – the challenge to categories is widely available. 'Joy is my name': throughout this dialogue, as adult and child make and remake each other's experience, sharing each other's projections, the parent knows too well that Joy is a *name*, the child that it is an immediate condition. Joy as pivotal object (as joy the child itself comes to play the pivotal object) causes a lesion, an easing away of concept from state, and state from person, the first intimations of metaphor. Separation happens without phallic violence: it is *space* which orders separation: and creates transitional ambiguities. The carefully arranged typographical column of 'Joy' (four repetitions of the word are placed at the same point in each successive line) divides the poem vertically. The poem aligns a series of 'o's which are ambiguously circles and noughts, indivisible continuities and blanks. The identity of both mother and child – for this does seem to be a female world – trembles round those indeterminate figures. The child names herself with a non-patriarchal name, the mother likewise. But we remember that the mother has no identity in law at this time, and with that sinister understanding the repetition of unpaired internal rhyme insists upon the missing rhyme word – 'joy', 'boy'. Such a collocation, a girl's name and a boy's sex, shocks the order of gender. But if 'joy' is a generic term for emotion and not fixed to gender, could it be that this challenging of categories enables the boy to achieve identity without the threat of phallic violence, just as the girl and the mother have momentarily created an emancipatory world by refusing conventional categories? Could the father have access to this world by becoming a nurse, a carer? The emancipatory moment opens – and closes. Though not before the enormity of the change that would be necessary for this alteration to occur is apparent. For if the repressive law of the father were to change and *were* to enact the mother's part without violence, this would imply, in Blake's world, different legal, social and economic structures, different power relations, both for boy child and for father, girl child and mother. God would be different. The angel standing beside the baby (in the pictorial engraving of the poem) would be different.

References

Blake, William, *The Marriage of Heaven and Hell* in *Works*, ed. W.H. Stevenson and David V. Erdman, London, 1971, pp. 101–24.

De Man, Paul, 'The Rhetoric of Temporality', in C.S. Singleton, ed., *Interpretation, Theory and Practice*, Baltimore, 1969.

Derrida, Jacques, 'Economimesis', *Diacritics*, XI, 1981, pp. 3–25.

Eagleton, Terry, *The Ideology of the Aesthetic*, Oxford, 1990.

Felski, Rita, *Beyond Feminist Aesthetics*, Harvard, 1989.

Forrest-Thomson, Veronica, *Collected Poems and Translations*, London, 1971.

Kant, Immanuel, *Critique of Judgement*, New York and London, 1951.

—, 'An Answer to the Question: What is Enlightenment?' in David Simpson, ed., *German Aesthetic and Literary Criticism*, Cambridge, 1984.

Kaplan, Cora, *Sea Changes: Culture and Feminism*, London, 1986.

The Kristeva Reader, ed. Toril Moi, Oxford, 1986.

Lloyd, David, 'Race Under Representation', *The Oxford Literary Review* ('Neocolonialism'), XIII, 1991, pp. 62–94.

Ricoeur, Paul, *The Rule of Metaphor: Multi-Disciplinary Studies of the Creation of Meaning in Language*, trans. Robert Czerny et al., London, 1978.

Vygotsky, L.S., *Mind in Society. The Development of Higher Psychological Processes*, ed. Michael Cole et al., Cambridge, Mass. and London, 1978.

Winnicott, D.W., *Playing and Reality*, Harmondsworth, 1974.

Contributors

Isobel Armstrong is Professor of English at Birkbeck College London. Among her recent publications are *Language as Living Form in Nineteenth-Century Poetry* (1982) and the *Routledge Critical History of Victorian Poetry* (1993). She is the co-editor of *Women: A Cultural Review*, and has recently edited *New Feminist Discourses: Essays in Feminist Criticism* (1992). She is working on an anthology of nineteenth-century women's poetry, a study of Romantic poetry by women, and a book on glass and the nineteenth century.

Gillian Beer is Professor of English at Cambridge University and Fellow of Girton College. Among her recent publications are *Darwin's Plots* (1983) and *Arguing with the Past* (1989). She is at present completing a study of islands and their place in the nineteenth-century imagination and theory.

Ross Chambers is Marvin Felheim Distinguished University Professor of French and Comparative Literature at the University of Michigan. Among his recent publications are *Story and Situation* (1984), *Mélancolie et opposition* (1988), and *Room for Maneuver* (1991). His work focuses on modern literature, critical theory and cultural politics.

Sarah Kay is Lecturer in French at Cambridge University and Fellow of Girton College. She has written books on *Subjectivity in Troubadour Poetry* (1990) and *The Romance of the Rose* (forthcoming). She is currently working on a comparative study of medieval French epic and romance.

Lawrence E. Klein is Associate Professor of History at the University of Nevada, Las Vegas. He has published several articles on the theory and practice of politeness in early modern Britain. His study *Shaftesbury and the Culture of Politeness: Moral Discourse and Cultural Politics in Early Eighteenth-Century England* is forthcoming.

Nancy K. Miller is Distinguished Professor of English at Lehman College and the Graduate Center, City University of New York. Editor of *The Poetics of Gender* (1986) and co-editor with Joan DeJean of *Displacements, Women, Tradition, Literature in French* (1991), her recent publications include *Subject to Change: Reading Feminist Writing* (1988) and *Getting Personal: Feminist Occasions and Other Autobiographical Acts* (1991).

Jan Montefiore is Lecturer in English and Women's Studies at the University of Kent. She is the author of *Feminism and Poetry* (1987) and of many essays on feminist critical theory and on the relationship between contemporary poetry, gender and tradition. She is currently completing a book on the regendering of the history of the 1930s.

Jennifer Patterson has recently completed a Ph.D. at University College London on fragmentation of the body in Surrealist poetry and painting. She is currently preparing a 'catalogue raisonné' of Surrealist texts which bear manuscript dedications.

Sandy Petrey is Professor of French and Comparative Literature at the State University of New York, Stony Brook. Editor of *The French Revolution 1789–1989, Two Hundred Years of Rethinking*, his other recent publications include *Realism and Revolution* and *Speech Acts and Literary Theory*.

Judith Still is Senior Lecturer in Critical Theory at the University of Nottingham. Co-editor of *Intertextuality* (1990), her most recent publication is *Justice and Difference in the Works of Rousseau*: Bienfaisance *and* Pudeur (1992). She has also translated Djanet Lachmet's *Lallia* and co-translated Luce Irigaray's *Elemental Passions* (1992) with Joanne Collie. She is currently working on feminine economies.

Clare Whatling is currently completing a Ph.D. at the University of Nottingham on the constructions of sex, sexuality and gender in twentieth-century female-authored texts. She has published articles on Julia Kristeva, Joan Nestle and on lesbian film theory.

Gregory Wood is Lecturer in English and Communication Studies at the Nottingham Trent University. He is the author of *Articulate Flesh: Male Homoeroticism in Modern Poetry* (1987), a collection of poems entitled *We Have the Melon* (1992) and numerous essays on literature by and about man-loving men. He is currently writing a book on Marcel Proust.

Michael Worton is Senior Lecturer in French at University College London. Co-editor of *Intertextuality* (1990), he has recently published *Michel Tournier: La Goutte d'Or* (1992) and *René Char: The Dawn Breakers/Les matinaux* (1992). He is currently editing a collection of essays on Michel Tournier and completing a study of Beckett's theatre.

Index